Roots of Elvis

Roots of Elvis

David Neale

iUniverse, Inc.
New York Lincoln Shanghai

Roots of Elvis

All Rights Reserved © 2003 by David Neale

No part of this book may be reproduced or transmitted in any form or by any means, graphic, electronic, or mechanical, including photocopying, recording, taping, or by any information storage retrieval system, without the written permission of the publisher.

iUniverse, Inc.

For information address:
iUniverse
2021 Pine Lake Road, Suite 100
Lincoln, NE 68512
www.iuniverse.com

ISBN: 0-595-29505-3

Printed in the United States of America

Contents

Introduction 1

Titles Index 7

Artists Index 147

Writers and Composers Index 165

Problem Originals 189

Not Included 193

Collecting Originals 197

Acknowledgements, etc. 203

Supplementary Index 209

Addendum 223

Introduction

Introduction

Where Do You Come From?

In 1958 I was a 9-year old boy in the Rhondda Valley, a coal-mining community in the south of Wales. Each week I was allowed to go to the cinema (the "pictures"). The choice was fairly limited: there was The Grand, further up the valley and the more local cinema, the name of which I never really knew, but it was a shorter walk, so that's where I usually went.

One week the main picture was *Loving You*, a musical starring a singer called Elvis Presley. The music was astonishing to me and the red and white cowboy outfit that Elvis wore during his performance of *Teddy Bear* could only be a dream for a boy from the Valleys, whose own cowboy outfit was no more than an unmatched set of hand-me-downs.

I persuaded my father to buy *Teddy Bear* on a 78-rpm record and played and played it over and over. Soon, however, my parents separated and I left the recorded voice of Elvis in Wales, as I moved across the border to England with my mother.

I still remembered Elvis, however, even though I had little opportunity to do much about it until a few years later, when two of my mother's work colleagues learnt of my liking and gave me copies of Elvis Monthly. Eventually my mother was able to buy me a reel-to-reel tape recorder and I soon built up a sizeable collection of Elvis music, thanks to the generosity of better-off fellow Elvis fans at school. As things improved financially, I even began buying the occasional Elvis record! I also became a member of the *Official Elvis Presley Fan Club of Great Britain and The Commonwealth* (yes, that was the impressive title at that time!).

Getting married in 1971 brought financial problems again, so Elvis had to take a back seat. Actually, I had to make quite a decision at the time: move to Belgium to get married, or save my money to go to Las Vegas with the British fan club the next year to see Elvis perform! Perhaps I made the wrong decision: I am still married, but I never did get to see Elvis! Thankfully, by the 1980s I was again able to buy Elvis records and within ten years was starting a CD collection, too, alongside an ever-growing library of Elvis books.

One of the CDs I bought was not of Elvis himself. Instead, it was a collection of "originals" released to coincide with a series of programmes on a Flemish radio station. The CD was called simply *The Originals* and contained twenty-two tracks, purportedly of the original versions of songs later recorded by Elvis. This sparked my interest: how many numbers in Elvis's huge catalogue had been originally recorded by someone else? Surely more than the twenty-two tracks on the CD, but could it be as many as fifty, or a hundred? I started my search in earnest in about 1994, relying on numerous books. I soon passed the fifty mark and was amazed when title number one hundred was reached a few months later. I began to toy with the idea of putting the information I had collected into book-form.

The total continued to rise and, with the advent of easy access to the World Wide Web, I passed the two hundred count and decided to share my findings by placing them in a Web page. My research continued and I also received some limited feedback from others who had discovered the Web page. By 2003, the list of titles had reached a phenomenal four hundred and I had to redesign the web page into a full site in order to allow faster loading and easier access. People were also asking me if the information on the Web was also available as a book, so I decided to take up my earlier idea again and you, dear reader, are now holding the result.

Find Out What's Happening

I do not pretend that I have exhausted my search for the originals of numbers also performed by Elvis Presley. I do believe that this is probably the most complete list on the subject, however. 450 titles are listed in the main body, with a few more in the *Problem Originals* section.

But what can you expect to find in this book?

Well, to start with, you will not find every song that Elvis Presley ever recorded included here. Elvis recorded an enormous amount of material in his 23-year career—it is difficult to know exactly how many titles he actually did record (does one include one-liners, home recordings, informal recordings, etc?), but probably close to 800 different titles can be found. Listed here are only those numbers originally recorded by someone else, so don't look for *Jailhouse Rock*, *King Creole*, or other more or less well know Elvis titles—these were first recorded by Elvis himself and so are not eligible for inclusion here.

Furthermore, this book does not provide information about numbers performed in an Elvis concert by someone else, on which Elvis's voice does not feature. Also not included are songs available only on audio- and videotape recordings. A list of such recordings is provided in the *Not Included* section.

As far as I have been able to ascertain, every full-length studio recording made by Elvis that had previously been recorded by someone else is included here. In addition to these full-length studio recordings, I also include home recordings, one-liners and other snippets that have been released on vinyl or CD. Such numbers are often only available on "unofficial" recordings (better known as bootlegs, of course!) and the relatively recent collectors series of Elvis CDs on the official Follow That Dream label.

My decision for selecting the original version indicated for each title is based on information gained from online and traditional sources. Some might argue that almost all Elvis numbers have an "original" as almost all studio recordings were presented initially as demos. These, however, I have chosen to ignore and provide only officially released recordings.

The range of music represented is quite extraordinary and is a testimony to Elvis's versatility: rock'n'roll, blues, rhythm and blues, gospel, folk, and even a bit of classical: who would have thought that names such as Bach, Beethoven and Brahms would appear in a book about the music of Elvis Presley!

As well as the main list, the *Titles Index*, which is sorted by title, two other lists are included: the *Artists Index* and the *Writers Index*. The *Artists Index* is sorted by the full name of the artist(s) rather than by surname: Jerry Reed, for example, is listed among the Js and not the Rs. The *Writers Index* lists all writers individually: in this way Leiber and Stoller are listed separately. Each entry in these indexes indicates the title concerned, so that further information can easily be located in the *Titles Index*.

Please feel free to pass on any suggestions, corrections, or additions to me via email at david.neale@pandora.be

Updates to this list can be found in my Elvis Presley The Originals site at http://users.pandora.be/davidneale/elvis/originals/

David Neale
Heusden, Belgium, August 2003

Titles Index

Titles Index

In addition to the title, each entry includes the name or names of its writers, the date on which Elvis recorded his own version (in the case of multiple recordings of the same number, the date of the best-known version is indicated), the name of the artist(s) who recorded the number first and the year in which that recording was made or released, together with additional information relating to the number, the original artist, or Elvis's version—sometimes a combination of the three.

I also indicate at least one LP or CD on which Elvis's version can be found. This is a weak part, for Elvis's catalogue seems to be in constant flux. It is therefore possible that a listed CD is no longer available or that the number is now available on a more easily located collection. Look upon this part of an entry as nothing more than a poor indication. If you really want to find a number and are unable to locate a source, send me an email and I'll see if I can help.

(Marie's The Name) His Latest Flame (Pomus/Shuman)
Recorded by Elvis on Monday, 26 June, 1961
Original: Del Shannon, 1961
Elvis's version can be heard on ELV1S 30 #1 Hits; From Nashville to Memphis (CD 2)

Recorded first by Del Shannon in May 1961, the month before Elvis recorded his version during an all-night session, starting at 6PM on the 25th June and continuing until 7:30 the next morning. Even before Del Shannon's version, failed attempts to record the number had been made by Bobby Vee and Bobby Darin. Sadly, Del Shannon committed suicide early in 1990. See also Runaway.

(Now And Then There's) A Fool Such As I (Trader)
Recorded by Elvis on Tuesday, 10 June, 1958
Original: Hank Snow, 1952
Elvis's version can be heard on Elvis' Gold Records Volume 2; The Complete 50's Masters 4; ELV1S 30 #1 Hits

Canadian Hank Snow was originally likened to Jimmie Rodgers and was therefore dubbed the Yodelling Ranger (Rodgers was the Yodelling Brakeman). As his voice changed, however, this soon became the Singing Ranger. Note that the track released on *ELVIS 30 #1 Hits* is not the original single release! See also *I'm Gonna Bid My Blues Goodbye* and *I'm Movin' On*.

(That's What You Get) For Lovin' Me (Lightfoot)
Recorded by Elvis on Monday, 15 March, 1971
Original: Peter, Paul and Mary, 1964
Elvis's version can be heard on Walk A Mile In My Shoes—The Essential 70's Masters Disc 3

Gordon Lightfoot did not record his own song until a year after Peter, Paul and Mary's hit version. Peter Yarrow, Noel "Paul" Stookey and Mary Tavers came together in 1961, apparently capitalising on the folk boom, but in reality harking back to the early 1950s and The Weavers. They enjoyed huge success until their break-up in 1970.

(There'll Be) Peace In The Valley (For Me) (Dorsey)
Recorded by Elvis on Sunday, 13 January, 1957
Original: Mahalia Jackson, 1937
Elvis's version can be heard on Elvis' Christmas Album; The Complete Million Dollar Session; The Complete 50's Masters 2

Written by Thomas A. Dorsey, known as "the father of gospel music," having written over 400 gospels after a much more secular start in the music business (for example, he recorded *Tight Like That* with Tampa Red in 1928!). Some sources credit him with inventing the term "gospel music." Dorsey wrote this number in 1939, basing it on the earlier spiritual, *We Shall Walk Through The Valley In Peace*. Mahalia Jackson was born in Louisiana in 1911 and moved to Chicago in 1927. She first sang in church choirs and in a quintet (the Johnson Singers). In the 1930s she became associated with Dorsey, who wrote *Peace In The Valley* for her. She subsequently had a successful international career as a soloist. Elvis also recorded Dorsey's *Take My Hand, Precious Lord*. Elvis's version of *Peace In The Valley*, however, owes more to Red Foley's 1951 version. Elvis included this number in his performance on the third Ed Sullivan show in which he starred, in January 1957.

500 Miles (West)
Recorded by Elvis in 1966
Original: Peter, Paul and Mary, 1962
Elvis's version can be heard on In A Private Moment

The full title of the song is *500 Miles From Home* and exactly who wrote it is something of a mystery: some sources show it as being "traditional," others give only Hedy West as the writer, while still others list it as having been written by Bobby Bare, Hedy West and Charlie Williams. Even the year of writing poses a problem, ranging from 1961 to 1963. The latter seems unlikely, as Peter, Paul and Mary had a hit with the song in 1962! But if Bobby Bare had a hand in writing the song, did they in fact record it before him—his version was a huge hit in 1963. Elvis's home recording is sung to a backing provided by the LP, *Sing A Song With The Kingston Trio*. Elvis's recording was an informal one, made on a household tape-recorder and never intended for release.

A Hundred Years From Now (Flatt/Scruggs (Hein/Royale?))

Recorded by Elvis on Thursday, 4 June, 1970
Original: Flatt & Scruggs, 1957
Elvis's version can be heard on Walk A Mile In My Shoes—The Essential 70's Masters Disc 3

Flatt & Scruggs recorded the original at Bradley Film & Recording Studio, 804 16th Avenue South, Nashville, Tennessee, during a three-hour session on March 24, 1957, starting at 10am. The producer was Don Law. There is some confusion about who wrote the number, however: Elvis's recordings list Flatt & Scruggs, as does Ernst Jorgensen's *A Life In Music*. However, Bear Family Records (1991) indicate that it was written by Hein and Royale. To confuse matters even further, Red River Dave (David L McEnery), a Texas country singer, published the song in his 1930's song portfolio titled *Songs Of The Mountains And Plains* as *I Won't Care (A Hundred Years From Now)*. But…there is a registration on both BMI and ASCAP for a song titled *A Hundred Years From Now* credited to Silvio Hein, George V Hobart and Edwin Royale!

A Thing Called Love (Hubbard)

Recorded by Elvis on Wednesday, 19 May, 1971
Original: Jerry Reed, 1968
Elvis's version can be heard on He Touched Me; Amazing Grace (CD 2)

Jerry Hubbard, the author, is the real name of Jerry Reed. He also wrote *Guitar Man, Talk About The Good Times* and *U.S. Male*, all recorded by Elvis.

After Loving You (Miller/Lantz)

Recorded by Elvis on Tuesday, 18 February, 1969
Original: Joe Henderson, 1962
Elvis's version can be heard on From Nashville to Memphis (5)

Elvis first recorded this number at home in 1966 and this home-recording was issued on *Platinum: A Life In Music* in 1997. The studio recording, however, was made at the American Studios and was originally released almost 20 years earlier on the *From Elvis In Memphis* album—perhaps the very best Elvis album. Joe Henderson's version was on Todd 1077.

Ain't That Loving You Baby (Otis/Hunter)
    Recorded by Elvis on Tuesday, 10 June, 1958
    Original: Eddie Riff, 1956
    Elvis's version can be heard on Elvis' Golden Records Vol.4; Reconsider Baby

According to Ernst Jorgensen in his book, *Elvis Presley: A Life In Music*, this song was written by Clyde Otis and Ivory Joe Hunter especially for the June 10, 1958 session. This, however, can't be, as the number was first recorded by Eddie Riff (real name: Edward Ruffin) in July 1956 and issued on Dover 102 before the end of that year with credits indicating Hunter/Otis. Elvis's version was not released until 1964. The single peaked at number 16 on Billboard's Hot 100 chart. An alternate take with a faster tempo was released in 1985 on the *Reconsider Baby* album.

All Shook Up (Blackwell)
    Recorded by Elvis on Saturday, 12 January, 1957
    Original: David Hill, 1956
    Elvis's version can be heard on Elvis' Golden Records; ELV1S 30 #1 Hits

David Hill was a rock singer from New York. Well, this is a pretty loose use of the word "rock," for he sounds very much like Pat Boone on this number—need I say more? In 1959 he had some success with the numbers *Two Brothers* and *Living Doll* (covered in the UK by Cliff Richard). Vicki Young also recorded *All Shook Up* in 1956 before Elvis, but her version, too, was overshadowed by Elvis's. This was Elvis's first number one hit in the UK. *All Shook Up* spent 30 weeks on the Hot 100 chart in the USA.

Allá En El Rancho Grande (Urange/del Moral/Ramos)
    Recorded by Elvis on Wednesday, 15 July, 1970
    Original: Tito Guízar, 1936
    Elvis's version can be heard on Walk A Mile In My Shoes—The Essential 70's Masters Disc 5

Not an "official" recording, but nevertheless released officially by BMG, this is just Elvis playing around during rehearsals for the film *That's The Way It Is*. The title translates as "Over there in the big ranch." The 1936 original comes from a film of the same title and was sung by the famous actor and singer, whose full name was Federico Arturo Guízar Tolentino.

Almost Always True (Wise/Weisman)
>Recorded by Elvis on Wednesday, 22 March, 1961
>Original: Joseph Saucier (Alouette), 1915
>Elvis's version can be heard on Blue Hawaii

Surely the tune for this number is taken from the French song, Alouette? The latter seems to have been a traditional Canadian song, taken from Canada to France by Canadian troops (presumably in the First World War), from where it became an international children's favourite.

Aloha Oe (Liliuokalani/Wilmott)
>Recorded by Elvis on Tuesday, 21 March, 1961
>Original: Royal Hawaiian Troubadours, 1905
>Elvis's version can be heard on Blue Hawaii

Aloha Oe means "Farewell to thee" or "Until we meet again." An appropriate title for a number written by the Hawaiian crown princess whilst in exile! Princess Kamekeha Liliuokalani composed Aloha Oe in 1878. She was Queen of Hawaii from 1891 until 1893. The Toots Paka Hawaiians recorded a version of the song in the original language in 1920. Prior to this, however, the "Hilo Hawaiians" (a pseudonym of the Arthur Pryor Band) issued the number in 1913—English or Polynesian, I don't know. Arthur Pryor was an ex John Sousa collaborator and a major force in early 20th century American music. I know still less about the even earlier version by The Royal Hawaiian Troubadours!

Alright, Okay, You Win (Wyche/Watts)
>Recorded by Elvis on Sunday, 29 September, 1974
>Original: Buddy & Ella Johnson, 1955
>Elvis's version can be heard on Dragonheart

Though originally recorded by Ella Johnson, singing with her brother's band, the song was made famous by Peggy Lee and has since become something of a standard. Elvis sang just one verse of the song during a concert in Detroit. Writer Wyche is associated with Elvis through another song, *A Big Hunk O' Love*, which he wrote with Aaron Schroeder.

Always On My Mind (Carson/James/Christopher)
>Recorded by Elvis on Wednesday, 29 March, 1972
>Original: Brenda Lee, 1972
>Elvis's version can be heard on The Essential Collection; Walk A Mile In My Shoes—The Essential 70's Masters Disc 2

Mark James, whose name appears in the writers credits, also wrote *It's Only Love, Moody Blue* and *Suspicious Minds*. Brenda Lee probably recorded her version of *Always On My Mind* after Elvis, but her version was released earlier. Elvis's version was coupled on a single with *Separate Ways*.

Amazing Grace (Traditional/Newton)
>Recorded by Elvis on Monday, 15 March, 1971
>Original: Rev. J. M. Gates, 1926
>Elvis's version can be heard on Walk A Mile In My Shoes—The Essential 70's Masters Disc 3; Amazing Grace (CD 1); He Touched Me

The tune is associated with the Scottish folk song *Loch Lomond* and the 17th century English hymn *Todlen Hame*. There is certainly a melodic resemblance with *Loch Lomond*, but I have never heard *Todlen Hame*. John Newton supplied the new words in the 18th century. Newton was the reformed master of a slave ship and not a particularly pleasant character in his earlier life.

Amen (Traditional)
>Recorded by Elvis on Wednesday, 20 March, 1974
>Original: The Impressions, 1964
>Elvis's version can be heard on Recorded Live On Stage In Memphis

RCA recorded *Amen* (sung together with *I Got A Woman*) on April 9, 1972 at the Coliseum, Hampton Roads, Virginia, though this has probably not been released. The song was certainly used in a 1940 film called *Maryland*, but the first released recorded version seems to have been by The Impressions, with a version credited to John W. Pate and Curtis Mayfield, which reached number 7 in the Billboard Hot 100 chart in 1964.

America The Beautiful (Bates)
>Recorded by Elvis on Saturday, 13 December, 1975
>Original: Frank Sinatra, 1945
>Elvis's version can be heard on Elvis Aron Presley

Katherine Lee Bates wrote the lyrics to this song in 1893 after visiting Pike's Peak and admiring the view from there. Her poem was published on July 4th, 1895. The music used for the song was written in 1888 by Samuel Ward as *Materna* and was originally used for the hymn, *O Mother Dear Jerusalem*. Elvis's recording was issued as a B-side of the single *My Way* in 1977.

An American Trilogy (Traditional/Newbury)
>Recorded by Elvis on Thursday, 17 February, 1972
>Original: Mickey Newbury, 1971
>Elvis's version can be heard on Walk A Mile In My Shoes—The Essential 70's Masters Disc 1; Recorded Live On Stage In Memphis

The three numbers used by Newbury to make up the Trilogy are: *Dixie*, written in 1859 by Dan Emmett; *Battle Hymn Of The Republic*, written in 1861 by Julia Howe (set to the tune of *John Brown's Body*); *All My Trials*, which is a traditional number whose composer is unknown, though the names of Rita Green and C.C. Carter are sometimes listed—versions of *All My Trials* were released in 1956 by Cynthia Gooding and Bob Gibson. The live Feb 17 recording of this number by Elvis was released as a single with *The First Time Ever I Saw Your Face*. Other live recordings by Elvis have also been released.

An Evening Prayer (Battersby/Gabriel)
>Recorded by Elvis on Tuesday, 18 May, 1971
>Original: Homer Rodeheaver, 1915
>Elvis's version can be heard on He Touched Me

Charles Gabriel provided the arrangement for this hymn written in 1911 by C. M. Battersby, which is based on the bible text, Psalm 19:12-13, "Forgive my hidden faults. Keep your servant also from willful sins." It has been recorded by numerous singers, including Jim Reeves, Mahalia Jackson and The Blackwood Brothers. Homer Rodehaver's original from 1915 was released on the Victor label.

And I Love You So (McLean)
>Recorded by Elvis on Tuesday, 11 March, 1975
>Original: Don McLean, 1970
>Elvis's version can be heard on Today; Elvis In Concert

Bobby Goldsboro recorded this song in 1971 and Perry Como in 1973; Como's release reached number 29 on Billboard's Hot 100 charts.

And The Grass Won't Pay No Mind (Diamond)
>Recorded by Elvis on Tuesday, 18 February, 1969
>Original: Neil Diamond, 1968
>Elvis's version can be heard on Back In Memphis; From Nashville to Memphis (4)

Both Elvis and Neil Diamond recorded this song in the same Memphis studio. Mark Lindsay, lead singer with Paul Revere and the Raiders had a version in 1970 that peaked at number 44 on the Billboard Hot 100 charts. Elvis also recorded Neil Diamond's *Sweet Caroline*.

Any Day Now (My Wild Beautiful Bird) (Bacharach/Hilliard)
> Recorded by Elvis on Friday, 21 February, 1969
> Original: Chuck Jackson, 1962
> Elvis's version can be heard on From Elvis in Memphis; From Nashville to Memphis (5)

The original version by Chuck Jackson reached number 23 in the Billboard Hot 100 chart and number 2 in the R&B chart, but the biggest hit version was Ronnie Milsap's 1982 release, which topped the Country chart and got to number 14 on the Hot 100 chart.

Apron Strings (Weiss/Schroeder)
> Recorded by Elvis on April (or later), 1959
> Original: Little David (Schroeder), 1959
> Elvis's version can be heard on Platinum: A Life In Music; In A Private Moment

Here's a strange little entry. Weiss and Schroeder probably wrote this song with Elvis in mind, but, presumably because of Elvis's army stint, never got around to giving it to him—at least, Elvis never got around to recording it officially: his is an informal home recording, never intended for release. Little David (also a Schroeder, so perhaps he was writer Aaron Schroeder's son) recorded the number for US release and somehow or other, the relatively new British excuse for a Rock'n'Roller, Cliff Richard, also got hold of the number and recorded it a little later. On the set *Platinum: A Life In Music* the number is included as part of a track called *The Bad Nauheim Medley*, (Elvis's house was in Bad Nauheim), which further includes *I'll Take You Home Again Kathleen, I Will Be True, It's Been So Long Darling* and *There's No Tomorrow*.

Are You Lonesome Tonight? (Turk/Handman)
> Recorded by Elvis on Monday, 4 April, 1960
> Original: Ned Jakobs, 1927
> Elvis's version can be heard on The Essential Collection; Golden Records Vol.3; Elvis In Concert; ELV1S 30 #1 Hits

The number is probably more associated with Al Jolson than with Ned Jakobs (who recorded it on 17 May 1927 for Brunswick), but Jolson did not make his recording until April 1950. Like Elvis, Jolson became a legend in his own time, even before he starred in the first "talkies"! Elvis's manager, Tom Parker, persuaded Elvis to record this number, a favourite of Mrs. Parker's! The arrangement used in Elvis's version is based on the 1950 recording of *Are You Lonesome Tonight* by the Blue Barron Orchestra. The spoken part is taken from a speech by Jacques in Shakespeare's *As You Like It*, Act II Scene VII.

Are You Sincere (Walker)
>Recorded by Elvis on Monday, 24 September, 1973
>Original: Wayne Walker, 1957
>Elvis's version can be heard on Raised On Rock; Walk A Mile In My Shoes—The Essential 70's Masters Disc 4

Wayne Walker recorded his own composition in 1957, but it was a Top Ten entry for Andy Williams on the Cadence Records label (Cadence 1340) the following year.

Ask Me (Modugno/Giant/Baum/Kaye)
>Recorded by Elvis on Monday, 27 May, 1963
>Original: Domenico Modugno, 1958
>Elvis's version can be heard on Collectors Gold; From Nashville to Memphis (3)

Italian Domenico Modugno had a massive hit in 1958 with *Volare* and now had a new number out called *Io*. The original title was printed on the label of the UK single release of *Ask Me*, between brackets after the English title. This caused some confusion to Albert Hand, then editor of *Elvis Monthly*, who wondered what the number 10 meant! Elvis recorded the number twice: the May 27th version was not released until 1991; the 1964 single version was recorded on January 12, 1964.

At The Hop (Singer/Madara/White)
>Recorded by Elvis in 1959
>Original: Danny And The Juniors, 1957
>Elvis's version can be heard on Greetings From Germany (unofficial CD)

The number was originally written as *Do The Bop*, but by the time it was ready to be recorded, the dance called the Bop was already history. Dick Clark suggested a quick title change to *At The Hop*, and the rest really is history! Not only did Danny And The Juniors have a number 1 smash with the song, but Elvis recorded it informally on a home tape recorded whilst in Germany doing his army stint. The recording has not been officially released.

Aubrey (Gates)
>Recorded by Elvis on Monday, 2 September, 1974
>Original: Bread, 1972
>Elvis's version can be heard on Desert Storm (unofficial CD)

The number was a number 15 hit in the USA for the group Bread. David Gates, responsible for both music and words, was lead singer with Bread. This was far from the group's first success after its formation in 1969; the group was internationally successful until their break-up in 1976. Elvis's recording is taken from a Las Vegas concert; the song is sung by Voice, his backing singers, while Elvis recites the words.

Auld Lang Syne (Burns)
>Recorded by Elvis on Friday, 31 December, 1976
>Original: Emile Berliner, 1890
>Elvis's version can be heard on New Year's Eve (FTD label)

Scottish poet Robert Burns wrote the words of *Auld Lang Syne* in about 1789 for use with a piece of Scottish music dating from 1687, *The Duke Of Bucclugh's Tune*. Guy Lombardo had the first recorded hit with the song. Elvis sang the song at the New Year's Eve concert in Pittsburgh on December 31, 1976.

Ave Maria (Bach/Bernard/Gounod)
>Recorded by Elvis on August, 1970
>Original: Alessandro Moreschi "The Last Castrato", 1902
>Elvis's version can be heard on The Hillbilly Cat "Live" (unofficial release)

Paul Bernard and Charles Gounod used Luke 1:28 as the inspiration for *Ave Maria* in 1859, adapting the words to J.S. Bach's First prelude. Alessandro Moreschi (apparently a somewhat physically challenged singer...) recorded the number on a cylinder in 1902 (Opal 5477). Elvis used the song in an unusual medley with *I Got A Woman* in the International Hotel, Las Vegas, in August 1970.

Baby Let's Play House (Gunter)
>Recorded by Elvis on Saturday, 5 February, 1955
>Original: Arthur Gunter, 1954
>Elvis's version can be heard on The Sun Sessions CD; The Complete 50's Masters 1

Elvis changed the words of the original slightly in his performance, singing "you may get a pink Cadillac," in place of Gunter's original "you may get religion." Elvis already had religion, the Cadillac would soon follow! There is some doubt about the recording date: 5 February is the date normally listed, but Elvis appeared at the Louisiana Hayride on that date; it is possible that the song was recorded earlier that same week.

Baby What You Want Me To Do (Reed)
>Recorded by Elvis on Thursday, 27 June, 1968
>Original: Jimmy Reed, 1960
>Elvis's version can be heard on NBC-TV Special

Jimmy Reed was born in 1925. Despite his limited prowess with both harmonica and guitar, he became the most successful Blues artist of the 1950s. Much of Reed's success was also due to his friend and guitarist, Eddie Taylor, and to his wife, known as Mama Reed, who wrote many of his songs. Elvis also recorded Reed's *Big Boss Man*.

Beyond The Reef (Pitman)
>Recorded by Elvis on Friday, 27 May, 1966
>Original: Napua Stevens, 1949
>Elvis's version can be heard on From Nashville to Memphis (3)

Jack Pitman, who composed this number, was a Canadian. He moved to Hawaii in 1943 and there composed *Beyond The Reef*, probably his most famous song, in 1948. Napua Stevens was a popular and successful Hawaiian recording artist. Following her local success, the number was picked up and recorded on the mainland of the USA by Jimmy Wakely together with Margaret Whiting and at just about the same time by Bing Crosby. An earlier, incomplete home recording of Elvis's version of this number was made in 1960; this was released in 2000 on the CD *In A Private Moment*.

Big Boss Man (Smith/Dixon)
>Recorded by Elvis on Sunday, 10 September, 1967
>Original: Jimmy Reed, 1961
>Elvis's version can be heard on From Nashville to Memphis (3); NBC-TV Special

Big Boss Man is actually a post-war revamp of the pre-war number *Stack o' Dollars*, written and performed on the Victor label by Sleepy John Estes in 1930. Elvis also recorded Reed's *Baby What You Want Me To Do*.

Bitter They Are, Harder They Fall (Gatlin)
>Recorded by Elvis on Monday, 2 February, 1976
>Original: Larry Gatlin, 1974
>Elvis's version can be heard on From Elvis Presley Boulevard, Memphis Tennessee

Help Me was also written by Gatlin. Larry Gatlin has yet another connection with Elvis, having briefly been a member of the Imperials gospel group in 1971. Gatlin's original was titled *Bigger They Are, Harder They Fall*.

Blessed Jesus (Hold My Hand) (Brumley)
>Recorded by Elvis on Tuesday, 4 December, 1956
>Original: Cori Sacri in Chiesa, 1933
>Elvis's version can be heard on The Complete Million Dollar Session

Albert Brumley is probably the best-known 20th century gospel music writer in America. He wrote his first and most successful gospel song in 1931—*I'll Fly Away*. Another Brumley song recorded by Elvis is *If We Never Meet Again*.

Blowin' In The Wind (Dylan)
>Recorded by Elvis in 1966
>Original: Bob Dylan, 1962
>Elvis's version can be heard on In A Private Moment

Elvis seems to have liked Bob Dylan's songs, and rightly so, of course. Unfortunately, RCA didn't seem to want Elvis to record anything too "advanced" in the sixties, concentrating instead on film scores—Elvis did his best, but was fighting a losing battle most of the time! Still, he did record Dylan's little-known *Tomorrow Is a Long Time*—a superb rendition, relegated to the insignificance of a "bonus track" on the otherwise fairly nondescript film album *Spinout*!

Anyway, back to *Blowin' In The Wind*! Sadly, Elvis did not make an official recording of the number, so we have only this informal home recording, never intended for release, made some time in 1966. Dylan's own version was recorded in July 1962, but was not released to the public until May 1963 as part of his *Freewheelin'* LP. Dylan's melody for *Blowin' In The Wind* was based on an earlier number called *No More Auction Block*. Bob Dylan might not have been the first person to record his own song—a demo version was probably made earlier by The New World Singers.

Elvis's home recording is sung to a backing provided by the LP, *Sing A Song With The Kingston Trio*.

Blue Christmas (Hayes/Johnson)
    Recorded by Elvis on Thursday, 5 September, 1957
    Original: Doye O'Dell, 1948
    Elvis's version can be heard on Elvis' Christmas Album; If Every Day Was Like Christmas; NBC-TV Special; The Complete 50's Masters 3

Although recorded in 1957 and part of the original *Elvis' Christmas Album*, the track was not released on single until 1964, when it reached the top of the Billboard special Christmas Singles chart. Doye O'Dell was born in 1912. One of his biggest hits was *Old Shep*, which he recorded in 1947 (later also recorded by Elvis). In the 1950s he became one of the many singing cowboys in films, though continued his recording career, which remained his most significant activity. Doye O'Dell died in January 2001.

Blue Eyes Crying In The Rain (Rose)
    Recorded by Elvis on Sunday, 8 February, 1976
    Original: Roy Acuff & His Smokey Mountain Boys, 1947
    Elvis's version can be heard on From Elvis Presley Boulevard, Memphis Tennessee

Author Fred Rose was co-founder of the Nashville-based Acuff-Rose music publishing company, together with performer Roy Acuff. Willie Nelson's 1975 release of the number reached the top of the Billboard Country chart.

Blue Hawaii (Robin/Rainger)
    Recorded by Elvis on Wednesday, 22 March, 1961
    Original: Bing Crosby, 1937
    Elvis's version can be heard on Blue Hawaii

The original was also from a film: *Waikiki Wedding*. Marilyn Monroe fans might like to know that co-writer Leo Robin also wrote *Diamonds Are A Girl's Best Friend*.

Blue Moon (Rodgers/Hart)
    Recorded by Elvis on Thursday, 19 August, 1954
    Original: Frankie Trumbauer & Band, 1934
    Elvis's version can be heard on The Complete 50's Masters 1; The Sun Sessions CD

The tune was used with the familiar *Blue Moon* words as the theme music for the radio series Hollywood Hotel, but was first heard in the Hollywood Revue Of 1933, where it was sung by Jean Harlow as *Prayer*. Shirley Ross used the tune when performing the song *The Bad In Every Man* in the 1934 film *Manhattan Melodrama*.

Blue Moon Of Kentucky (Monroe)

    Recorded by Elvis on Tuesday, 6 July, 1954
    Original: Bill Monroe, 1946
    Elvis's version can be heard on The Complete 50's Masters 1; The Sun Sessions CD

Bill Monroe with Flatt and Scruggs, who played guitar and banjo respectively in his bluegrass group, recorded the original version of this classic in 3/4 time—waltz tempo. But Monroe's waltz tempo original was light years away from Elvis's quantum leap into rockabilly. Elvis was worried that Bluegrass giant Bill Monroe would be offended by his tampering with the number, but Monroe soon recorded his own version in Elvis's 4/4 rhythm. Elvis recorded several Bill Monroe originals, including *I Hear A Sweet Voice Calling*, *Little Cabin On The Hill*, *Summertime Has Passed And Gone*, *Sweetheart You Done Me Wrong* and perhaps even *Uncle Pen*.

Blue Suede Shoes (Perkins)

    Recorded by Elvis on Monday, 30 January, 1956
    Original: Carl Perkins, 1956
    Elvis's version can be heard on Elvis Presley; G.I. Blues; The Complete 50's Masters 1

Carl Perkins was born in 1932, the son of a poor share-cropper. He wrote *Blue Suede Shoes* after having heard a boy tell his date not to step on his blue suede shoes. The song was written on a potato sack. He recorded the number at Sun, but a near-fatal car accident and the subsequent long period of recovery, which initiated a struggle with alcoholism, stunted his aspirations to become a major star. Nevertheless, he wrote a number of other strong songs, including *Dixie Fried*. Carl Perkins died in 1998. Elvis covered his own cover of Perkins' *Blue Suede Shoes* in 1960, when a new recording was made for the film *G.I. Blues*.

Blueberry Hill (Lewis/Stock/Rose)

    Recorded by Elvis on Saturday, 19 January, 1957
    Original: Gene Autry, 1940
    Elvis's version can be heard on Loving You; The Complete 50's Masters 3

Autry, a singing cowboy, performed this number in the 1940 film *The Singing Hill*. Glenn Miller recorded a version that same year, but the number is undoubtedly most associated with Fats Domino, whose 1956 version made it to the top of the R&B charts.

Bosom Of Abraham (Johnson/McFadden/Brooks)
>Recorded by Elvis on Wednesday, 9 June, 1971
Original: Golden Gate Quartet, 1938
Elvis's version can be heard on Amazing Grace (CD 2)

The version by the Golden Gate Quartet was called *Rock My Soul*. The Trumpeteers released a version called *Bosom Of Abraham* (Score 5031) in 1949. The Jordanaires released a version in 1954 (Decca 29188).

Bossa Nova Baby (Leiber/Stoller)
>Recorded by Elvis on Tuesday, 22 January, 1963
Original: Tippy and the Clovers, 1962
Elvis's version can be heard on Double Features: It Happened At The World's Fair & Fun In Acapulco

The Bossa Nova was of Brazilian origin. However, *Fun In Acapulco*, in which the number was used, was a film whose action supposedly took place in Mexico!

Bridge Over Troubled Water (Simon)
>Recorded by Elvis on Friday, 5 June, 1970
Original: Simon and Garfunkel, 1970
Elvis's version can be heard on That's The Way It Is

The original reached number 1 in the US Hot 100 and received a Grammy Award for Record of the Year in 1970. Although released as a performance by Simon and Garfunkel, only Art Garfunkel actually sang on the number, but then, it was only Paul Simon who wrote it, so fair's fair! Elvis's recording was made in a studio—the "live" applause was overdubbed.

Brown Eyed Handsome Man (Berry)
>Recorded by Elvis on Tuesday, 4 December, 1956
Original: Chuck Berry, 1956
Elvis's version can be heard on The Complete Million Dollar Session

Chuck Berry will go down in history as the Bard of Rock'n'Roll: no other songwriter was quite able to match Berry's masterful ability to summarise in a few verses and with such brilliant phrasing the hopes and wishes of youth. Elvis covered numerous Berry numbers—see also *Johnny B. Goode*; *Long Live Rock And Roll (School Days)*; *Maybellene*; *Memphis, Tennessee*; *Promised Land*; *Too Much Monkey Business*.

Burning Love (Linde)
    Recorded by Elvis on Tuesday, 28 March, 1972
    Original: Arthur Alexander, 1972
    Elvis's version can be heard on Walk A Mile In My Shoes—The Essential 70's Masters Disc 1; ELV1S 30 #1 Hits

Author Dennis Linde recorded his own version of this number in 1973. J. D. Sumner and The Stamps provided backing vocals on Elvis's recording of Burning Love. This was the first time that Elvis used this group, though he had admired them since before himself becoming a star. Note that the version on *ELV1S 30 #1 Hits* is indicated as being a "mixed and mastered" version, so presumably it is based on the original single take, despite the fact that it is six seconds longer...

By And By (Tindley)
    Recorded by Elvis on Friday, 27 May, 1966
    Original: Blind Willie Johnson, 1930
    Elvis's version can be heard on How Great Thou Art; Amazing Grace (CD 1)

Charles H. Tindley was born in 1851 and died in 1936. He wrote this number in 1905 as *We'll Understand It Better By and By*. He might have recorded the number himself, but this can't be confirmed. Tindley also wrote the song *I'll Overcome Some Day*, which later became know as *We Shall Overcome*. Furthermore, he wrote the gospel number *Stand By Me*. Many sources imply that this is the song with which Ben E. King had a hit in the 1960s, but that was a different number. However, Elvis also recorded Tindley's *Stand By Me* for his own *How Great Thou Art* gospel collection. As for Blind Willie Johnson—one of the greats of early Blues! If you want to feel shivers, listen to his recording *Dark Was The Night*—quite superb.

Can't Help Falling In Love (Peretti/Creatore/Weiss)
    Recorded by Elvis on Thursday, 23 March, 1961
    Original: A. Delcroix, 1903
    Elvis's version can be heard on Blue Hawaii; ELV1S 30 #1 Hits

Based on *Plaisir d'Amour* (Pleasure of Love), a song dating from 1785, with original words by Jean-Pierre Claris de Florian and music by Johann Paul Aegidius Martini (Schwarzendorf). The words first appeared in de Florian's novel *Célestine* and, because of its context there, the song was also know as *Romance du Chevrier* (Romance of the goatherd). It was later adapted in English as *The Joy of Love*. Recorded innumerable times by everyone and his mother, the very earliest recording seems to have been made by A. Delcroix (listed on label as "Mons. A. Delcroix"—very French!) on Odeon 33089 in 1903. *Can't Help Falling In Love* is an adaptation of the original tune with new words, written for the film *Blue Hawaii*, by George Weiss.

Carry Me Back To Old Virginia (Bland)
Recorded by Elvis on Monday, 10 April, 1972
Original: Alma Gluck, 1915
Elvis's version can be heard on Carry Me Back To Old Virginia (unofficial)

Originally titled *Carry Me Back To Old Virginny*, the number was written in 1875 by the African American minstrel James Bland, who wrote over 700 songs, including *Oh Dem Golden Slippers*. It became the state song of Virginia in 1940, but was given the status of "state song emeritus" in 1997 when the Virginia Senate decided that a new song was required. Elvis sang just one line of the song during a concert in Richmond, Virginia.

Cattle Call (Owens)
Recorded by Elvis on Wednesday, 29 July, 1970
Original: Tex Owens, 1934
Elvis's version can be heard on One Night In Vegas

Cattle Call was written in 1934 by country artist Tex Owens and recorded by him on 28 August of that year. It became a number one country hit for Eddy Arnold with Hugo Winterhalter And His Orchestra in 1955. It is believed that Elvis sang *Cattle Call* at some of his concerts in the 1950s. Two recordings of Elvis rehearsing the number are available: the first dates from 29 July 1970 and is included in the *Platinum, A Life In Music* set, but it is just a 25 second snippet; the second at 1m.16s is considerably longer and can be found on the Follow That Dream release, *One Night In Vegas*.

Cindy, Cindy (Drake/Shirl (based on traditional))
Recorded by Elvis on Thursday, 4 June, 1970
Original: Lulu Belle and Scotty, 1934
Elvis's version can be heard on Love Letters From Elvis; Walk A Mile In My Shoes—The Essential 70's Masters Disc 3

Based on a number called *Get Along Home Cindy*, recorded by Lulu Belle and Scotty in the 1930s. This duo also sang the original of Elvis's *Have I Told You Lately That I Love You*. Various other versions of this traditional number have been recorded, most with different lyrics to those supplied to Elvis. Amongst these: Ricky Nelson (with same title as Elvis's, in 1959) and Trini Lopez (1968 as *I'm Coming Home Cindy*).

Clambake (Weisman/Wayne)

    Recorded by Elvis on Wednesday, 22 February, 1967
    Original: Henry Whitter (harmonica solo), 1924
    Elvis's version can be heard on Double Features: Kissin' Cousins, Clambake and Stay Away Joe

There can be little doubt that the chorus of this number is a simple rewrite of the traditional *Shortnin' Bread*. Whitter recorded for the Okeh and Victor labels. The original title, *Shortnin' Bread* appears in numerous forms, including "Shortenin'" and "Shortening" and "Saltin'"; one recording lists it as *Salt Rising Bread*. There seems to be utter confusion about the origins of the song!

Come Along (Hess (but Traditional))

    Recorded by Elvis on Wednesday, 12 May, 1965
    Original: Alabama Barn Stormers (Riley Puckett & Hugh Cross), 1927
    Elvis's version can be heard on Frankie and Johnny

This number was used in Elvis's film *Frankie and Johnny*, with composing credits going to David Hess. It was the first track recorded for the film. However, the tune seems to be the same as an older number called *Gonna Raise A Ruckus Tonight*, recorded first by Puckett and Cross in 1927. The melody is still older, however, and can only be indicated as "traditional." Robert Emmett Dolan arranged the tune and Johnny Mercer provided the words to create *We'll Raise A Ruckus Tonight*, which was finally published in 1934 (this is getting complicated!). How similar the words in Elvis's version are to the "original," I have no idea, but the phrase "gonna raise a ruckus tonight" is still there!

Come What May (Tableporter)

    Recorded by Elvis on Saturday, 28 May, 1966
    Original: Etta James, 1957
    Elvis's version can be heard on From Nashville to Memphis (3)

Although it is normally reported that this is a Clyde McPhatter number, it seems that the first recording was actually by Etta James, who made it in August 1957 (about a year before McPhatter's version), and released it on Modern 1022.

Cottonfields (Ledbetter)
>Recorded by Elvis on Wednesday, 15 July, 1970
>Original: Leadbelly (Huddie Ledbetter), 1940
>Elvis's version can be heard on That's The Way It Is (3-CD set)

This song is referred to in *Go, Cat, Go!* (the biography of Carl Perkins, by Carl Perkins and David McGee) as being part of Elvis's repertoire during a performance in 1954 at a high school gymnasium in Bethel Springs, Tennessee, some fifteen miles from Jackson. A recording was made in July 1970 during the filming for *That's The Way It Is*.

Crazy Arms (Mooney/Seals)
>Recorded by Elvis on Tuesday, 4 December, 1956
>Original: Ray Price, 1956
>Elvis's version can be heard on The Complete Million Dollar Session

Recorded during the jam session at the Sun Studios, known as The Million Dollar Quartet. Jerry Lee Lewis (The Killer) was at the session, along with Carl Perkins and Elvis (Johnny Cash was there for at least some time, but it is not certain that he was actually caught on tape). Jerry Lee recorded *Crazy Arms* too, of course.

Crying In The Chapel (Glenn)
>Recorded by Elvis on Monday, 31 October, 1960
>Original: Darrell Glenn, 1953
>Elvis's version can be heard on How Great Thou Art; Amazing Grace (CD 1); ELV1S 30 #1 Hits

Darrell's father, Artie Glenn wrote *Crying In The Chapel*. Elvis's version was recorded in 1960 during the *His Hand In Mine* sessions, but was not released until 1965, when it reached the number one spot in several national charts, including the UK. Why the delay? Well, the publishing rights of *Crying In The Chapel* were held by Artie Glenn, who refused to share the rights with Hill & Range. Release was therefore held back until Hill & Range were able to acquire full rights to the number.

Crying Time (Owens)
>Recorded by Elvis on Thursday, 16 July, 1970
>Original: Buck Owens, 1964
>Elvis's version can be heard on From Hollywood To Vegas (unofficial release).

The B-side of Buck Owens' hit *I've Got A Tiger By The Tail*, *Crying Time*, is sung by Elvis during a studio rehearsal in the film *That's The Way It Is*. The song has never been officially released on CD, but does appear on the *That's The Way It Is* DVD.

Danny Boy (Weatherly)
>Recorded by Elvis on Thursday, 5 February, 1976
>Original: Ernestine Schumann-Heink, 1918
>Elvis's version can be heard on From Elvis Presley Boulevard, Memphis Tennessee; Walk A Mile In My Shoes—The Essential 70's Masters Disc 4

Fred Weatherly provided the words to *Danny Boy*, but the melody was first published in George Petrie's *The Petrie Collection Of The Ancient Music Of Ireland* in 1855. The nameless piece bore the annotation that it originated in Londonderry and so became known as *The Londonderry Air*. Ernestine Schumann-Heink was a German contralto with the New York Metropolitan Opera.

Dark Moon (Miller)
>Recorded by Elvis in 1966
>Original: Bonnie Guitar, 1957
>Elvis's version can be heard on A Golden Celebration; The Home Recordings

Dark Moon was written by Ned Miller (see also *From A Jack To A King*) in 1957. Several artists recorded the number that year, but Bonnie Guitar's version seems to have been the first. She was beaten in the charts, however, by Gale Storm, who reached number 4 in Billboard's Top 100, Bonnie only getting as far as number 6.

Elvis's version is an informal recording, probably made in 1966. It was discovered by the late Joan Deary of RCA records when she searched Graceland after Elvis's death, in the hope of finding some overlooked recordings.

Delilah (Reed/Mason)
>Recorded by Elvis in May 1976
>Original: Tom Jones, 1968
>Elvis's version can be heard on Elvis Among Friends (unofficial CD)

Quite a number of Elvis's "recordings" are little more than just a few lines of a song. This is an example, and here Elvis didn't even sing enough for the compiler of the CD to get the title correct! The CD lists *I Saw The Light*, so one would expect to hear Elvis singing the Hank Williams song (he had quite a penchant for them); instead he sings just the opening lines of Welsh singer Tom Jones's more raucous number (which, admittedly, begins with the words, "I saw the light..."). The story goes that Elvis used to warm up his voice with this number. Nothing at all official about either the release or the recording, which was made during a Lake Tahoe concert and sounds as if the mike was held under the table!

Detroit City (Tillis/Dill)
>Recorded by Elvis on Friday, 11 September, 1970
>Original: Mel Tillis, 1963
>Elvis's version can be heard on Real Fun On Stage...And In The Studio (unofficial)

Probably best known in the version by Bobby Bare (later covered by Welsh singer Tom Jones), the original was recorded by Mel Tillis, who wrote the number together with Danny Dill. Elvis sang three lines in a concert in the Olympia Arena, Detroit, in 1970, before a crowd of 16,000. Perhaps his friend Tom Jones was in the audience!

Don't Forbid Me (Singleton)
>Recorded by Elvis on Tuesday, 4 December, 1956
>Original: Pat Boone, 1956
>Elvis's version can be heard on The Complete Million Dollar Session; Today, Tomorrow And Forever

Recorded during the jam session at the Sun Studios, known as "The Million Dollar Quartet." Jerry Lee Lewis (The Killer) was at the session, along with Carl Perkins and Elvis (Johnny Cash was there for at least some time, but it is not certain that he was actually caught on tape). Pat Boone was the establishment's attempt to tone down Rock'n'Roll and it almost succeeded, Boone selling more records than anyone other than Elvis in the late 1950s. With Boone's willing approval, lyrics were cleaned up and movement on stage was kept to a minimum. Elvis allowed the black part of the music to shine through, whereas Boone tried to whitewash it away.

Don't It Make You Wanna Go Home (South)
>Recorded by Elvis on Wednesday, 29 July, 1970
>Original: Joe South, 1969
>Elvis's version can be heard on The Brightest Star on Sunset Boulevard (unofficial release)

Elvis never recorded a full version of this number, which, given its lyrics, is a great shame, as it could almost have been written for him. An official release, *That's The Way It Is Special Edition* also has Elvis singing four lines of the song, following the *Little Sister/Get Back* medley on CD 3, but this is not indicated in the track list. Joe South's original reached number 27 in the US charts in 1969.

Don't Think Twice, It's All Right (Dylan)
>Recorded by Elvis on Sunday, 16 May, 1971
>Original: Bob Dylan, 1963
>Elvis's version can be heard on Walk A Mile In My Shoes—The Essential 70's Masters Disc 4

Dylan's number was probably based on the Appalachian traditional *Who'll Buy Your Chickens When I'm Gone* first recorded by Paul Clayton. Robert Shelton, however, points to *Scarlet Ribbons For Her Hair* as the source for *Don't Think Twice*.

Down By The Riverside (Traditional/Giant/Baum/Kaye)
>Recorded by Elvis on Tuesday, 4 December, 1956
>Original: Elkins-Payne Jubilee Singers, 1923
>Elvis's version can be heard on The Complete Million Dollar Session; Double Features: Frankie and Johnny & Paradise, Hawaiian Style

Elvis sung along on this traditional gospel number with Carl Perkins and Jerry Lee Lewis during the Million Dollar Quartet jam session at the Sun Studios in December 1956. It would be almost 10 years, however, before he recorded a more secular version of the number for the soundtrack of the film *Frankie and Johnny*, where it was coupled with *When The Saints Go Marchin' In*.

Down In The Alley (Stone)
>Recorded by Elvis on Thursday, 26 May, 1966
>Original: Jesse Stone and The Clovers, 1953
>Elvis's version can be heard on Reconsider Baby; From Nashville to Memphis (3)

Elvis also recorded Stone's *Like A Baby* in 1960 and *Down In The Alley* in 1966.

Drums Of The Islands (Polynesian Culture Center/Tepper/Bennett)
>Recorded by Elvis on Monday, 26 July, 1965
>Original: Traditional Polynesian,?
>Elvis's version can be heard on Paradise, Hawaiian Style

The melody of this number is based on an old Tongan chant *Bula Lai*, so the rhythm pattern for this song dates from before the colonisation of the islands and is therefore of Pacific origin. The melody is copyrighted by The Polynesian Culture Center, who are therefore credited for the song together with Tepper and Bennett.

Early Morning Rain (Lightfoot)
>Recorded by Elvis on Monday, 15 March, 1971
>Original: Peter, Paul and Mary, 1965
>Elvis's version can be heard on Elvis Now; Elvis In Concert; Elvis in Nashville

Writer Gordon Lightfoot recorded his own version in 1966.

Earth Angel (Belvin/Williams/Hodge)
>Recorded by Elvis on April 1959 (perhaps later)
>Original: Jesse & Marvin, 1954
>Elvis's version can be heard on A Golden Celebration

Jesse & Marvin recorded their version prior to The Penguins. The Penguins, however, scored a number one in the R&B charts with this number. Co-author Curtis Williams was leader of The Penguins. Elvis's recording is a home recording, made in Goethestrasse, Bad Nauheim, Germany, during his army service.

El Paso (Robbins)
> Recorded by Elvis on Thursday, 30 March, 1972
> Original: Marty Robbins, 1959
> Elvis's version can be heard on Between Takes (unofficial recording)

Marty Robbins is something of a legend in the world of Country and Western: he was the last performer to sing at the Grand Ole Opry's Ryman Auditorium and the first to perform at the new Opryland. He wrote *El Paso* in 1959, but Columbia Records were initially reluctant to release it as a single because of its length. Public demand was so great following its LP appearance on *Gunfighter Ballads and Trail Songs*, however, that the single was released in late 1959 and became an international best-seller. In 1960 the song received a Grammy Award for Best Country and Western Performance. Elvis is not known to have officially recorded *El Paso*, but he did sing a line or two occasionally during some of his concerts in the 1970s.

End Of The Road (Berlin)
> Recorded by Elvis on Tuesday, 4 December, 1956
> Original: Fats Waller, 1927
> Elvis's version can be heard on The Complete Million Dollar Session

Originally titled *Waiting At The End Of The Road* and used as the theme for the film *Hallelujah* in 1929, when Waller re-recorded the number. That same year saw recordings by the Colonial Club Orchestra and none other than the Paul Whiteman Orchestra. Quite a heritage! Elvis does not actually sing on the recording made during the Million Dollar Quartet session!

Everybody Loves Somebody (Taylor/Lane)
> Recorded by Elvis on Monday, 23 February, 1970
> Original: Frank Sinatra, 1948
> Elvis's version can be heard on On Stage January 26th/February 23rd 1970—True Love Travels On a Gravel Road

Elvis sang about 4 lines of *Everybody Loves Somebody* during the closing show of one of his stints in Las Vegas. Dean Martin was in the audience at the time, and it was he who had a huge hit with the song in 1964. Perhaps Elvis thought that Deano had made the original recording, but then, Elvis didn't have the benefit of this book! It seems that another of the Rat Pack, Mr. Frank Sinatra himself, had already recorded the song quite some time before. Indeed, other artists had also recorded the number prior to Dean Martin, including Peggy Lee and Dinah Washington.

Faded Love (Wills/Wills)
>Recorded by Elvis on Sunday, 7 June, 1970
>Original: Bob Wills & His Texas Playboys, 1946
>Elvis's version can be heard on I'm 10,000 Years Old: Elvis Country; Walk A Mile In My Shoes—The Essential 70's Masters Disc 3

Bob's big success with *Faded Love* came in 1950, but his original recording of the number was made on the Tiffany label four years earlier. The song was originally just a fiddle tune, made up by Bob Wills' father, John Wills. Later Bob provided the words together with his bother, Billy Jack.

Fairytale (Pointer/Pointer)
>Recorded by Elvis on Monday, 10 March, 1975
>Original: The Pointer Sisters, 1974
>Elvis's version can be heard on Today; Elvis In Concert

The Pointer Sisters' original version was awarded a Grammy in the category Best Vocal Performance by a Duo or Group.

Farther Along (Stone)
>Recorded by Elvis on Friday, 27 May, 1966
>Original: Stamps Quartet, 1940s
>Elvis's version can be heard on The Complete Million Dollar Session; How Great Thou Art; Amazing Grace (CD 1)

W. B. Stone wrote this number in 1937. Elvis originally recorded this number during the jam session at the Sun Studios, known as The Million Dollar Quartet. He included it in the *How Great Thou Art* sessions, almost ten years later. The Stamps Quartet was originally formed in 1924 and, after numerous changes of personnel, became a regular with Elvis, both in the studio and on stage in the 1970s.

Feelings (Albert)
>Recorded by Elvis on Monday, 1 November, 1976
>Original: Morris Albert, 1975
>Elvis's version has yet to be released.

Brazilian singer/songwriter Morris Albert scored a big hit in South and Central America with his number *Feelings* before it was released in the USA, where it reached the top ten. It went on to become a worldwide hit. The Paris Appeals Court convicted Albert of plagiarism in 1987, forcing him to pay half a million dollars to French composer Louis Gasté who had accused Albert of using his composition *Pour Toi* as the basis of *Feelings*. *Pour Toi* was written for the film *Le Feu Aux Poudres* and was originally recorded in 1957 by Dario Moreno. It is said that *Feelings* was the last song recorded by Elvis during a studio session (October 31-November 1, 1976), but that it was never completed.

Fever (Cooley/Davenport)
  Recorded by Elvis on Sunday, 3 April, 1960
  Original: Little Willie John, 1958
  Elvis's version can be heard on Elvis Is Back!; Aloha From Hawaii Via Satellite

Talented Little Willie John's career was cut short in 1966 when he was convicted of manslaughter. He died in prison just two years later. The Davenport in the composer credits is a pseudonym for none other than Otis Blackwell. Davenport was the name of Blackwell's stepfather and was used because Little Willie John recorded for one music publisher, while Blackwell was under contract to another. Though Elvis almost certainly knew Little Willie John's version (Elvis's knowledge of black music was extensive), his own version is clearly based on Peggy Lee's (also from 1958), which has different lyrics and the same emphasis on the bass-line.

Find Out What's Happening (Crutchfield)
  Recorded by Elvis on Sunday, 22 July, 1973
  Original: Bobby Bare, 1968
  Elvis's version can be heard on Raised On Rock

Elvis fans might well remember the 1958 hit *All American Boy*, a parody of Elvis's joining the army, by Bill Parsons. Well, it wasn't Bill Parsons who sang it, but Bobby Bare—and Bare also wrote it! He recorded it as a sort of demo for Parsons, but the demo was then released with Parsons' name on it!

Five Sleepy Heads (Tepper/Bennett)
  Recorded by Elvis on Tuesday, 20 June, 1967
  Original: Arthur Rubinstein, 1947
  Elvis's version can be heard on Double Features: Easy Come, Easy Go; Speedway

Tepper and Bennett? Add German classical composer Johannes Brahms, for this song is a sort of pop version of his lullaby, *Guten Abend, Gute Nacht*. Brahms was born in Hamburg, Germany on 7 May 1833 and died in Vienna, Austria, on 3 April 1897. "The song was written in honor of the birth of a child of Brahms's friends Bertha and Artur Faber in 1868. Years earlier, Brahms had briefly fallen in love with Bertha when she was a young visitor to his female choir in Hamburg, and during the playful courtship she used to sing him a lilting 3/4-time Viennese melody. The romance ended, but the friendship endured, and the melody that Brahms later composed for the private lullaby was a creative counterpoint to the earlier love song that the child's mother would remember singing to the composer. When he presented the gift to the Fabers, Brahms included this note to her husband: "Frau Bertha will realize that I wrote the 'Wiegenlied' for her little one. She will find it quite in order…that while she is singing Hans to sleep, a love song is being sung to her." Bertha was the first person to sing Brahms's Lullaby." From *Johannes Brahms: A Biography*, by Jan Swafford (1997, Alfred A. Knopf, Inc.)

Flip, Flop And Fly (Calhoun/Turner)

    Recorded by Elvis on Saturday, 28 January, 1956

    Original: Joe Turner, 1955

    Elvis's version can be heard on A Golden Celebration; Recorded Live On Stage In Memphis

Charles Calhoun is a pseudonym of Jesse Stone, who was also responsible for other Elvis originals *Money Honey* and *Shake Rattle And Roll*. Elvis sang *Flip, Flop And Fly* together with *Shake, Rattle and Roll* on the CBS *Stage Show* TV programme—a white man singing black music with the original words, just like a black man (white covers always "toned down" the originals). Was this the start of integration? Elvis continued to use the number in his live performances in the 1970s.

Folsom Prison Blues (Cash)

    Recorded by Elvis on Friday, 14 August, 1970

    Original: Johnny Cash, 1955

    Elvis's version can be heard on The Entertainer (unofficial release)

Johnny Cash had a big hit on Billboard's Country chart in 1955, reaching number 5. It was his second release on the Sun label and was recorded in July 1955. He rerecorded the number in 1968 and scored another big hit, receiving a Grammy Award for best country and western male vocal in 1969. Elvis coupled *Folsom Prison Blues* with *I Walk The Line*, another Cash hit, at some of his Las Vegas and Lake Tahoe shows.

Fool (Sigman/Last)
> Recorded by Elvis on Tuesday, 28 March, 1972
> Original: Wayne Newton, 1969
> Elvis's version can be heard on Walk A Mile In My Shoes—The Essential 70's Masters Disc 2

Although Wayne Newton was the first to record a version of this number with the name *Fool* in 1972, the real "original" was made by composer and bandleader James Last. His version, titled *No Words*, appeared on his 1971 LP, *Star Portrait*.

Fool, Fool, Fool (Nugetre)
> Recorded by Elvis on January or February, 1955
> Original: The Clovers, 1951
> Elvis's version can be heard on The Complete 50's Masters 5 (Rare and Rockin') Disc 5

This number was recorded for radio in Lubbock, Texas. Elvis visited Lubbock on January 6 and February 13, 1955, so it was probably recorded on one of these dates. The number was a chart-topper for The Clovers in 1951. Nugetre? Written in reverse, it spells Ertegun—Ahmet Ertegun was the boss of Atlantic Records and he wrote several decent numbers, including Big Joe Turner's *Chains of Love* and Ben E. King's *Don't Play That Song*. Ertegun competed with RCA and others for Elvis's Sun contract in 1955, but was unable to offer more than US$25,000 ("That was everything we had, including my desk," he said to Elvis biographer Jerry Hopkins). And just to put this into perspective, Atlantic had just bought another contract they absolutely had to have, that of Ray Charles, for which they paid US$2,500.

Fools Fall In Love (Leiber/Stoller)
> Recorded by Elvis on Saturday, 28 May, 1966
> Original: The Drifters, 1957
> Elvis's version can be heard on From Nashville to Memphis (3)

The Drifters were formed in 1953, with ex-Dominoes singer Clyde McPhatter as front man. By the time they recorded this number, however, McPhatter had left the group and Johnny Moore (ex Three Blazers) sang the lead. Elvis's version was originally released as the B-side of *Indescribably Blue*.

Fools Rush In (Where Angels Fear To Tread) (Mercer/Bloom)
>Recorded by Elvis on Tuesday, 18 May, 1971
>Original: Mildred Bailey, 1940
>Elvis's version can be heard on Elvis Now

Both Glenn Miller and Tommy Dorsey also recorded this number in 1940—Frank Sinatra provided the vocals on Dorsey's version. Elvis's version copied the arrangement of the 1963 recording of Ricky Nelson, on which James Burton played lead guitar. An informal home recording, dating from 1966, of Elvis singing this number at a much gentler pace, was released officially on the CD *In A Private Moment*.

For Ol' Times Sake (White)
>Recorded by Elvis on Monday, 23 July, 1973
>Original: Tony Joe White, 1973
>Elvis's version can be heard on Raised On Rock; Walk A Mile In My Shoes Disc 2

Tony Joe White recorded the original for inclusion on his LP, *Homemade Ice Cream*. Elvis also recorded Tony Joe White's *Polk Salad Annie* and *I've Got A Thing About You Baby*.

For The Good Times (Kristofferson)
>Recorded by Elvis on Monday, 27 March, 1972
>Original: Kris Kristofferson, 1970
>Elvis's version can be heard on Elvis as Recorded at Madison Square Garden; Walk A Mile In My Shoes—The Essential 70's Masters Disc 4

Composer Kris Kristofferson may have cut the original, but Ray Price scored the biggest hit that same year, 1970, when he reached number one in the C&W charts. The version on the album *Elvis as Recorded at Madison Square Garden* was recorded on June 10, 1972, whereas the studio version that appears on *Walk A Mile In My Shoes—The Essential 70's Masters Disc 4* was recorded on March 27, 1972. See also *Help Me Make It Through The Night* and *Why Me Lord*.

Frankie And Johnny (Gottlieb/Karger/Weisman)
>Recorded by Elvis on Thursday, 13 May, 1965
>Original: Charlie Porter And The North Carolina Ramblers (?), 1926
>Elvis's version can be heard on Frankie And Johnny

A reference to Frankie and Johnny is made in the 1926 recording *Leavin' Home* by Charlie Porter And The North Carolina Ramblers. The oldest known publication of the tune dates from 1904, under the title *He Done Me Wrong (The Death Of Bill Bailey)*, written by Hughie Cannon, and the song was first published as *Frankie And Johnny* in 1912, with composer and lyricist credits going to The Leighton Brothers and Ren Shields. The songs origins, however, go back much further, but would require their own book to be fully investigated. The number, then, is a traditional, though the version for the film seems to have merited its own writers' credits.

Froggy Went a'Courtin' (Peretti/Creatore/Rodgers)
    Recorded by Elvis on Wednesday, 29 July, 1970
    Original: Jimmie Rodgers, 1958
    Elvis's version can be heard on Walk A Mile In My Shoes—The Essential 70s Masters, CD 5

Probably based on a much earlier folk song, Rodgers "wrote" this number together with Peretti and Creatore, who are more associated with Elvis as part of the team that came up with *Can't Help Falling In Love*. Jimmie Rodgers should not be confused with the Singing Brakeman of the 1920s and 1930s, of the same name and, incidentally, a favourite of Gladys Presley, Elvis's mother.

From A Jack To A King (Miller)
    Recorded by Elvis on Wednesday, 22 January, 1969
    Original: Ned Miller, 1957
    Elvis's version can be heard on Back In Memphis; From Nashville to Memphis (4)

Ned Miller recorded this song in 1957, when it was released as a single, but failed to chart. It was reissued in 1962, then reaching number 2 on the Billboard Country chart and number 6 on the Hot 100 chart.

Funny How Time Slips Away (Nelson)
    Recorded by Elvis on Saturday, 10 June, 1972
    Original: Billy Walker, 1961
    Elvis's version can be heard on I'm 10,000 Years Old: Elvis Country; Walk A Mile In My Shoes—The Essential 70's Masters Disc 3; Elvis as Recorded at Madison Square Garden

Composer Willie Nelson recorded his own version in 1962. A concert version by Elvis recorded at Shreveport, Louisiana on June 7, 1975 is listed in the box set *Elvis Aron Presley*.

Gentle On My Mind (Hartford)
>Recorded by Elvis on Tuesday, 14 January, 1969
>Original: John Hartford, 1967
>Elvis's version can be heard on From Elvis in Memphis; From Nashville to Memphis (4)

Surely one of the highlights of the *From Elvis In Memphis* album, which itself must rank as one of Elvis's very best. If you want only one Elvis album in your collection, get this one and forget about the rest. I can stick the headphones on, set the CD player to replay, and listen to this number over and over again. A real gem! John Hartford was something of an eccentric; as well as being a musician and composer, he was also an author and riverboat captain and could dance a mean soft-shoe shuffle. He died in 2001.

Get Back (Lennon/McCartney)
>Recorded by Elvis on Wednesday, 12 August, 1970
>Original: The Beatles, 1969
>Elvis's version can be heard on Elvis Aron Presley (silver box set); Live In Las Vegas

Although listed as a Lennon-McCartney composition, it was Paul McCartney who was solely responsible for *Get Back*, composed at a difficult time for The Beatles and in an attempt to "get back" to their roots. The recording featured Paul on lead vocal and Billy Preston on organ, who was also credited on the record label. Elvis sometimes coupled *Get Back* with *Little Sister* during live appearances in the 1970s. A recording of Elvis rehearsing the number on 29 July 1970 also exists.

Ghost Riders In The Sky (Jones)
>Recorded by Elvis on Wednesday, 15 July, 1970
>Original: Stan Jones, 1949
>Elvis's version can be heard on The Way It Was

Having failed to get music publishing companies interested in his songs, Stan Jones recorded several of them, including this one, himself. Composer Eden Ahbez (best known for the hit *Nature Boy*) heard *Ghost Riders in the Sky* and brought it to Burl Ives, who cut it for Columbia Records. It was later picked up by Bing Crosby, Gene Autry, and Vaughn Monroe, as well as dozens of others, and Jones had a new career and major Hollywood representation. Elvis's recording is taken from a rehearsal and was not originally intended for release; indeed, it was not released officially for over thirty years!

Girl Next Door Went A Walkin' (Rice/Wayne)
>Recorded by Elvis on Monday, 4 April, 1960
>Original: Thomas Wayne, 1959
>Elvis's version can be heard on Elvis Is Back!; From Nashville to Memphis (1)

Thomas Wayne, co-writer and original recording artist, was a graduate of L.C. Humes High School, just like Elvis! His original single carried the title *Girl Next Door*; early pressings of *Elvis Is Back!* listed the number as *The Girl Next Door* and later pressings as *The Girl Next Door Went a-Walking*.

Girls! Girls! Girls! (Leiber/Stoller)
>Recorded by Elvis on Tuesday, 27 March, 1962
>Original: The Coasters, 1960
>Elvis's version can be heard on Double Features: Kid Galahad & Girls! Girls! Girls!

The Coasters, one of *the* groups of the 50s and early 60s, recorded many Leiber and Stoller numbers. *Little Egypt* was another Leiber and Stoller number that both the Coasters and Elvis recorded.

Give Me More, More, More Of Your Kisses (Price/Frizzell)
>Recorded by Elvis in 1955(?)
>Original: Lefty Frizzell, 1951
>Elvis's version can be heard on Uncle Pen (unofficial 2-track CD)

Frizzel was a real innovator in style and presentation and a major influence on others singers. After a less than successful spell as a boxer, Frizzell turned to singing, with considerably more success: in 1951 he held the number one position in the Country charts for more than half the year. And Elvis's rhinestone-encrusted jumpsuits can also be traced back to Lefty! Frizzell was the first singer to wear rhinestones on stage, in an outfit designed by none other than Nudie Cohen, the man who created Elvis's gold lamé suit. Lefty Frizzell died in 1975. He was inducted into the Country Music Hall of Fame in 1982. As for Elvis's version of this number, well, it appeared on a rather mysterious 2-song CD put out on the Suedes label (KAYS 1955-578-1), which might be a recording of Elvis performing the number live on a radio show. The cover reads, "We cannot make any statements about the identity of the singer, firstly because of legal reasons and secondly because we really don't know." But take a look at the entry for *Uncle Pen*, below!

Good Rockin' Tonight (Brown)
>Recorded by Elvis on Friday, 10 September, 1954
>Original: Roy Brown with The Bob Ogden Orchestra, 1947
>Elvis's version can be heard on The Sun Sessions CD; The Complete 50's Masters 1

Was Roy Brown's *Good Rockin' Tonight* the first Rock'n'Roll record? Brown first offered his number to Wynonie Harris, who turned it down. Brown recorded it himself and the number reached the R&B Top 20, so Wynonie Harris then recorded it and scored a number one R&B hit in 1948. Pat Boone sang the only version to get into the American top 100. Sorry, but can you really imagine Pat Boone singing *Good Rockin' Tonight*...?

Good Time Charlie's Got The Blues (O'Keefe)
>Recorded by Elvis on Thursday, 13 December, 1973
>Original: Danny O'Keefe, 1967
>Elvis's version can be heard on Good Times; Walk A Mile In My Shoes—The Essential 70's Masters Disc 4

Composer Danny O'Keefe recorded this number on no less than three separate occasions! The original dates from 1967, on the Jerden label; then came a version on the Cotillion label in 1971; finally O'Keefe recorded his hit version for the Signpost label in 1972. Elvis did not sing the lines "I got my pills to ease the pain, Can't find a thing to ease my brain."

Got My Mojo Working (Foster)
>Recorded by Elvis on Friday, 5 June, 1970
>Original: Ann Cole, 1957
>Elvis's version can be heard on Love Letters From Elvis; Walk A Mile In My Shoes—The Essential 70's Masters Disc 3

Ann Cole originally recorded with her own gospel group, the Colemanaires, under her own name, Cynthia Coleman, but changed names when she started recording R&B numbers in the 50s. *Got My Mojo Working* might be associated with Muddy Waters, but he learned the number from Ann Cole, who sang it as part of the warm-up act at Muddy's concerts. Both artists recorded the song at about the same time, but Muddy's version had the benefit of better distribution and so became the bigger hit.

Green, Green Grass Of Home (Putman)
> Recorded by Elvis on Tuesday, 11 March, 1975
> Original: Johnny Darrell, 1965
> Elvis's version can be heard on Today; Walk A Mile In My Shoes—The Essential 70's Masters Disc 2

Curly Putman's own version also dates from 1965, but Johnny Darrell's recording was first. That same year also saw versions by Porter Wagoner, Jerry Lee Lewis, and Ferlin Husky. Welshman Tom Jones's UK number one version was recorded in 1966. It was Jones's version that persuaded Elvis to record the number.

Guadalajara (Pepe Guízar)
> Recorded by Elvis on Wednesday, 23 January, 1963
> Original: Pepe Guízar, 1938
> Elvis's version can be heard on Double Features: It Happened At The World's Fair & Fun In Acapulco

Pepe Guízar wrote the number in 1938 and then went on to perform it in the film *Caminos de Ayer* (also called *La Mano de Dios*).

Guitar Man (Hubbard)
> Recorded by Elvis on Sunday, 10 September, 1967
> Original: Jerry Reed, 1967
> Elvis's version can be heard on Elvis in Nashville; From Nashville to Memphis (3); NBC-TV Special

Jerry Reed and Jerry Hubbard are one and the same—Hubbard is the real name. Jerry played guitar on Elvis's recording of this number. See also *A Thing Called Love*, *U.S. Male* and *Talk About The Good Times*.

Hands Off (Bowman/McShann)
> Recorded by Elvis on Autumn 1960
> Original: Jay McShann, 1955
> Elvis's version can be heard on The Home Recordings

This was McShann's biggest hit, featuring Priscilla Bowman on vocals. According to the sleeve-notes of *The Home Recordings*, this number was recorded in Perugia Way, Bel Air; the book, *A Life In Music*, however, gives Monovale Drive, Hollywood, as the recording location. The number itself isn't original, being a rewrite of a country song called *Keep Your Hands Off Of It (Birthday Cake)*.

Happy Birthday (Hill/Hill/Coleman)

    Recorded by Elvis on Thursday, 21 August, 1969
    Original: Leningrad Philharmonic and Academic Choir (but see note), 1927
    Elvis's version can be heard on Collectors Gold

Yes, *Happy Birthday To You*. But that's not how the song started out! The sisters Mildred and Patty Hill wrote the original song for children and published it in 1893 as *Good Morning To All*. Robert Coleman published the song again in 1924 without the sisters' permission, adding a second verse—*Happy Birthday To You*. This verse became so popular that everyone forgot about the first! Enter sister number three, Jessica Hill: she, together with Patty (Mildred died in 1916), sued for and won ownership of the song. The family now legally owns the song and is entitled to a royalty payment each time it is played for commercial purposes! The version on *Collectors Gold* was sung in concert in Las Vegas for James Burton. Some unofficial releases also provide renditions of the song by Elvis in concert: at Fort Worth for sound engineer Bruce "Goose" Jackson, 3 June 1976 (*Cajun Tornado*) and on Tuesday, May 3, 1977, he sang it at a concert in Saginaw for Linda Thompson (*Springtime in Saginaw*). So what's all this got to do with the Leningrad Philharmonic, I hear you ask? Well, composer Shostakovich included the tune in the trumpet solo of his *Symphony Number 2*, written to celebrate the tenth anniversary of the October Revolution! This was a performance, rather than a recording, but it looks good, doesn't it? As for the first recording, this was probably made by Shirley Temple in her 1934 film, *Baby Take a Bow* (her first film, incidentally).

Happy, Happy Birthday Baby (Lopez/Sylvia)

    Recorded by Elvis on Wednesday, 28 May, 1958
    Original: Tune Weavers, 1957
    Elvis's version can be heard on Forever Young, Forever Beautiful (unofficial release)

Gilbert Lopez and his sister, Margo Sylvia, wrote *Happy, Happy Birthday Baby* in 1952. Together with their cousin, Charlotte Davis, and Margo's husband, John, they formed the Tune Weavers and recorded the number in 1957, reaching number 5 on Billboard's Top 100 and number 4 on the R&B chart. The recording of Elvis singing the song was made by his friend, Eddie Fadal, when Elvis was visiting his home in Waco Texas, during his national service.

Harbor Lights (Grosz/Kennedy)
    Recorded by Elvis on Monday, 5 July, 1954
    Original: Ray Fox Orchestra, vocal Barry Gray, 1937
    Elvis's version can be heard on The Sun Sessions CD; The Complete 50's Masters 1

Harbor Lights is not an American, but a British original, so the correct spelling of the original is *Harbour Lights*. The first American spelling version was also recorded in 1937 by Claude Thornhill.

Hava Nagila (Nathanson)
    Recorded by Elvis on Wednesday, 15 July, 1970
    Original: Harry Belafonte, 1959
    Elvis's version can be heard on Electrifying (Bilko 5100 unofficial CD)

Based on a traditional tune, perhaps originating in the Ukraine. The tune itself is in the public domain, so anyone can publish, arrange and play about with it, though an exact reproduction of the originally published lead sheet (1932) would be an infringement of so-called mechanical rights.

Have I Told You Lately That I Love You (Wiseman)
    Recorded by Elvis on Saturday, 19 January, 1957
    Original: Lulu Belle & Scotty, 1945
    Elvis's version can be heard on The Complete 50's Masters 3

The Scotty of the original duo is Scott Wiseman, composer of *Have I Told You Lately*. He wrote this number after his wife said the phrase whilst visiting him in hospital in Chicago in 1944. Lulu Belle and Scotty were known as The Sweethearts Of Country Music.

Hawaiian Wedding Song (King/Hoffman/Manning)
    Recorded by Elvis on Wednesday, 22 March, 1961
    Original: Andy Williams, 1958
    Elvis's version can be heard on Blue Hawaii

The original title of this number, written in 1926 by Charles King, was *Ke Kali Nei Au*. Charles King made a recording of his own song in 1926. Bing Crosby recorded an English language version in 1951, but new English lyrics were provided by Al Hoffman and Dick Manning in 1958, providing Andy Williams with a hit at the time when Hawaii became the fiftieth State of the USA. These are the lyrics used in Elvis's version of the number.

He (Richards/Mullen)
>Recorded by Elvis in 1960
>Original: Al Hibbler, 1955
>Elvis's version can be heard on In A Private Moment

Al Hibbler's original reached number 4 in the US charts in 1955 (The McGuire Sisters' cover of the same period got to number 10). Hibbler was born in Mississippi in 1915. He sang with the Duke Ellington Band through the 1940s, leaving in 1951 to pursue a solo career. He often sang in an idiosyncratic manner (as was the case with this number) and sometimes used a Cockney accent. Hibbler died in 2001.

He Is My Everything (Frazier)
>Recorded by Elvis on Wednesday, 9 June, 1971
>Original: Jack Greene, 1968
>Elvis's version can be heard on He Touched Me; Amazing Grace (CD2)

Jack Greene had a big hit in 1966 with his original version of Frazier's *There Goes My Everything* (see below)—notice anything about the title? Pretty similar, isn't it? That's because composer Dallas Frazier simply rewrote the lyrics to his earlier secular success to come up with this modern gospel number.

He Knows Just What I Need (Lister)
>Recorded by Elvis on Sunday, 30 October, 1960
>Original: Mosie Lister, 1955
>Elvis's version can be heard on His Hand In Mine; Amazing Grace (CD 1)

Mosie Lister was the leader of the Statesmen Quartet, an influential white gospel group. He also wrote *His Hand In Mine* and *Where No One Stands Alone*, also recorded by Elvis.

He Touched Me (Gaither)
>Recorded by Elvis on Tuesday, 18 May, 1971
>Original: Bill Gaither Trio, 1963
>Elvis's version can be heard on He Touched Me; Amazing Grace (CD2)

One of the most successful songwriters in all of Christian music, Bill Gaither was an original member of the renowned gospel music act the Gaither Trio (made up of Gaither, his brother Bill, and sister Mary Ann). Bill's wife, Gloria, later replaced Mary Ann in the group, which was inducted into the Gospel Music Association Hall of Fame in 1999. In addition to recording with the trio, Bill and Gloria recorded as a duo and as part of the Gaither Vocal Band. Bill Gaither released a solo CD in 2002 entitled *He Touched Me.*

He'll Have To Go (Allison/Allison)
>Recorded by Elvis on Sunday, 31 October, 1976
>Original: Billy Brown, 1959
>Elvis's version can be heard on Moody Blue; Walk A Mile In My Shoes—The Essential 70's Masters Disc 4

A number perhaps most associated with "Gentleman" Jim Reeves, who scored a C&W number one with it in 1959, but rockabilly artist Billy Brown recorded it first on Columbia 41380.

Hearts Of Stone (Ray/Jackson)
>Recorded by Elvis on Saturday, 15 January, 1955
>Original: The Jewels, 1954
>Elvis's version can be heard on Sunrise

A fairly recent Elvis "find," having first appeared officially on the 1999 *Sunrise* double-CD set—a very early and very scratchy live recording, possibly made in Lubbock, Texas, at a concert attended by Buddy Holly.

Help Me (Gatlin)
>Recorded by Elvis on Wednesday, 12 December, 1973
>Original: Connie Smith, 1973
>Elvis's version can be heard on Promised Land; Amazing Grace (CD2)

It is possible that Larry Gatlin recorded his own version of his composition in 1972, but I have been unable to verify this. Johnny Cash featured the song in a film that year, but did not record it until considerably later. Connie Smith had enormous success as a country singer, but then chose to devote her life to her family and faith. She has, however, recently attempted a come-back.

Help Me Make It Through The Night (Kristofferson)
>Recorded by Elvis on Monday, May 17, 1971
>Original: Sammi Smith, 1970
>Elvis's version can be heard on Elvis Now

Sammi Smith's 1970 recording reached number one in the C&W charts. See also *For The Good Times* and *Why Me Lord*, both numbers by Kris Kristofferson.

Here Comes Santa Claus (Autry/Haldeman)
Recorded by Elvis on Friday, 6 September, 1957
Original: Gene Autry, 1947
Elvis's version can be heard on Elvis' Christmas Album; If Every Day Was Like Christmas

When Gene Autry took part in a Christmas parade in Hollywood in November 1947, he heard children shouting "Here Comes Santa Claus" all along the route. By December he and Oakley Haldeman had written the song and Autrey's own recording was in the Billboard Best Selling Singles top ten.

Hey Jude (Lennon/McCartney)
Recorded by Elvis on Wednesday, 22 January, 1969
Original: The Beatles, 1968
Elvis's version can be heard on Elvis Now; From Nashville to Memphis (4)

For contractual reasons, John Lennon's name appears in the writer credits, but the number was the sole work of Paul McCartney. He wrote it in the car whilst on his way to visit Lennon; the original title was *Hey Jules,* the Jules in question being Lennon's son, Julian.

Hide Thou Me (Crosby)
Recorded by Elvis in 1966
Original: Chuck Wagon Gang, 1941
Elvis's version can be heard on In A Private Moment

Frances Jane Crosby is probably the world's most prolific hymn-writer, though she is better known as Fanny Crosby and also had hymns published under many pseudonyms. During her lifetime, she wrote more than 8,000 (yes, eight thousand) hymns, including *Hide Thou Me* (from 1880), a hymn usually sung to the same tune as *Rock Of Ages,* dating from 1899, though the original music was composed by Rev. Robert Lowry, who often collaborated with Crosby.

Elvis's version was recorded at home in Rocca Place, California, and was never intended for commercial release.

High Heel Sneakers (Higginbotham)
>Recorded by Elvis on Monday, 11 September, 1967
>Original: Tommy Tucker, 1964
>Elvis's version can be heard on Reconsider Baby; From Nashville to Memphis (3)

Or even *Hi-Heel Sneaker*, which was how the title of the original was written. Presumably assuming that his given name was not a commercial asset, Robert Higginbotham took Tommy Tucker as his performing name. Atlantic wasn't interested in this number and sold the rights to Chess, who promptly released the song. Alter ego Robert Higginbotham continued as a jazz musician, who played organ, piano, drums, bass and clarinet in a variety of bands. Tucker/Higginbotham died of food poisoning on January 22, 1982.

High Noon (Do Not Forsake Me Oh My Darlin') (Tiomkin/Washington)
>Recorded by Elvis on Sunday, 10 September, 1967
>Original: Frankie Laine, 1952
>Elvis's version can be heard on Platinum, A Life In Music

Just a one-liner by Elvis during the recording of *Guitar Man*. The song *Do Not Forsake Me Oh My Darlin'* was the theme song for the 1952 film *High Noon*. The film won seven Academy Awards, including one for Best Song for its theme.

His Hand In Mine (Lister)
>Recorded by Elvis on Sunday, 30 October, 1960
>Original: The Statesmen, 1953
>Elvis's version can be heard on His Hand In Mine; Amazing Grace (CD 1)

Mosie Lister, who wrote this number, did the arrangements for The Statesmen, but did not sing in the group. The Statesmen Quartet was formed by Hovie Lister in 1948 and was originally made up of Mosie Lister, Bobby Strickland, Bervin Kendricks and Gordon Hill. Jake Hess, a great favourite of Elvis and possibly an influence on his singing style, replaced Mosie Lister after a few months and sang lead on their original version of this number.

Hot Dog (Leiber/Stoller)
>Recorded by Elvis on Friday, 18 January, 1957
>Original: Young Jessie, 1956
>Elvis's version can be heard on Loving You; The Complete 50's Masters Disc 3

Young Jessie recorded this number in 1956, but it was not issued until much later, probably the 80s (although I have heard that there was a release on the

Modern label that same year—proof, anyone?). A different number by the same name was recorded by Buck Owens under the pseudonym Corky Jones.

Hound Dog (Leiber/Stoller)
>Recorded by Elvis on Monday, 2 July, 1956
>Original: Willie Mae "Big Mama" Thornton, 1952
>Elvis's version can be heard on Elvis' Golden Records; Recorded Live On Stage In Memphis ELV1S 30 #1 Hits

Rock'n'Roll in a nutshell: one of the truly great rock songs, written by one of the truly great rock writing teams and performed by the truly great performer, Elvis. But before him came Big Mama Thornton's version, which itself sold more than two million copies! Although released in 1953, the original recording was actually made in 1952. Its release was delayed, however, because of Johnny Otis's assertion that he should share in the authors' rights. Although Thornton had the original, Elvis did not base his version on hers. Rather, it would seem that he was heavily influenced by the performance of the number by Freddie Bell and The Bellboys, which he saw during his first stint in Las Vegas.

How Do You Think I Feel (Walker/Pierce)
>Recorded by Elvis on Saturday, 1 September, 1956
>Original: Jimmie Rodgers Snow, 1954
>Elvis's version can be heard on Elvis; The Complete 50's Masters 2

Jimmie Rodgers Snow was Hank Snow's son. Red Sovine also had a version of *How Do You Think I feel* issued in 1954. I am not sure whether he or Jimmie Rogers Snow recorded it first.

How Great Thou Art (Boberg/Hine)
>Recorded by Elvis on Wednesday, 25 May, 1966
>Original: George Beverly Shea, 1955
>Elvis's version can be heard on How Great Thou Art; Amazing Grace (CD 1); Elvis In Concert

This number comes originally from Sweden, with English words by Stuart K. Hine. The number was originally a 9-verse poem called *O Store Gud* and was written in 1886 by Pastor Carl Boberg, inspired during a visit to a country estate in the south-east of Sweden, when he was caught in a huge thunderstorm which was followed by clear and brilliant sunshine and he then heard birds singing nearby. Several years later the words were set to a traditional Swedish folk melody. A German version was created in 1907 and some 5 years later a Russian version. English lyrics were provided for the first three verses by the Rev. Stuart Hine in about 1933 and for the fourth verse in 1947. Elvis loved singing this number in concert. (Note that I came across all sorts of stories and dates when trying to find the origins of this number. I present here a synthesis that seems to approach the truth!)

How The Web Was Woven (Clive Westlake/David Most)
Recorded by Elvis on Friday, 5 June, 1970
Original: Jackie Lomax, 1969
Elvis's version can be heard on That's The Way It Is; Walk A Mile In My Shoes—The Essential 70's Masters Disc 1

This number was recorded by Lomax as his final single for the Beatles' Apple label. It was selected and produced by George Harrison. Lomax's single had another Elvis connection: the B-side, *Thumbin' a Ride*, was written by Leiber and Stoller!

How's The World Treating You (Atkins/Bryant)
Recorded by Elvis on Saturday, 1 September, 1956
Original: Eddy Arnold, 1953
Elvis's version can be heard on Elvis; The Complete 50's Masters 2

No less than Chet Atkins wrote this number, together with Eddy Arnold (he's the "Bryant") and Arnold's version got to number 4 in the Country Chart. Eddy Arnold was a big name in Country music, with over 140 hits to his credit. Tom Parker managed Arnold before he saw the gold in Elvis. Elvis seems to have seen some gold in Arnold, though—he covered seven of his numbers, this being the first.

Hurt (Crane/Jacobs)
Recorded by Elvis on Thursday, 5 February, 1976
Original: Roy Hamilton, 1954
Elvis's version can be heard on From Elvis Presley Boulevard, Memphis Tennessee; Elvis In Concert

Roy Hamilton is the typical big ballad singer that Elvis really liked. In addition to *Hurt*, Elvis also recorded *You'll Never Walk Alone*, Hamilton's first record and a major success in 1954.

I Apologize (Hoffman/Goodhart/Nelson)
    Recorded by Elvis on?
    Original: Bing Crosby; Nat Shilkret, 1931
    Elvis's version has not been released.

I Apologize is probably most associated with Billy Eckstine, who had a million-selling hit with it in 1951. The number was, however, written by Al Hoffman, Al Goodhart and Ed Nelson in the 1930s, when both Bing Crosby and Nat Shilkret scored hits with it. There is no certainty that Elvis recorded *I Apologize* officially, though it is rumoured that he may have done so during his Sun days. In 1962 he sang a small part of the song, which can be heard before an alternate take of *Beyond The Bend* and in 1974 he also sang a part on stage in Lake Tahoe.

I Asked The Lord (Lange/Duncan)
    Recorded by Elvis on 1959 (After April)
    Original: Kate Smith, 1930
    Elvis's version can be heard on *A Golden Celebration*; *The Home Recordings*

RCA released this number on *A Golden Celebration* as *He's Only A Prayer Away*. Elvis recorded the number on a Grundig reel-to-reel consumer tape recorder in his rented house in Goethestrasse, Bad Nauheim, during his military service in Germany. A number of artists had recorded the song earlier, including Kate Smith and Mahalia Jackson. But is Kate Smith's the original recording? Difficult to ascertain!

I Believe (Drake/Graham/Shirl/Stillman)
    Recorded by Elvis on Saturday, 12 January, 1957
    Original: Jane Froman, 1953
    Elvis's version can be heard on *Elvis' Christmas Album*; *The Complete 50's Masters 2*; *Amazing Grace* (CD 1)

This was probably the first number to become a hit as a result of television exposure. Jane Froman first sang the number in her TV series *Jane Froman's USA* in 1952 and recorded the number early the following year, when it reached number 11 on the Billboard Best Selling Singles chart.

I Believe In The Man In The Sky (Howard)
>   Recorded by Elvis on Sunday, 30 October, 1960
>   Original: The Statesmen, 1955
>   Elvis's version can be heard on His Hand In Mine; Amazing Grace (CD 1)

Lead singer of The Statesmen was Jake Hess, a great favourite of Elvis and possibly an influence on his singing style.

I Can Help (Swan)
>   Recorded by Elvis on Tuesday, 11 March, 1975
>   Original: Billy Swan, 1974
>   Elvis's version can be heard on Today; Walk A Mile In My Shoes—The Essential 70's Masters Disc 4

A number one success for Swan. Billy Swan was once employed as a guard at Graceland. He also had a stint as a janitor, together with Kris Kristofferson, at Columbia Record Studios in Nashville!

I Can't Help It (If I'm Still In Love With You) (Williams)
>   Recorded by Elvis on April 1959(?)
>   Original: Hank Williams, 1951
>   Elvis's version can be heard on Platinum: A Life In Music (CD2)

From the blurb on the box of *Platinum: A Life In Music*: "Tapes recorded at Graceland about 1961 give us a further idea of what Elvis sounded like away from the recording studios and movie stages. We also get a sense of, what he listened to and sang for his own pleasure. *I Can't Help It* was one of Hank Williams greatest hits and one that Elvis undoubtedly heard as a kid." Well, pure speculation, but quite possible, of course. Jorgensen's *A Life In Music* gives the recording date as April 1959. What is certain is that Hank Williams was a pioneer and one of the greats of C&W music and Elvis recorded several of his numbers, both formally and informally. Indeed, this number exists on an earlier, but very unofficial, recording, which was made at Eddie Fadal's home in Waco, Texas: on that recording, Elvis plays piano and joins in on the chorus, as Anita Wood takes the lead.

I Can't Stop Loving You (Gibson)

> Recorded by Elvis on Monday, 25 August, 1969
> Original: Don Gibson, 1958
> Elvis's version can be heard on Aloha From Hawaii Via Satellite; From Nashville to Memphis (5)

Not a Ray Charles original, though I'm sure that most readers would have supplied his name for this number. Don Gibson wrote and recorded *I Can't Stop Loving You* as the B-side of his country blockbuster *Oh, Lonesome Me*.

I Don't Care If The Sun Don't Shine (David)

> Recorded by Elvis on Friday, 10 September, 1954
> Original: Patti Page, 1950
> Elvis's version can be heard on The Sun Sessions CD; The Complete 50's Masters 1

This song was originally submitted for the score of the Disney cartoon *Cinderella*, but was not used in the film. Elvis was not really a rocker at heart (though he might well have been a rocker in his soul…). His musical tastes were many and varied, but he seemed to have a predilection for apparent opposites: Blues singers and Crooners! His own version of *I Don't Care*…seems to be based on that of his very favorite crooner, Dean Martin! The story goes that when Elvis decided to record it for Sun, he could not remember all of the song, so Marion Keisker, assistant to Sun producer Sam Phillips, wrote additional lyrics. The song's publisher insisted that Marion sign a disclaimer that her name would not be on the label nor would she receive royalties. Marion agreed. It was released as the B-side of the *Good Rockin' Tonight* single.

I Feel So Bad (Willis)

> Recorded by Elvis on Sunday, 12 March, 1961
> Original: Chuck Willis, 1954
> Elvis's version can be heard on Golden Records Vol.3; From Nashville to Memphis (1)

Elvis's version of this number closely follows Chuck Willis's 1954 recording in both style and arrangement. Note that Lightnin' Hopkins recorded a number called *I Feel So Bad* in 1946, but that it is a completely different song!

I Got A Woman (Charles/Richard)
>Recorded by Elvis on Tuesday, 10 January, 1956
>Original: Ray Charles, 1954
>Elvis's version can be heard on Elvis Presley (Rock 'n' Roll No.1); Recorded Live On Stage In Memphis

Ray Charles recorded this number as *I've Got A Woman*. According to Renald Richard, Charles's bandleader at the time, they wrote the number after hearing and singing along to a gospel number, whilst driving to Nashville from a gig in South Bend, Indiana. Charles liked the tune and asked Richard if he could do something with it; the next morning, *I've Got A Woman* was written. The original gospel song was probably an Alex Brown hymn that began, "I've got a saviour, way over Jordan, He's saved my soul, oh yeah…" In 1951 the Bailey Gospel Singers recorded a version as *I've Got A Savior (Across Town)*.

I Gotta Know (Evans/Williams)
>Recorded by Elvis on Sunday, 3 April, 1960
>Original: Cliff Richard, 1959
>Elvis's version can be heard on Elvis Is Back; From Nashville to Memphis (CD1)

How Cliff Richard came to record *I Gotta Know* seems to be a mystery even to its composer, Paul Evans. He was given the choice of letting Fabian or Elvis record the song (now who remembers Fabian?) and chose Elvis, only later to learn that the song had already been recorded by British Elvis wannabe, Cliff Richard, in the September of the previous year, 1959. Elvis's version was used as the B-side of *Are You Lonesome Tonight?* but even as a B-side made it to number 14 in the charts!

I Hear A Sweet Voice Calling (Monroe)
>Recorded by Elvis on Tuesday, 4 December, 1956
>Original: Bill Monroe, 1947
>Elvis's version can be heard on The Complete Million Dollar Session

Bill Monroe is referred to as "the father of Bluegrass." He was born in 1911 and died in 1984 and might have been related to Marilyn Monroe through common descent from US President James Moore! Elvis recorded several Bill Monroe originals, including *Blue Moon Of Kentucky, Little Cabin On The Hill, Summertime Has Passed And Gone, Sweetheart You Done Me Wrong* and perhaps even *Uncle Pen*.

I Just Can't Help Believin' (Mann/Weil)
Recorded by Elvis on Tuesday, 11 August, 1970
Original: Barry Mann, 1968
Elvis's version can be heard on That's The Way It Is; Walk A Mile In My Shoes—The Essential 70's Masters Disc 1

Barry Mann, co-writer of the number, probably recorded his version before that of Bobby Vee. The latter version, however, appears on the Belgian CD *The Originals*, EVA 7895622. To add to the confusion, BJ Thomas seems to have had the first success with the number, reaching number 9 in the US Billboard charts in 1970.

I Just Can't Make It By Myself (Ward)
Recorded by Elvis on Tuesday, 4 December, 1956
Original: Blackwood Brothers, 1950s
Elvis's version can be heard on The Complete Million Dollar Session

Songwriter Clara Ward wrote mostly for the Ward Singers, but it seems that the Blackwood Brothers (favourites of Elvis) originally recorded this number in the 1950s. Ward perhaps based the song on an earlier "traditional." Exactly when the Blackwoods recorded their version as yet remains a mystery, however!

I Love Only One Girl (Tepper/Bennett)
Recorded by Elvis on Wednesday, 29 June, 1966
Original: Band of the Grenadier Guards (Canada), 1927(?)
Elvis's version can be heard on Double Features: Spinout and Double Trouble

The melody used in this Elvis track is an old French song, *Auprès de Ma Blonde*, which apparently dates back to the time of Louis XIV, when it was sung by the French infantry—hardly surprising, as the lyrics are somewhat bawdy and are certainly more suited to a bunch of soldiers than to its use as a children's song ("It feels good to sleep next to my blond girl…")!

I Love You Because (Payne)
Recorded by Elvis on Monday, 5 July, 1954
Original: Leon Payne, 1949
Elvis's version can be heard on Elvis Presley (Rock 'n' Roll No.1); The Sun Sessions CD; The Complete 50's Masters 1

In his book *The Originals*, Arnold Rypens professes that this number is derived from *When You Were Sweet Sixteen* from the 1938 film *Little Miss*

Broadway. Whatever the truth of this proposition, the song *I Love You Because* was written and first recorded by blind Texas hillbilly singer Leon Payne, who had a hit with it on Capitol in 1949. Payne later returned the compliment by covering Elvis's adaptation of *My Baby Left Me* under the name Rock Rogers.

I Need You So (Hunter)
    Recorded by Elvis on Saturday, 23 February, 1957
    Original: Ivory Joe Hunter, 1950
    Elvis's version can be heard on The Complete 50's Masters 3

Ivory Joe Hunter was born in 1911. He performed in his own radio shows in Texas, but only gained major success when he moved to California in the 1940s. He ran his own record company, Ivory and Pacific, with which he had several number 1s on the R&B charts in the early 1950s. He disliked being labelled solely an R&B artist, however, and was equally at home with pop, ballads, gospel, and C&W. Ivory Joe Hunter died of lung cancer in 1974. See also *I Will Be True*.

I Need Your Loving (Every Day) (Gardner/Robinson)
    Recorded by Elvis on Saturday, 14 August, 1971 (?)
    Original: Gardner and Dee Dee Ford, 1962
    Elvis's version can be heard on From Hollywood To Vegas (unofficial release).

Written by Don Gardner and Bobby Robinson in 1962, *I Need Your Loving (Every Day)* was recorded that same year by Gardner and Dee Dee Ford. The song reached number 20 on Billboard's Hot 100 and number 4 on the R&B charts. It is reported that Elvis sang *I Need Your Loving (Every Day)* at a few of his 1970 concerts.

I Really Don't Want To Know (Barnes/Robertson)
    Recorded by Elvis on Sunday, 7 June, 1970
    Original: Don Robertson, 1953
    Elvis's version can be heard on I'm 10,000 Years Old: Elvis Country; Elvis In Concert; Walk A Mile In My Shoes—The Essential 70's Masters Disc 1

Pianist-composer Don Robertson was born in Peking—his father was a diplomat. His piano-playing style was a major influence in Nashville during the fifties and his writing produced numerous country successes for a plethora of artists. He even scored a big hit himself with his own *Happy Whistler* in 1959. Elvis recorded several Don Robertson compositions. This particular number was a big hit for Eddy Arnold in 1954, when it reached number 2 in the US Country charts.

I Shall Be Released (Dylan)
>
> Recorded by Elvis on Thursday, 20 May, 1971
> Original: Bob Dylan, 1967
> Elvis's version can be heard on Walk A Mile In My Shoes Disc 4

Elvis did more than justice to the few Bob Dylan songs he recorded. Such a pity then, that this number was never "officially" recorded and exists only as an all-too-short less than one minute piece of Elvis apparently musing to himself in the studio.

I Shall Not Be Moved (Morris (?))
>
> Recorded by Elvis on Tuesday, 4 December, 1956
> Original: Little Jimmy Dickens, 1950
> Elvis's version can be heard on The Complete Million Dollar Quartet Session

The oldest of 13 children, Jimmy Dickens was born in West Virginia, in 1920. He joined the Grand Ole Opry in 1948. At just 4'11" (1m 50cm) he gained the nickname "Little" and became best known for novelty songs, such as *May The Bird of Paradise Fly Up Your Nose*. The number *I Shall Not Be Moved* is also known as *We Shall Not Be Moved*. A query follows the writer credits because various sources list various writers (Jorgensen lists "Traditional," the online Folk Index lists Akley...). Elvis sung along on this traditional gospel number with Carl Perkins and Jerry Lee Lewis during the Million Dollar Quartet jam session at the Sun Studios in December 1956.

I Understand (Just How You Feel) (Best)
>
> Recorded by Elvis on Wednesday, 28 May, 1958
> Original: Four Tunes, 1954
> Elvis's version can be heard on Forever Young, Forever Beautiful; The Home Recordings

The first million-seller for The Four Tunes, *I Understand (Just How You Feel)* was written by Pat Best. The number was a US top ten hit in 1954 and became a hit again in 1964 when it was recorded by British group, Freddie and The Dreamers. The recording of Elvis singing the song was made by his friend, Eddie Fadal, when Elvis was visiting his home in Waco Texas, during his national service.

I Walk The Line (Cash)
>   Recorded by Elvis on Friday, 14 August, 1970
>   Original: Johnny Cash, 1956
>   Elvis's version can be heard on The Entertainer (unofficial release)

Johnny Cash wrote *I Walk The Line*, his first million seller, himself. Together with The Tennessee Two, Luther Perkins and Marshall Grant, he recorded for Sun Records from 1954 until switching to Columbia in 1957. Elvis coupled *I Walk The Line* with *Folsom Prison Blues*, another Cash hit, at some of his Las Vegas and Lake Tahoe shows in the 1970s.

I Want You With Me (Harris)
>   Recorded by Elvis on Sunday, 12 March, 1961
>   Original: Bobby Darin, 1958
>   Elvis's version can be heard on Something For Everybody; From Nashville To Memphis (1)

Although Bobby Darin recorded this number in July 1958, it was not released until September 1960, on his *For Teenagers Only* LP on the Atco label.

I Was Born About Ten Thousand Years Ago (Traditional/adapted Elvis Presley)
>   Recorded by Elvis on Thursday, 4 June, 1970
>   Original: Kelly Harrell, 1925
>   Elvis's version can be heard on Elvis Now; Walk A Mile In My Shoes (The Essential 70's Masters) CD 3

This is an old traditional number, which is also known as *The Bragging Song*. The title has appeared in numerous forms, depending on the recording artist or music book publisher. These tend to be variations of *I was born(ed) (about) four thousand (10,000/4,000) years ago*. RCA first released Elvis's recording as a series of linking excerpts on the wonderful *Elvis Country* LP—almost a concept album.

I Washed My Hands In Muddy Water (Habcock)
>   Recorded by Elvis on Sunday, 7 June, 1970
>   Original: Joe Babcock, 1964
>   Elvis's version can be heard on Elvis Country; Walk A Mile In My Shoes: The Essential 70's Masters (CD 3)

Joe Babcock sang high harmony behind Marty Robbins for years, as part of the Glaser Brothers. Later he did studio work with the Jordanaires and formed the vocal group The Nashville Edition. He eventually sang on more than 10,000 recordings, including Elvis's own *Kentucky Rain* and *Suspicious Minds*. Babcock is still performing.

I Will Be Home Again (Benjamin/Leveen/Singer)

    Recorded by Elvis on Sunday, 3 April, 1960
    Original: Golden Gate Quartet, 1945
    Elvis's version can be heard on Elvis Is Back; From Nashville to Memphis (1)

Elvis presumably still felt something of the soldier away from home when he sang this number as a duet with Charlie Hodge for the fantastic *Elvis Is Back!* album, recorded just after his discharge in 1960. The Golden Gate Quartet must have had the same sort of sentiments when they recorded their version of this Benny Benjamin and Lou Singer song on 16 March 1945, released on the Columbia label.

I Will Be True (Hunter)

    Recorded by Elvis on Wednesday, 19 May, 1971
    Original: Ivory Joe Hunter, 1952
    Elvis's version can be heard on Walk A Mile In My Shoes—The Essential 70's Masters Disc 4

Ivory Joe Hunter was born in 1911. He performed in his own radio shows in Texas, but only gained major success when he moved to California in the 1940s. He ran his own record company, Ivory and Pacific, with which he had several number 1s on the R&B charts in the early 1950s. He disliked being labelled solely an R&B artist, however, and was equally at home with pop, ballads, gospel, and C&W. Ivory Joe Hunter died of lung cancer in 1974. See also *I Need You So*.

I Wonder, I Wonder, I Wonder (Hutchins)

    Recorded by Elvis in 1960
    Original: Eddy Howard, 1946
    Elvis's version can be heard on In A Private Moment

I have been able to find little about this song, other than that it was a hit for Eddy Howard and The Four Aces in about 1947, with Howard perhaps performing the original version. Howard had a varied musical career—radio singer, band crooner, band leader, solo artist…He had ten Top 20 hits between 1946 and 1952, this being one of them. But was there an earlier version and who wrote it? Elvis's recording was an informal one, made on a consumer tape-recorder and never intended for release.

I'll Be Home For Christmas (Gannon/Kent/Ram)
>Recorded by Elvis on Saturday, 7 September, 1957
>Original: Bing Crosby with the John Scott Trotter Orchestra, 1943
>Elvis's version can be heard on Elvis' Christmas Album; If Every Day Was Like Christmas; The Complete 50's Masters 3

Bing Crosby's influence in the first half of the 20th century was similar to that of Elvis's in the second half: huge record sales, the most popular radio star, a massive box-office draw and the ability to sing in a variety of styles. He was born in 1903 as Harry Lillis Crosby, the Bing coming from his childhood nickname Bingo, a comic-strip character of which he was fond. Bing Crosby died in October 1977.

I'll Be There (Darin)
>Recorded by Elvis on Thursday, 23 January, 1969
>Original: Bobby Darin, 1960
>Elvis's version can be heard on From Nashville to Memphis (4)

I'll Be There seems to be a popular title for a song, though the Ray Price (1954) and The Jackson 5 (1970) versions are two totally different numbers. Gerry and The Pacemakers (who also had a hit with *You'll Never Walk Alone*) recorded this track in 1963, including the verse that Elvis left out: "I'll miss you and in my dreams I'll kiss you/Then wish you luck in your new affair/So baby if you miss me/All you gotta do is call me/Don't you worry darling, I'll be there."

I'll Hold You In My Heart (Dilbeck/Horton/Arnold)
>Recorded by Elvis on Thursday, 23 January, 1969
>Original: Eddy Arnold, 1947
>Elvis's version can be heard on From Elvis in Memphis; From Nashville to Memphis (4)

Eddy Arnold's original spent no less than 21 weeks at the top of Billboard's Country chart in 1947, a joint record with Hank Snow's *I'm Movin' On* (also recorded by Elvis) and Webb Pierce's *In The Jailhouse Now*. Tom Parker managed Eddy Arnold before he moved on to better things with Elvis (better for Parker, of course!)

I'll Never Fall In Love Again (Donegan/Currie)
> Recorded by Elvis on Wednesday, 4 February, 1976
> Original: Lonnie Donegan, 1962
> Elvis's version can be heard on From Elvis Presley Boulevard, Memphis Tennessee

Hands up everyone who thought that Welshman Tom Jones had the original version—be honest! The full title is *(It Looks Like) I'll Never Fall In Love Again* and should not be confused with Burt Bacharach's *I'll Never Fall In Love Again* which is a totally different number, dating from 1968. Lonnie Donegan, the great British skiffle hero, was born in Scotland in 1931. He enjoyed huge success in the 1950s and early part of the 1960s. He died in November 2002.

I'll Never Let You Go (Little Darlin') (Wakely)
> Recorded by Elvis on Friday, 10 September, 1954
> Original: Jimmy Wakely, 1943
> Elvis's version can be heard on Elvis Presley (Rock 'n' Roll No.1); The Sun Sessions CD; The Complete 50's Masters 1

Jimmy Wakely got his break into showbusiness in 1940, when his trio was hired to play in Gene Autry's radio show. He left after two years to pursue his own career in music and films, appearing in well over 30 as a cowboy actor. Wakely died in 1982.

I'll Never Stand In Your Way (Rose/Heath)
> Recorded by Elvis on Monday, 4 January, 1954
> Original: Joni James, 1953
> Elvis's version can be heard on Platinum: A Life In Music

Fred Rose and Hy Heath wrote *I'll Never Stand In Your Way* in 1953, the same year that Joni James recorded the number. Her version was closely followed by that of Ernie Lee. On January 4, 1954, Elvis visited the Memphis Recording Service to make his second personal recording, coupling *I'll Never Stand In Your Way* with *It Wouldn't Be The Same Without You*. It is possible that Elvis recorded *I'll Never Stand In Your Way* at Sun Records, but this has not been confirmed.

I'll Remember You (Lee)
    Recorded by Elvis on Friday, 10 June, 1966
    Original: Kuiokolani Lee, 1966(?)
    Elvis's version can be heard on Aloha From Hawaii Via Satellite; From Nashville to Memphis (3)

Kui Lee was born in 1932, a mixture of Hawaiian, Chinese, and Scottish ancestry. He loved Hawaii and is said to have written this beautiful number when leaving it for one of his trips to work as an entertainer in mainland USA. He died on 3 December, 1966.

I'll Take You Home Again, Kathleen (Westendorf)
    Recorded by Elvis on After April 1959
    Original: Will Oakland, 1912
    Elvis's version can be heard on Elvis (the Fool album); Walk A Mile In My Shoes—The Essential 70's Masters Disc 4

Thomas Westendorf wrote this number in 1876, basing his tune on *Barney, Take Me Home Again*. Elvis made a home-recording of this number in 1959, whilst staying in Goethestrasse, Bad Nauheim, Germany, during his military service, and also made a studio recording on 19 May 1971.

I'm Beginning To Forget You (Phelps)
    Recorded by Elvis on April 1959
    Original: Jim Reeves, 1959
    Elvis's version can be heard on A Legendary Performer, Volume 4

Jim Reeves was born in 1923. A "singing disk-jockey," he turned to a full-time singing career in about 1949, but his big break came in 1952 when he stood in for Hank Williams, who had failed to turn up for a show. He became hugely successful in the USA and around the world (especially in South Africa, where he also recorded in Afrikaans). Jim Reeves died on 31 July 1964 when the plane he was piloting crashed outside Nashville during a storm. According to the notes in the 1997 release *Platinum: A Life In Music*, this number was recorded in 1961. Later research has shown that it was actually recorded during Elvis's army service in Germany at his home in Bad Nauheim.

I'm Comin' Home (Rich)
>Recorded by Elvis on Sunday, 12 March, 1961
>Original: Carl Mann, 1960
>Elvis's version can be heard on Something For Everybody; From Nashville to Memphis (2)

Born in 1942, Carl Mann started singing professionally in the late 1950s. He seemed to specialise in making rockabilly versions of popular songs. He recorded for Phillips International, a label owned by Sam Phillips—another Elvis connection! His two main successes came with *Pretend* and *Mona Lisa*. Although the original was not a hit, Elvis copied the performance very closely.

I'm Gonna Bid My Blues Goodbye (Snow)
>Recorded by Elvis on Tuesday, 4 December, 1956
>Original: Hank Snow, 1940s
>Elvis's version can be heard on The Complete Million Dollar Session

Canadian Hank Snow was originally likened to Jimmie Rodgers and was therefore dubbed the Yodelling Ranger (Rodgers was the Yodelling Brakeman). As his voice changed, however, this soon became the Singing Ranger.

I'm Gonna Sit Right Down And Cry (Over You) (Thomas/Biggs)
>Recorded by Elvis on Tuesday, 31 January, 1956
>Original: Joe Thomas, 1953
>Elvis's version can be heard on Elvis Presley (Rock 'n' Roll No.1); The Complete 50's Masters 1

Ray Price, a favourite of Elvis's, also recorded this number, using it for the B-side of his 1954 hit single, *You'll Never Walk Alone*, a number also recorded by Elvis!

I'm Gonna Walk Dem Golden Stairs (Holt)
>Recorded by Elvis on Monday, 31 October, 1960
>Original: The Jordanaires, 1949
>Elvis's version can be heard on His Hand In Mine; Amazing Grace (CD 1)

Cully Holt, who wrote this number, was the original bass singer for the Jordanaires. The group went on to back just about everybody in Country music, along with numerous other recording artists, too, one of whom was, of course, Elvis Presley!

I'm Leaving It Up To You (Harris/Terry)
> Recorded by Elvis on Tuesday, 8 February, 1972
> Original: Don Harris and Dewey Terry, 1957
> Elvis's version can be heard on Leavin' It Up To You (unofficial release)

Don Harris and Dewey Terry composed and recorded *I'm Leaving It Up To You* in 1957. Its big chart success, however, came in 1963, when Dale (Houston) and Grace (Broussard) scored a number one US hit with their cover. Elvis did not make a studio recording of *I'm Leaving It Up To You*, but sang it occasionally in his 1970 concerts.

I'm Movin' On (Snow)
> Recorded by Elvis on Wednesday, 15 January, 1969
> Original: Hank Snow, 1949
> Elvis's version can be heard on From Elvis in Memphis; From Nashville to Memphis (4)

Hank Snow's original spent no less than 21 weeks at the top of Billboard's Country chart in 1950. See also *(Now And Then There's) A Fool Such As I* and *I'm Gonna Bid My Blues Goodbye*.

I'm So Lonesome I Could Cry (Williams)
> Recorded by Elvis on Sunday, 14 January, 1973
> Original: Hank Williams, 1949
> Elvis's version can be heard on Aloha From Hawaii Via Satellite; Walk A Mile In My Shoes—The Essential 70's Masters Disc 5

A recording made by Hank Williams on 30 August, 1949. According to Elvis, "Probably the saddest song I've ever heard." Could be, could be.

I'm With The Crowd (But So Alone) (Tubb/Story)
> Recorded by Elvis on Tuesday, 4 December, 1956
> Original: Ernest Tubb, 1951
> Elvis's version can be heard on The Complete Million Dollar Session

The number is listed on *The Complete Million Dollar Session* as *I'm In The Crowd (But Oh So Alone)*. Carl Story copyrighted song in his own name July 30, 1947. Elaine Tubb was added to the copyright May 25, 1948. Tubb was born in 1914. Success largely eluded him, until he wrote and recorded *Walking The Floor Over You* in 1942. This led to his first appearance at the Grand Ole Opry that same year and the following year he became a regular performer there, appearing right up to his death in 1984.

I've Got A Thing About You Baby (White)
>Recorded by Elvis on Sunday, 22 July, 1973
>Original: Billy Lee Riley, 1971
>Elvis's version can be heard on Good Times; Walk A Mile In My Shoes—The Essential 70's Masters Disc 2

Tony Joe White also recorded this number for use on an LP, but I believe that Billy Lee Riley's version was recorded earlier. Elvis also recorded Tony Joe's *Polk Salad Annie* and *For Ol' Times Sake*.

I've Got Confidence (Crouch)
>Recorded by Elvis on Tuesday, 18 May, 1971
>Original: Andrae Crouch and The Disciples, 1971
>Elvis's version can be heard on Amazing Grace (CD2)

I've Got Confidence is a modern gospel number. It was recorded by its composer, together with his group The Disciples and was issued on their album *I've Got Confidence*.

I've Lost You (Howard/Blaikley)
>Recorded by Elvis on Thursday, 4 June, 1970
>Original: Matthews' Southern Comfort, 1969
>Elvis's version can be heard on That's The Way It Is; Walk A Mile In My Shoes—The Essential 70's Masters Disc 1

Ian Matthews was a former member of Fairport Convention. Ken Howard and Alan Blaikley were prolific writers of hits for British groups of the sixties and seventies. Matthews' Southern Comfort are probably best remembered for their number *Woodstock*.

I, John (Johnson/McFadden/Brooks)
>Recorded by Elvis on Wednesday, 9 June, 1971
>Original: Mighty Faith Increasers, 1962
>Elvis's version can be heard on Amazing Grace

Here's a song that doesn't let its origins be easily found! This version was written in 1961 and the earliest recording that I can find was released in 1962 on an LP called *A Festival Of Spiritual Songs* on the King label by the Mighty Faith Increasers. The track was then called *I John Saw A Mighty Number*. Not all sources agree on the authorship of the number, though this might well be the result of an error in Jorgensen's *A Life In Music*, where the number is listed on p.205 as having been written by William Gaither. Similarly-titled songs

(*John Saw a Mighty Number*, *John Saw De Holy Number*, etc.) were already included in the earliest collections of negro Spirituals, dating from the 1870s. Recordings made prior to 1961 exist with such titles, but I have been unable to determine exactly how close they are to *I, John*, which indeed seems to be a mixture of several traditional spirituals. It is based on the biblical text Revelation 21.

If I Loved You (Hammerstein/Rodgers)
Recorded by Elvis on Autumn 1960
Original: John Raitt, 1945
Elvis's version can be heard on In A Private Moment

Elvis made a home recording of this number in the autumn of 1960, when staying on the west coast of the USA. A second home recording, made in 1966, has been released on a CD called, appropriately, *The Home Recordings*. The tape containing this latter version was made at Rocca Place, Hollywood, though was only discovered in Graceland in 1996. *If I Loved You* was written for the 1945 musical *Carousel*. Elvis officially recorded the number *You'll Never Walk Alone* from the same musical.

If I'm A Fool (For Loving You) (Kesler)
Recorded by Elvis on Friday, 21 February, 1969
Original: Jimmy Clanton, 1964
Elvis's version can be heard on From Nashville to Memphis (5)

Jimmy Clanton is perhaps best remembered, if at all, for his starring role in Alan Freed's 1959 film *Go, Johnny, Go*. He was drafted in 1961 but fared less well than Elvis, having just one post-service hit, *Venus In Blue Jeans*, in late 1962. The latter number was, of course, the inspiration for that great British eccentric and rocker Screaming Lord Sutch's own *Monster In Black Tights*!

If That Isn't Love (Rambo)
Recorded by Elvis on Sunday, 16 December, 1973
Original: The Rambos, 1969
Elvis's version can be heard on Amazing Grace (CD2)

Dottie Rambo, who wrote this number, formed The Rambos together with husband Buck and released her composition on Vista. It is said that Dottie Rambo has written more than 1,500 songs!

If The Lord Wasn't Walking By My Side (Slaughter)
>Recorded by Elvis on Friday, 27 May, 1966
>Original: Claiborne Brothers Quartette, 1963
>Elvis's version can be heard on How Great Thou Art; Amazing Grace (CD1)

Henry Slaughter, who wrote this number in 1961 was a pianist with The Imperials. The story goes that Elvis was so pleased with his own recording, on which he duets with Jake Hess, that he had the Meditation Garden in Graceland built.

If We Never Meet Again (Brumley)
>Recorded by Elvis on Sunday, 30 October, 1960
>Original: Albert E. Brumley, 1945
>Elvis's version can be heard on His Hand In Mine; Amazing Grace (CD 1)

Albert Brumley is probably the best-known 20th century gospel music writer in America. He wrote his first and most successful gospel song in 1931—*I'll Fly Away*. Another Brumley song recorded by Elvis, though unofficially during the Million Dollar Quartet session, is *Blessed Jesus Hold My Hand* (see above).

If You Don't Come Back (Leiber/Stoller)
>Recorded by Elvis on Saturday, 21 July, 1973
>Original: The Drifters, 1963
>Elvis's version can be heard on Raised On Rock

The Drifters were originally formed in 1953, with no less than Clyde McPhatter as the lead singer of the quartet. Their debut single, *Money Honey* (also recorded by Elvis) became a number one in the USA, with the label reading "Clyde McPhatter and The Drifters." Other successes followed, despite McPhatter's having to leave the group to do national service (and after that he decided on a solo career). Problems between the group and its manager, who owned the name, led to the group being fired in 1958 and the members of another group, The Five Crowns, being given the name. This new Drifters group gained perhaps even more success than the original. At one time, Ben E. King was the lead singer, but it is Johnny Moore (ex leader of The Three Blazers) who takes the lead on *If You Don't Come Back*.

If You Love Me (Let Me Know) (Rostill)
>Recorded by Elvis on Friday, 6 June, 1975
>Original: Olivia Newton John, 1974
>Elvis's version can be heard on Elvis In Concert; Moody Blue

John Rostill was a former member of the famous British guitar group, The Shadows. He died in 1973, aged just 31. See also *Let Me Be There*. Olivia Newton John is a right mixture: she was born in England of a Welsh father and a German mother; she was taken to Australia when she was 5 years old. After winning an Australian talent contest, she moved back to England in 1965 to try for a career in entertainment. After a not too auspicious start, she finally made the big time.

In My Father's House (Hanks)
>Recorded by Elvis on Sunday, 30 October, 1960
>Original: The Blackwood Brothers, 1954
>Elvis's version can be heard on His Hand In Mine; Amazing Grace CD 1

Elvis's 70s bass singer, the late J.D. Sumner, was a member of the Blackwood Brothers from 1954 until 1965. Their lead singer was Jake Hess, a great favourite of Elvis and possibly an influence on his singing style. The Blackwood Brothers group was formed as a quartet in 1934 and then consisted of three brothers, Roy, Doyle and James together with R.W. Blackwood, Roy's son. Jake Hess later went on to form The Imperials.

In The Garden (Miles)
>Recorded by Elvis on Friday, 27 May, 1966
>Original: Ada Jones & George Ballard, 1914
>Elvis's version can be heard on How Great Thou Art; Amazing Grace (CD 1)

C. Austin Miles wrote this number, whose complete title is *(He Walks With Me) In The Garden*, in 1912 after music publisher Adam Geibel asked him to write a hymn text that would be "sympathetic in tone, breathing tenderness in every line; one that would bring hope to the hopeless, rest for the wary, and downy pillows to dying beds." Well, it's a nice song and Elvis sings it wonderfully!

Is It So Strange (Young)
> Recorded by Elvis on Saturday, 19 January, 1957
> Original: Faron Young, 1956
> Elvis's version can be heard on The Complete Million Dollar Session; The Complete 50's Masters CD 3

Faron Young was born in 1932. He dropped out of college in 1950 to work in radio and soon joined The Louisiana Hayride, shortly moving to The Grand Ole Opry. His first number 1 hit came in 1955 with *Live Fast, Love Hard, Die Young*. Faron Young enjoyed considerable success, but followed the advice in his first big hit and finally shot himself in 1985. Elvis recorded this number unofficially, as part of The Million Dollar Quartet in December 1956. The official recording of this number occurred several weeks later.

It Ain't No Big Thing (But It's Growing) (Merritt/Joy/Hall)
> Recorded by Elvis on Saturday, 6 June, 1970
> Original: Charlie Louvin, 1968
> Elvis's version can be heard on Walk A Mile In My Shoes—The Essential 70's Masters (CD 3)

In 1955 Elvis was the opening act for a show starring Charlie Louvin as part of the Louvin Brothers. Elvis's recording came about after he picked up a guitar during a session and started playing the intro to the number.

It Is No Secret (What God Can Do) (Hamblen)
> Recorded by Elvis on Saturday, 19 January, 1957
> Original: Stuart Hamblen, 1952
> Elvis's version can be heard on Elvis' Christmas Album; The Complete 50's Masters 3; Amazing Grace (CD 1)

Elvis's version was originally released as part of the *Peace In The Valley* EP in 1957. Stuart Hamblen was a western film star and the leader of a C&W band before his conversion to Christianity. He then went on to write and record several gospel numbers, of which this is undoubtedly the most well known (another of his numbers recorded by Elvis is *Known Only To Him*). He also had his own radio programme, *Cowboy Church Of The Air* from 1938 until 1952. The story goes that Stuart Hamblen got the idea for the song from John Wayne, who said the title to him as Hamblen was leaving his home in a depressive mood.

It Keeps Right On A Hurtin' (Tillotson)
> Recorded by Elvis on Thursday, 20 February, 1969
> Original: Johnny Tillotson, 1962
> Elvis's version can be heard on From Elvis in Memphis; From Nashville to Memphis (5)

Elvis co-star Shelley Fabares (*California Holiday, Clambake, Girl Happy*) recorded this number in 1962. Perhaps she mentioned it to him on the film set…Tillotson's original reached number 3 in Billboard's Hot 100 chart and number 4 in the Country chart. Tillotson recorded the number whilst doing his army service (in fact, he recorded a full album!) and some advertisements for the record showed him in army uniform, naming him Private Johnny Tillotson!

It Wouldn't Be The Same Without You (Wakely/Rose)
> Recorded by Elvis on Monday, 4 January, 1954
> Original: Al Rogers And His Rocky Mountain Boys, 1950 (?)
> Elvis's version can be heard on Sunrise

Elvis visited the Memphis Recording Service to make his second personal recording in January 1954, coupling *I'll Never Stand In Your Way* with *It Wouldn't Be The Same Without You*. As far as I can ascertain, Al Rogers only ever had two records released, both on 78s, but for two different companies, Capitol and MGM; his version of *It Wouldn't Be The Same Without You* was released on MGM 10709 as the B-side of *Shuffle-Boogie Bellhop*.

It's A Sin (Rose/Turner)
> Recorded by Elvis on Sunday, 12 March, 1961
> Original: Eddy Arnold, 1947
> Elvis's version can be heard on Something For Everybody; From Nashville to Memphis (1)

Eddy Arnold's original stayed at the number 1 position of the US Country charts for five weeks. Tom Parker managed Eddy Arnold for several years before dropping him (or was it a case of Arnold dropping Parker…?) when he saw great big dollar signs in the shape of Elvis Presley.

It's A Sin To Tell A Lie (Mayhew)
>Recorded by Elvis in 1966
>Original: Fats Waller, 1935
>Elvis's version can be heard on In A Private Moment

Billy Mayhew copyrighted his number, *It's A Sin To Tell A Lie*, in 1933, so it is possible that an earlier recording than that of Fats Waller's exists. About the same time as Fats, Ruth Etting also released her version—perhaps it was recorded earlier. The number has been recorded by just about everyone, from Billie Holliday to Vera Lynn—quite a contrast! Elvis's home recording, however, is based more on that of the wonderful Ink Spots, a group he was very fond of—and rightly so!—and he even provides a Bill Kenny-like recitation.

It's Been So Long Darling (Tubb)
>Recorded by Elvis on After April 1959
>Original: Ernest Tubb, 1945
>Elvis's version can be heard on Platinum, A Life In Music; In A Private Moment

This was a number one on the Country Chart for Tubb and one of his biggest hits during his long career. On the set *Platinum: A Life In Music* the number is included as part of a track called *The Bad Nauheim Medley*, (Elvis's house was in Bad Nauheim), which further includes *I'll Take You Home Again Kathleen*, *I Will Be True*, *Apron Strings* and *There's No Tomorrow*.

It's Impossible (Rivgauche/Wayne)
>Recorded by Elvis on Wednesday, 16 February, 1972
>Original: Perry Como (?), 1971
>Elvis's version can be heard on Walk A Mile In My Shoes—The Essential 70's Masters Disc 5

Well, yes, Como's version is the original with this title, but the song actually dates back to 1965 and Belgium, no less! There it was sung for the first time on the BRT radio by Lili Castel during an international music competition, though it would seem that no record was made at the time. The text was then translated into the first English incarnation *The Way Of Love* and recorded by delicious Kathy Kirby (and later by Cher and none other than Welsh diva Shirley Bassey!). A Spanish version, *Somos Novios*, written in 1968 by Mexican singer-songwriter Armando Manzanero for the film of the same name, was recorded in 1970 by Vikki Carr. Only then did Perry Como's version *It's Impossible* see the light of day, with English lyrics provided by Sid Wayne. Hence the question mark!

It's Now Or Never (Capurro/di Capua/Mazzucchi/Schroeder/Gold)
>Recorded by Elvis on Sunday, 3 April, 1960
>Original: Giuseppe Anselmi, 1907
>Elvis's version can be heard on From Nashville to Memphis (1); ELV1S 30 #1 Hits

What counts as an original? Elvis liked a 1949 Tony Martin number called *There's No Tomorrow* and recorded private versions of the song whilst on army service in Germany. But *There's No Tomorrow* was itself based on a much older Italian number called *O Sole Mio*, which was written in 1898 by Di Capua when he was travelling in the Ukraine. In 1973, documents were presented to the Italian court, showing that Mazzucchi was co-author of the number. New lyrics were provided for Elvis by Aaron Schroeder and Wally Gold and a demo was made by David Hill.

It's Only Love (James/Tyrell)
>Recorded by Elvis on Thursday, 20 May, 1971
>Original: B.J. Thomas, 1969
>Elvis's version can be heard on Walk A Mile In My Shoes—The Essential 70's Masters Disc 1

B.J. (Billy Joe) Thomas enjoyed considerable success in the USA from the mid 1960s to the late 1980s in both pop and country fields. He also had some international success, notably with his recording of *Raindrops Keep Falling On My Head*. Since the late 1980s he has been active in the field of Christian music. Mark James also wrote *Always On My Mind*, *Moody Blue* and *Suspicious Minds*.

It's Over (Rodgers)
>Recorded by Elvis on Sunday, 14 January, 1973
>Original: Jimmie Rodgers, 1966
>Elvis's version can be heard on Aloha From Hawaii Via Satellite; Walk A Mile In My Shoes—The Essential 70's Masters Disc 5

The song is not to be confused with Roy Orbison's 1961 success with the same title. Nor is the original artist to be confused with the "real" Jimmie Rodgers, "The Singing Brakeman." Another cover by Elvis of a Jimmie Rodgers original was *Froggy Went a'Courtin'*.

Jambalaya (On The Bayou) (Williams)
>Recorded by Elvis on Saturday, 7 June, 1975
>Original: Hank Williams (?), 1952
>Elvis's version can be heard on A Profile CD 3: Lake Charles 4/5/75 (unofficial release)

A question mark on this Hank Williams original. Surely everyone knows that *Jambalaya* and Hank are inseparable, with his studio recording dating from 13 June, 1952. Maybe so, at least with that title, but *Jambalaya* is based on a slightly earlier number by Julius Lamperez, recording under the name Papa Cairo And His Boys, in 1949. The original title was *Big Texas*, so perhaps *Jambalaya (On The Oilfield)* would have been more appropriate.

Jesus Walked That Lonesome Valley (Traditional)
>Recorded by Elvis on Tuesday, 4 December, 1956
>Original: Morris Brown Quartet, 1940
>Elvis's version can be heard on The Complete Million Dollar Session

This number is listed in *The Complete Million Dollar Session* as *Walk That Lonesome Valley*. The version recorded in 1940 by the Morris Brown Quartet was released as *You Got To Walk That Lonesome Valley*.

Jingle Bells (Pierpont)
>Recorded by Elvis in 1959 (1960?)
>Original: Edison Male Quartette, 1898
>Elvis's version can be heard on Home Recordings

J.S. Pierpont (or was it Pierpoint? Both are used extensively) wrote the number as *The One-Horse Open Sleigh* in order to cheer up the local Sunday-school evening meeting. The 1898 recording was issued on an Edison brown wax cylinder, number 2218.

Elvis can be heard playing a small part of the song on piano prior to *I Asked The Lord*.

Johnny B. Goode (Berry)
>Recorded by Elvis on Sunday, 24 August, 1969
>Original: Chuck Berry, 1958
>Elvis's version can be heard on Aloha From Hawaii Via Satellite; Elvis In Concert

Chuck wasn't above being influenced: it's well known that his *Maybellene* was based on the much older *Ida Red*, for example. His guitar playing in *Johnny B.*

Goode, especially the fantastic runs, are similar to those used by Freddy Slack in his 1942 recording of *I Got A Break Baby*. Let this not detract, however, from the pure poetry of Chuck's lyrics.

Joshua Fit The Battle (arr. Elvis Presley)
    Recorded by Elvis on Monday, 31 October, 1960
    Original: Paul Robeson, 1925
    Elvis's version can be heard on His Hand In Mine; Amazing Grace (CD 1)

Robeson's recording was titled *Joshua Fit De Battle of Jericho* and was released in 1925 on Vic 19743. It is also indicated as *Joshua Fought The Battle of Jericho* and *Joshua Fit The Battle of Jericho*. The number is invariably listed as "Traditional" or "Traditional African American," or something similar, but I have found at least one indication of it having been written in 1865, but perhaps this refers to the first publication of the words (and music?).

Judy (Redell)
    Recorded by Elvis on Monday, 13 March, 1961
    Original: Teddy Redell, 1960
    Elvis's version can be heard on Something For Everybody; From Nashville to Memphis (2)

For some reason, Teddy Redell never made it as the big-time Rock'n'Roll singer he promised to be. Nevertheless, he continues to appear in Rock 'n' Roll and Rockabilly shows around the world.

Just A Closer Walk With Thee (unknown)
    Recorded by Elvis on ca. 1956
    Original: Red Foley, 1950
    Elvis's version can be heard on Just A Closer Walk With Thee (Czech CD on Memory label)

This gospel number was probably recorded in the studio in 1956 by Elvis; a home recording also exists, made in Waco in 1958. There is some speculation that *Tell Me Why*, recorded by Elvis in 1957 (see below), was also based on this tune. It is thought that *Just A Closer Walk With Thee* is a comparatively recent song, perhaps dating from the evangelical crusades of the 1930s, though its origins have already been lost. Red Foley's recording was one of the first religious hits in Country music (see also *When God Dips His Love In My Heart* and *Tell Me Why*.)

Just A Little Bit *(Thornton/Bass/Washington/Brown/Thompson)*
>Recorded by Elvis on Sunday, 22 July, 1973
>Original: Rosco Gordon, 1960
>Elvis's version can be heard on Raised On Rock; Walk A Mile In My Shoes—The Essential 70's Masters Disc 4

Rosco Gordon was born in Memphis, Tennessee, in 1928. He recorded his first single, *Booted*, at Sun Studios, but Sam Phillips sold the track to Chess, who released it in 1951. The writing credits shown here for *Just A Little Bit* are those normally provided, but they are probably incorrect! Gordon's friend, Jimmy McCracklin, was working on a song, which Gordon finished as *Just A Little Bit*. His demo was released by another label, but the owner of his own label, Ralph Bass, had copyrighted the song under his own name. Gordon finally received the rights to his song in 1990. Roscoe Gordon died in July 2002. UK fans might remember a version by The Undertakers, recorded in 1964 and their only hit.

Just A Little Talk With Jesus *(Derricks)*
>Recorded by Elvis on Tuesday, 4 December, 1956
>Original: Cleavant Derricks (?), 1937
>Elvis's version can be heard on The Complete Million Dollar Session

The Reverend Cleavant Derricks was born in 1910 at Chattanooga, Tennessee. He studied at Cadek Conservatory of Music in Knoxville and at the State University and American Baptist Theological Seminary in Nashville. He wrote more than 300 songs, including *Just A Little Talk with Jesus* and *When God Dips His Love In My Heart*, both recorded by Elvis. Elvis visited the Sun studios on December 4th and ended up in a jam session, which has become legendary as the Million Dollar Quartet. Actually, the quartet was a trio (Johnny Cash, the fourth, was present while pictures were being taken, but left before the recordings started): Elvis, his friend Carl Perkins, and new Sun artist Jerry Lee Lewis. The three ended up in an informal jam session, which Sam Phillips wisely committed to tape. Most of the numbers sung were, like *Just a Little Talk/Walk with Jesus*, gospels.

Just Because *(Robin)*
>Recorded by Elvis on Tuesday, 14 September, 1954
>Original: Nelstone's Hawaiians, 1929
>Elvis's version can be heard on Elvis Presley (Rock 'n' Roll No.1); The Complete 50's Masters 1

Cliff Carlisle's *You'll Miss Me* is subtitled *Just Because* and is perhaps the semi-original version of *Just Because*. The tune of a march called *Washington and Lee*

Swing from 1910 is also a clear influence. The first "real" version, however, seems to be that of Nelstone's Hawaiians. The group consisted of Hubert Nelson (vocal and steel guitar) and James D. Touchstone (vocal and guitar), both from southern Alabama. The Shelton Brothers' version of *Just Because* was a big hit on the Decca label in 1935 and was listed with writers Shelton, Shelton and Robin—don't know why, as it is clearly the same number as that of Nelstone's Hawaiians!

Just Call Me Lonesome (Griffin)

    Recorded by Elvis on Monday, 11 September, 1967
    Original: Red Foley; Eddy Arnold, 1955
    Elvis's version can be heard on From Nashville to Memphis (3)

Surprisingly little is known about Rex Griffin, though he was quite a prolific writer of country songs. His early numbers were influenced by his admiration of Jimmie Rodgers. He recorded 36 tracks for Decca between 1935 and 1939. Griffin was born in 1912 and is believed to have died in 1959.

Just Let Me Make Believe (Blackwell)

    Recorded by Elvis in 1966
    Original: Roy Orbison, 1966
    Elvis's version can be heard on From The Bottom Of My Heart Vol.2 (unofficial release)

The big question is, however, is it really Elvis singing on the recording?! If it is, then he is certainly not taking lead vocal. Former Elvis body-guard/security advisor Dick Grob claimed that Elvis gave him this home recording, which Grob put up for sale in the mid-1990s.

Keep Your Hands Off Of It (Foster)

    Recorded by Elvis on Friday, 5 June, 1970
    Original: Damita Jo, 1961
    Elvis's version can be heard on Walk A Mile In My Shoes—The Essential 70's Masters Disc 3

The original was only a very minor hit, getting no higher than 75 in the US Hot 100. Elvis seems to have liked it, however, even though he apparently did not make an "official" recording of it—his version is a studio jam. Damita Jo's version was called *Keep Your Hands Off Of Him* and it reached the lower reaches of the Cashbox Top 100 in February 1961.

Keeper Of The Key *(Stewart/Howard/Devine/Guynes)*
> Recorded by Elvis on Tuesday, 4 December, 1956
> Original: Wynn Stewart, 1956
> Elvis's version can be heard on The Complete Million Dollar Session

Wynn Stewart began recording in 1954 for the Intro label. By 1956 he had moved to Capitol, where he recorded *Keeper Of The Key*, a number he had helped to write. Stewart died in 1985. Elvis sings only background vocals on this number, the lead being taken by Carl Perkins.

Known Only To Him *(Hamblen)*
> Recorded by Elvis on Monday, 31 October, 1960
> Original: Stuart Hamblen, 1952
> Elvis's version can be heard on His Hand In Mine; Amazing Grace (CD 1)

Numerous artists, including The Statesmen, have recorded this gospel favourite. Jake Hess, lead singer with The Statesmen, sang this number at Elvis's funeral. Stuart Hamblen was a film actor and popular radio personality. He wrote a number of gospels, including *It Is No Secret (What God Can Do)*, also recorded by Elvis.

Lady Madonna *(Lennon/McCartney)*
> Recorded by Elvis on Monday, 17 May, 1971
> Original: The Beatles, 1967
> Elvis's version can be heard on Walk A Mile In My Shoes—The Essential 70's Masters Disc 3

In his book *The Originals*, Arnold Rypens professes to recognise elements of the Humphrey Lyttleton Band's 1956 EMI recording of *Bad Penny Blues* (notably the piano) in *Lady Madonna*.

Lawdy Miss Clawdy *(Price)*
> Recorded by Elvis on Friday, 3 February, 1956
> Original: Lloyd Price, 1952
> Elvis's version can be heard on The Complete 50's Masters 2

With Fats Domino on piano, Lloyd Price took his own composition to the top of the R&B charts in 1952.

Lead Me, Guide Me (Akers)
>Recorded by Elvis on Monday, 17 May, 1971
>Original: Doris Akers, 1954
>Elvis's version can be heard on He Touched Me; Amazing Grace (CD 2)

Doris Akers was born in 1923. She wrote her first gospel song when she was just 10 years old (*Keep The Fire Burning In Me*). In additiion to *Lead Me, Guide Me*, Doris Akers also wrote the Elvis favourite *Sweet, Sweet Spirit*. Doris died in 1995.

Let It Be Me (Delanoë/Bécaud)
>Recorded by Elvis on Tuesday, 17 February, 1970
>Original: Gilbert Bécaud, 1955 (as *Je t'Appartiens*)
>Elvis's version can be heard on On Stage; Walk A Mile In My Shoes—The Essential 70's Masters Disc 5

Originally a French number, dating from 1955, the first English version was recorded in 1957 by Jill Corey and Jimmy Carroll, as *Let It Be Me*. Many more followed...

Let Me Be There (Rostill)
>Recorded by Elvis on Wednesday, 20 March, 1974
>Original: Olivia Newton John, 1973
>Elvis's version can be heard on Moody Blue; Recorded Live On Stage In Memphis

John Rostill was a former member of the famous British guitar group, The Shadows. He died in 1973, aged just 31. See also *If You Love Me (Let Me Know)*. Olivia Newton John is a right mixture: she was born in England of a Welsh father and a German mother; she was taken to Australia when she was 5 years old. After winning an Australian talent contest, she moved back to England in 1965 to try for a career in entertainment. After a not too auspicious start, she finally made the big time, with *Let Me Be There* being the real turning point.

Lighthouse (Hinson)
>Recorded by Elvis on Friday, 31 March, 1972
>Original: The Original Hinsons, 1971
>Elvis's version can be heard on The Complete On Tour Sessions Vol. 2 (unofficial CD)

Ronny Hinson wrote this modern gospel in 1970 and recorded it with his own group the following year. The song went on to win numerous gospel music awards. Elvis's version is an informal recording, never intended for release.

Like A Baby (Stone)
> Recorded by Elvis on Sunday, 3 April, 1960
> Original: Vikki Nelson, 1953
> Elvis's version can be heard on Elvis Is Back!

Jesse Stone often wrote for the Clovers and Elvis recorded his *Down In The Alley*, which they also recorded. It seems that Vikki Nelson had just one recording session, which took place in 1953.

Little Cabin On The Hill (Monroe/Flatt)
> Recorded by Elvis on Thursday, 4 June, 1970
> Original: Bill Monroe's Bluegrass Boys, 1948
> Elvis's version can be heard on The Complete Million Dollar Session; I'm 10,000 Years Old: Elvis Country; Walk A Mile In My Shoes—The Essential 70's Masters Disc 3

The title on the label of Bill Monroe's recording was *Little Cabin Home On The Hill*. Elvis's first recorded version of this number was made on December 4th 1956, when he imitated Bill Monroe during the informal Million Dollar Quartet session. Elvis recorded several Bill Monroe originals, including *Blue Moon Of Kentucky, I Hear A Sweet Voice Calling, Summertime Has Passed And Gone, Sweetheart You Done Me Wrong* and perhaps even *Uncle Pen*.

Little Darlin' (Williams)
> Recorded by Elvis on Sunday, 24 April, 1977
> Original: The Gladiolas, 1956
> Elvis's version can be heard on Moody Blue

Writer Maurice Williams was leader of The Gladiolas. Ernie Young recorded the Gladiolas' version after having asked them to sing their worst song. Elvis seems to have enjoyed the song a lot: not only did he sing it during concerts, when he clearly had great fun with the number, performing it very tongue-in-cheek, but he also sang it at home and several informal recordings of such performances exist, the earliest dating from 1958.

Little Egypt (Leiber/Stoller)
>Recorded by Elvis on Monday, 2 March, 1964
>Original: The Coasters, 1961
>Elvis's version can be heard on Double Features: Viva Las Vegas & Roustabout; Roustabout; Command Performances—Disc 2

The Coasters, one of *the* groups of the 1950s and early 1960s, recorded many Leiber and Stoller numbers. *Girls! Girls! Girls!* was another Leiber and Stoller number that both the Coasters and Elvis recorded.

Long Black Limousine (Stovall/George)
>Recorded by Elvis on Monday, 13 January, 1969
>Original: Gordon Terry, 1962
>Elvis's version can be heard on From Elvis in Memphis; From Nashville to Memphis (4)

Wynn Stewart recorded *Long Black Limousine* in 1958, though this original version was not released until May 2000, when it appeared on the *Wishful Thinking* box set (Bear Family number BCD 15886). Apart from Gordon Terry's apparently earliest official release (on RCA) the number has also been recorded by Glen Campbell (1962), Jody Miller (1968), Bobby Bare (60's), Rose Maddox (1962) and George Hamilton IV (60's).

Long Live Rock And Roll (School Days) (Berry)
>Recorded by Elvis on Friday, 6 June, 1975
>Original: Chuck Berry, 1957
>Elvis's version can be heard on Unsurpassed Masters 4: Las Vegas Hilton 13/12/75

Elvis covered numerous Berry numbers—see also *Johnny B. Goode*; *Brown Eyed Handsome Man*; *Maybellene*; *Memphis, Tennessee*; *Promised Land*; *Too Much Monkey Business*.

Long Tall Sally (Johnson/Penniman/Blackwell)
>Recorded by Elvis on Sunday, 2 September, 1956
>Original: Little Richard, 1956
>Elvis's version can be heard on Elvis (Rock 'n' Roll no.2); Recorded Live On Stage In Memphis

Little Richard was born Richard Penniman in 1935. That's the same Penniman as in the writers' credits. Little Richard made his first recordings in 1951—a set of eight urban blues tracks for Atlanta, but with no success. In

1955, however, he started recording for Specialty and had his first R&B hit with *Tutti Frutti*, quickly followed by *Long Tall Sally*, which was also a Top 10 hit. Hit after hit followed on both sides of the Atlantic. His chart success faded in the early 1960s, but Little Richard's frantic, raucous style is still remembered and he remains one of the true originals of Rock 'n' Roll. The recording date indicates the "official" recording date, though Elvis was recorded singing this number earlier, when appearing at the Frontier Hotel in Las Vegas, on 6 May. Elvis covered no less than four Little Richard originals in 1956. In addition to *Long Tall Sally*, see also *Ready Teddy*, *Rip It Up*, and *Tutti Frutti*.

Love Coming Down (Chesnut)

Recorded by Elvis on Friday, 6 February, 1976
Original: Razy Bailey, 1975
Elvis's version can be heard on From Elvis Presley Boulevard, Memphis Tennessee; Walk A Mile In My Shoes—The Essential 70's Masters Disc 4

Jerry Chesnut also wrote *The Wonders You Perform*, *T-R-O-U-B-L-E* and *Woman Without Love*, all recorded by Elvis.

Love Letters (Young/Heyman)

Recorded by Elvis on Thursday, 26 May, 1966
Original: Dick Haymes, 1945
Elvis's version can be heard on Love Letters From Elvis; From Nashville to Memphis (3)

Having succeeded Frank Sinatra in both the Harry James and the Tommy Dorsey orchestras, Dick Haymes went solo and turned to acting as well as singing. This number comes from a film of the same name in which he played.

Love Me (Leiber/Stoller)

Recorded by Elvis on Saturday, 1 September, 1956
Original: Willie and Ruth, 1954
Elvis's version can be heard on Elvis' Golden Records; Recorded Live On Stage In Memphis

Jerry Leiber and Mike Stoller stand amongst the really important Rock'n'Roll writers, and Elvis recorded a number of their compositions. However, they apparently wrote *Love Me* as a country music parody and called it one of the worst songs they'd written. Presumably this was before they had heard Elvis's version!

Love Me Tender (Aura Lee) (Fosdick/Poulton)
>Recorded by Elvis on Friday, 24 August, 1956
>Original: Frances Farmer, 1936
>Elvis's version can be heard on The Complete 50's Masters 2; ELV1S 30 #1 Hits

The poem *Aura Lee* was written in 1861 during the American Civil War. It was a fovourite of the South and later received new words to become the West Point anthem, *Army Blue*. It had been recorded as a song on numerous occasions before Elvis sang it with new words by Vera Matson (a pseudonym used by Ken Darby—actually his wife's name!) for his first film, *The Reno Brothers*—the title of the film was then changed to cash in on the popularity of Elvis's rendition. Frances Farmer's version also featured in the 1936 film *Come and Get It*.

Loving Arms (Jans)
>Recorded by Elvis on Thursday, 13 December, 1973
>Original: Dobie Gray, 1973
>Elvis's version can be heard on Good Times; Walk A Mile In My Shoes—The Essential 70's Masters Disc 2

Dobie Gray had a huge success in 1965 with the number *The In Crowd* and is probably still best known for that performance.

MacArthur Park (Webb)
>Recorded by Elvis on Saturday, 29 June, 1968
>Original: Richard Harris, 1968
>Elvis's version can be heard on The Burbank Sessions, Volume 2

The real MacArthur Park is situated at the end of Wilshire Boulevard in Los Angeles. Jim Webb composed the song and actor Richard Harris recorded it as part of *A Tramp Shining*, an album consisting solely of Webb songs, in January 1968. Released as a single of over seven minutes playing time, *MacArthur Park* became a massive international hit. It was awarded a Grammy for Best Arrangement Accompanying Vocalist(s) of 1968. Elvis sang a few lines of *MacArthur Park* during the taping of the 1968 NBC TV Special. Though not officially released, this extract can be heard on an unofficial recording.

Make Believe (Hammerstein/Kern)
>Recorded by Elvis on Autumn 1960
>Original: The Paul Whiteman Orchestra (vocals Bing Crosby), 1928
>Elvis's version can be heard on The Home Recordings

According to the sleeve-notes of *The Home Recordings,* this number was recorded in Perugia Way, Bel Air; the book, *A Life In Music,* however, gives Monovale Drive, Hollywood, as the recording location. *Make Believe* was written for the musical *Showboat,* which was based on the Edna Ferber novel of the same name, and was premiered in 1927 as a Ziegfeld production.

Make The World Go Away (Cochran)
>Recorded by Elvis on Sunday, 7 June, 1970
>Original: Ray Price, 1963
>Elvis's version can be heard on I'm 10,000 Years Old: Elvis Country; Walk A Mile In My Shoes—The Essential 70's Masters Disc 3

Songwriter Hank Cochran also wrote Patsy Cline's *I Fall To Pieces.* Ray Price's 1963 original of *Make The World Go Away* appeared first on his *Night Life* LP. The number was recorded that same year by Timi Yuro and Skeeter Davis.

Mama Don't Dance (Loggins/Messina)
>Recorded by Elvis on Wednesday, 20 March, 1974
>Original: Kenny Loggins and Jim Messina (as Your Mama Don't Dance), 1972
>Elvis's version can be heard on Recorded Live On Stage In Memphis

Elvis performed this number in Memphis as part of the ultimate Rock'n'Roll medley, *Long Tall Sally/A Whole Lotta Shakin' Goin' On/Mama Don't Dance/Flip, Flop and Fly/Jailhouse Rock/Hound Dog.*

Mansion Over The Hilltop (Stanphill)
>Recorded by Elvis on Sunday, 30 October, 1960
>Original: Red Foley, 1953
>Elvis's version can be heard on His Hand In Mine; Amazing Grace (CD 1)

Ira Stanphill wrote over 400 gospel songs and was a well-known singing evangelist. See other Foley originals recorded by Elvis: *Just A Closer Walk With Thee; Just Call Me Lonesome; Old Shep; (There'll Be) Peace In The Valley (For Me).*

Mary In The Morning (Cymbal/Rashkow)
> Recorded by Elvis on Friday, 5 June, 1970
> Original: Al Martino, 1967
> Elvis's version can be heard on That's The Way It Is; Walk A Mile In My Shoes—The Essential 70's Masters Disc 3

Al Martino made a little bit of history in 1952 when his first success, *Here In My Heart*, took him to the top spot of the UK singles charts, the first American artist to do so. He signed his first record deal in 1950, after having won Arthur Geoffrey's *Talent Scout Show*.

Maybellene (Berry)
> Recorded by Elvis on Saturday, 20 August, 1955
> Original: Chuck Berry, 1955
> Elvis's version can be heard on The Complete 50's Masters 5 (Rare and Rockin')

Elvis covered numerous Berry numbers—see also *Brown Eyed Handsome Man*; *Johnny B. Goode*; *Long Live Rock And Roll (School Days)*; *Memphis, Tennessee*; *Promised Land*; *Too Much Monkey Business*.

Memphis, Tennessee (Berry)
> Recorded by Elvis on Sunday, 12 January, 1964
> Original: Chuck Berry, 1959
> Elvis's version can be heard on Elvis For Everyone; From Nashville to Memphis (3)

There's a story that Elvis had some friends around and played them the acetate of his new recording, *Memphis Tennessee*. Presumably he wanted to release it as a single. Unfortunately, one of the guests, Johnny Rivers, liked the number, recorded and released it quickly, and had a number 2 Hot 100 hit with it. Elvis covered numerous Berry numbers—see also *Brown Eyed Handsome Man*; *Johnny B. Goode*; *Long Live Rock And Roll (School Days)*; *Maybellene*; *Promised Land*; *Too Much Monkey Business*.

Men With Broken Hearts (Williams)
>   Recorded by Elvis on Tuesday, 11 August, 1970
>   Original: Hank Williams (as Luke The Drifter), 1950
>   Elvis's version can be heard on The Essential 70's Masters (5); Live In Las Vegas (2)

Relatively hard-to-find "spoken-word poem" by the great Hank Williams, which he recorded on 21 December 1952. Williams himself counted it among his favorite songs, and Elvis occasionally recited parts of it during his concert performances in the late 1960s and 1970s. It has been covered by just a handful of artists.

Merry Christmas Baby (Baxter/Moore)
>   Recorded by Elvis on Saturday, 15 May, 1971
>   Original: Three Blazers, 1949
>   Elvis's version can be heard on Elvis Sings The Wonderful World Of Christmas; If Every Day Was Like Christmas

A real bluesy Christmas number! Compare Elvis's enjoyment in performing this number with similar enjoyment in his own original *Santa Claus Is Back In Town*! He enjoyed singing these numbers (and what about D.J. Fontana's opening on the latter!). Then listen to his boredom in numbers such as *Silver Bells* and, would you believe, *Winter Wonderland*. No wonder the man had problems! Anyway, This number just goes to show what a great Blues singer Elvis could have been (well, *was*, but didn't get enough chance to show it!). See also *Reconsider Baby* in this respect.

Milkcow Blues Boogie (Traditional?)
>   Recorded by Elvis on Friday, 10 December, 1954
>   Original: James Kokomo Arnold, 1934 (as Milk Cow Blues)
>   Elvis's version can be heard on The Sun Sessions CD; The Complete 50's Masters 1

So who did write this number? Some sources list "Traditional," presumably meaning they don't know, others indicate Sleepy John Estes, and still others give Kokomo Arnold himself the credit. Certainly not traditional was Elvis's breaking into the number after a few seconds to announce, "Hold it fellahs. That don't move me—let's get real, real gone for a change," before increasing the tempo, with Scotty and Bill tagging along. Anyone who thinks that Elvis copied other artists' recordings in order to break into the business has clearly not listened to Elvis's early renditions. His own version of this song, for example, bears almost no resemblance to Kokomo Arnold's original. Rather, it seems to indicate that Elvis had listened to thousands of pieces, some of which had left traces somewhere in his memory, traces he used to create something very different.

Milky White Way (Coleman/Gray)
>Recorded by Elvis on Sunday, 30 October, 1960
>Original: The Trumpeteers, 1947
>Elvis's version can be heard on His Hand In Mine; Amazing Grace (CD 1)

The Trumpeteers original release of this number reached number 8 in the R&B charts. The lead singer, Joseph Armstrong, was also a member of the Golden Gate Quartet.

Miracle Of The Rosary (Denson)
>Recorded by Elvis on Saturday, 15 May, 1971
>Original: Lee Denson, 1960
>Elvis's version can be heard on Elvis Now

Denson wrote and recorded the original version of this track, which was released on Enterprise 9086 in 1960.

Mona Lisa (Livingston/Evans)
>Recorded by Elvis on April, 1959
>Original: Nat King Cole, 1950
>Elvis's version can be heard on The Home Recordings

Nat "King" Cole was not just an accomplished vocalist, but was also an amazing pianist. He enjoyed enormous prestige, initially as an accompanyist or as a member of a band (he performed with Lionel Hampton, for example) and later as a performer in his own right, enjoying success after success. A heavy smoker, he died of lung-cancer in 1965. Elvis's recording was made on a consumer tape-recorder in his home in Goethestrasse, Bad Nauheim, Germany, during his military service.

Money Honey (Stone)
>Recorded by Elvis on Tuesday, 10 January, 1956
>Original: The Drifters, 1953
>Elvis's version can be heard on Elvis Presley (Rock 'n' Roll no.1); The Complete 50's Masters 1

Clyde McPhatter was the lead singer of The Drifters when they recorded this number. Elvis's version was recorded during his first RCA session, with RCA technicians attempting to recreate the Sun sound. Clyde McPhatter joined

Billy Ward and the Dominoes in 1950, but left to form the Drifters in 1953. Elvis recorded the Drifters' *Fools Fall In Love* and *If You Don't Come Back*. Other McPhatter originals recorded by Elvis are *Without Love* and *Such A Night*. McPhatter died on June 13, 1971; he was inducted into the Rock'n'Roll Hall of Fame in 1987.

Moody Blue (James)

Recorded by Elvis on Wednesday, 4 February, 1976
Original: Mark James, 1974
Elvis's version can be heard on Moody Blue; Walk A Mile In My Shoes— The Essential 70's Masters Disc 2

Mark James also wrote *It's Only Love*, *Suspicious Minds* and *Always On My Mind*.

Moonlight Sonata (Beethoven)

Recorded by Elvis in 1966
Original: Ignaz Jan Paderewski, 1923
Elvis's version can be heard on In A Private Moment

Huh! Elvis does Beethoven? Yes, honestly! Although a self-taught pianist, Elvis was quite a dab-hand on the ivories, apparently. The Moonlight Sonata, or *Sonata quasi una Fantasia*, was composed by The Deaf One in 1801. It consists of three movements, Adagio Sostenuto, Allegretto, and Presto.

Elvis's somewhat abbreviated version was recorded at home and was never intended for official release. However, this was not the only time that Elvis is known to have played the number for his own pleasure—he was "caught" doing so in a rehearsal room during the filming of his 1968 TV Special and worked on it each night with the Special's arranger, Billy Goldenberg. It was only after some of Elvis's "friends" interrupted them and made some insulting remarks about classical music that Elvis seemed to lose interest.

Ignacy (Ignaz and sometimes Ignace) Paderewski lived from 1860 to 1941 and was something of a superstar long before the word had been invented. He had flowing red hair, was an excellent pianist (the best-paid ever) and a wonderful speaker. He prepared USA President Wilson's Treaty of Versailles and acted as prime-minister of the newly independent Poland for two years from 1919 (he signed the peace treaty which led to Poland's independence). In 1936 he appeared in the film *Moonlight Sonata*. He gave all his money away and died a poor man in New York, once more calling for a free Poland. He was awarded a state burial in Arlington Cemetery and was buried again in 1992 in Poland. His heart, however, is kept at the Church of The Black Madonna in Doylestown, Pennsylvania.

Moonlight Swim (Dee/Weisman)

    Recorded by Elvis on Wednesday, 22 March, 1961
    Original: Nick Noble, 1957
    Elvis's version can be heard on Blue Hawaii

Nick Noble had a US top 40 entry with his single of *Moonlight Swim* in late 1957.

More (Newell/Ortolani/Oliviero)

    Recorded by Elvis on Thursday, 20 August, 1970
    Original: Riz Ortolani, 1963.
    Elvis's version can be heard on The Monologue LP

More was the theme to the 1963 Italian film *Mondo Cane*. It was written by Norman Newell, Riz Ortolani and N. Oliviero, winning an Oscar for Best Song. The original Italian title was *Ti Guardero' Nel Cuore*. Elvis sang a few lines of the song on a number of occasions in concert.

Must Jesus Bear The Cross Alone (Shepherd/Beecher/Allen)

    Recorded by Elvis on Friday, 31 March, 1972
    Original: Sam Cooke and The Soul Stirrers, 1956
    Elvis's version can be heard on Amazing Grace (CD 2)

The hymn, *Must Jesus Bear the Cross Alone?* originally read "Shall Simon bear the cross alone, and other saints be free." Thomas Shepherd, the author, used his hymn after preaching about Simon Peter, who was believed to have been crucified upside down. Later, the hymn was altered to refer to Jesus. The hymn was written in 1693. Henry Beecher added further verses in the 19th century. George Allen provided the music usually associated with the hymn in 1844, although it is sometimes also sung to the tune of *Amazing Grace*. Sam Cooke is known as "the inventor of soul music," but prior to his solo career, he led the Gospel group, The Soul Stirrers. Their version was titled *Must Jesus Bear This Cross Alone?* Cooke was murdered in 1964. Elvis's concert version was sung as a medley together with *Turn Your Eyes Upon Jesus* and *Nearer My God To Thee*.

My Babe (Dixon)

    Recorded by Elvis on Monday, 25 August, 1969
    Original: Little Walter Jacobs, 1955
    Elvis's version can be heard on Elvis Sings The Blues; In Person

Marion "Little Walter" Jacobs is generally considered the greatest blues harmonica player ever. He started playing harmonica as a child, was living basically on the street when he was 12 and by the time he was 17, in 1947, had travelled to Chicago from his native New Orleans, Louisiana, where he started playing and recording with Muddy Waters. Little Walter had a history of drink and drug problems and died from injuries sustained in a Chicago street fight, aged just 37, in 1968. Listen to the gospel number *This Train Don't Carry No Gamblers* The similarity between this number and *My Babe* is remarkable and I suspect that *My Babe* is derived from *This Train*.

My Baby Left Me (Crudup)
Recorded by Elvis on Monday, 30 January, 1956
Original: Arthur "Big Boy" Crudup, 1949
Elvis's version can be heard on For LP Fans Only; Recorded Live On Stage In Memphis

Arthur Crudup was born in 1905. He did not learn to play guitar until he was 32. His records enjoyed considerable success in the Southern states of the USA during the 1940s and early 1950s, but he disappeared from the recording scene in 1954. He enjoyed a career revival with the renewed interest in Blues music in the mid 1960s. Arthur Crudup died in 1974. See also *So Glad You're Mine* and *That's All Right Mama*.

My Boy (Boutayre/François)
Recorded by Elvis on Thursday, 13 December, 1973
Original: Richard Harris (?), 1971
Elvis's version can be heard on Good Times; Walk A Mile In My Shoes—The Essential 70's Masters Disc 2

Richard Harris certainly recorded the original English-language version of this number, but the real original dates to 4 years earlier, when Claude François wrote and recorded *Parce-que Je T'Aime Mon Enfant* (*Because I Love You, My Child*). See *My Way* for another Gallic surprise!

My Country, 'Tis Of Thee (Smith)
Recorded by Elvis on Wednesday, 29 July, 1970
Original: Columbia Band, 1901
Elvis's version can be heard on Electrifying (Bilko 5100 unofficial CD)

The melody is the same as that used for *God Save The King/Queen* and dates perhaps back to the 17th century. Words were later provided by Samuel Smith. The first known performance was in September 1745 at the Drury Lane Theatre, London. The tune has been used in numerous countries as national anthem, including Prussia and Russia. Elvis's recording is an informal one made during rehearsals and never intended for release—indeed it has never been officially released and can be found only on the unofficial CD indicated above.

My Happiness (Peterson/Bergantine)
   Recorded by Elvis on June 1953
   Original: Jon and Sondra Steele, 1948
   Elvis's version can be heard on The Great Performances; The Complete 50's Masters 1

The Rosetta Stone of modern music, the beginning of history, the start of time—this is the first song Elvis recorded and it was done on his own initiative. Many have reported that it was meant as a birthday present for his mother, but this is unlikely as her birthday was some months previous. A gift for his mother, possibly, but Elvis more than likely wanted two things from this initiative: to hear how he sounded on record and to impress Sam Phillips. Phillips wasn't too impressed, however, so Elvis returned later to cut a second personal disk. He still had to wait a year before Phillips called him in for an audition, though, but this $4 *My Happiness*, backed with *That's When Your Heartaches Begin*, was really the start of it all!

My Heart Cries For You (Faith/Sigman)
   Recorded by Elvis in 1966
   Original: Guy Mitchell, 1950
   Elvis's version can be heard on A Golden Celebration

My Heart Cries For You gave Guy Mitchell his first million seller when it reached number 2 in 1951, after having been released in December 1950. Several other artists recorded the song about the same time, including Vic Damone and Dinah Shore. The song was written by Carl Sigman and Percy Faith, an adaptation of the melody from *Chanson de Marie Antoinnette*, purported to have been written by the 18th century French queen. Elvis's version is an informal recording, made in Rocca Place, Hollywood. It was discovered on an acetate by Joan Deary of RCA records when she searched Graceland after Elvis's death, in the hope of finding some overlooked recordings.

My Way (Revaux/François/Thibaut)
>Recorded by Elvis on Thursday, 10 June, 1971
>Original: Paul Anka (?), 1969
>Elvis's version can be heard on Aloha From Hawaii Via Satellite; Walk A Mile In My Shoes—The Essential 70's Masters Disc 4

In fact, Paul Anka deserves two question marks. The song was originally recorded in French by Claude François as *Comme d'Habitude* (see also *My Boy*) in 1967—that's the first question mark cleared up. So why a second? Well, none other than young David Bowie recorded an earlier English translation, titled *Even A Fool Learns To Know*, in 1968. Who said it was Frank's song? Anyway, Anka bought the rights to the song after having heard the French version and when Sinatra asked him to write a song for him (Sinatra was toying with the idea of early retirement), he offered him *My Way*. Incidentally, Claude François recorded the English version shortly before he was killed when a hair-drier fell into his bath water!

Mystery Train (Parker/Phillips)
>Recorded by Elvis on Monday, 11 July, 1955
>Original: Herman "Little Junior" Parker, 1953
>Elvis's version can be heard on The Sun Sessions CD; The Complete 50's Masters 1

The original record release was credited to Little Junior's Blue Flames. The number was probably based on a Carter Family song from 1930, called *Worried Man Blues*.

Nearer My God To Thee (Flower/Mason)
>Recorded by Elvis on Friday, 31 March, 1972
>Original: Harry Macdonough, 1901
>Elvis's version can be heard on Amazing Grace (CD2)

Poet Sarah Flower (Sarah Fuller Flower Adams) wrote the verses used in this hymn in 1841. Different tunes are used with the words, depending on location and persuasion: in the UK the tune *Horbury* composed by John Dykes, is preferred, but in the US Lowell Mason's *Bethany* is used, so I assume this is what Elvis sings. There is confusion about which, if any, of the tunes was played on the *Titanic* as it was sinking. The version by Elvis is a rehearsal recording, never intended for release.

Never Been To Spain (Axton)
    Recorded by Elvis on Saturday, 10 June, 1972
    Original: Hoyt Axton, 1971
    Elvis's version can be heard on Elvis as Recorded at Madison Square Garden; Walk A Mile In My Shoes—The Essential 70's Masters Disc 5

Hoyt's mother, Mae Axton, wrote Elvis's own original *Heartbreak Hotel*. *Never Been To Spain* was a big hit in 1971 for Three Dog Night. Hoyt himself seems also to have been a bit of an actor, having appeared in a number of films, including Spielberg's *The Gremlins*. Hoyt Axton died in 1999.

No More (Robertson/Blair)
    Recorded by Elvis on Tuesday, 21 March, 1961
    Original: Musique De La Garde Républicaine, 1899
    Elvis's version can be heard on Blue Hawaii

The song on which *No More* was based is *La Paloma*, written By Sebastián Yradier, a Basque and student of the Madrid Conservatory, who was influenced by the music of Havana, Cuba, during his travels in the 1850s. He wrote the song and performed it for the first time in Havana in 1855; it was first published in 1859.

O Come, All Ye Faithful (Wade/Oakley)
    Recorded by Elvis on Sunday, 16 May, 1971
    Original: John McCormack & William H. Reitz and male chorus, 1915
    Elvis's version can be heard on Elvis Sings The Wonderful World Of Christmas; If Every Day Was Like Christmas

Englishman John Francis Wade wrote the words and music for *Adeste Fideles*; these were published together in 1782. The original Latin words were translated into English by Frederick Oakley in 1841. Although crooner Bing Crosby recorded *O Come All Ye Faithful* with English words in the 1940s, McCormack and Co. beat him by some thirty years with the original "original" version!

Ode To Billie Joe (Gentry)
    Recorded by Elvis on Monday, 11 September, 1967
    Original: Bobbie Gentry, 1967
    Elvis's version can be heard on From Nashville to Memphis CD 3

Don't look for this title on the *From Nashville To Memphis* CD mentioned above, as it is not listed! Elvis gives us just a couple of lines, sung comically, before getting into *Hi-Heel Sneakers*. Bobbie Gentry, born Roberta Streeter in

1944, never matched the success of her self-penned first hit, Ode To Billie Joe. But what a song! It won her four Grammy Awards in 1967: Best New Artist, Best Female Vocal Performance, Best Contemporary Female Solo Vocal Performance and Best Arrangement Accompanying A Vocalist. And Elvis seems to have liked the song, too!

Oh Happy Day (Traditional)
>Recorded by Elvis on Friday, 7 August, 1970
>Original: Elsie Baker & Elizabeth Wheeler, 1913
>Elvis's version can be heard on Peace In The Valley (3-CD set)

This traditional song became very popular in 1969 when The Edwin Hawkins Singers, featuring Dorothy Morgan, scored an international multi-million seller with the number. The Singers had recorded *Oh Happy Day* in 1967, together with seven other traditional gospel songs, in an effort to raise funds for the choir, then known as the Northern California State Youth Choir. The song received a Grammy award for Best Soul Gospel song of 1969. The first known recording, however, dates from April 1913 on Victor 17343, with composing credit given to Goetz.

Elvis never made a studio recording of *Oh Happy Day*," but he sang it occasionally in concert and thought about using it in his 1968 TV special. A pity he didn't!

Oh How I Love Jesus (Whitfield)
>Recorded by Elvis in 1966
>Original: Frederick Whitfield, ca.1900
>Elvis's version can be heard on In A Private Moment

Frederick Whitfield was an Anglican clergyman who lived from 1829-1904. In 1855 he published this hymn while still a student at Trinity College in Dublin, Ireland. Whitfield was born and raised in England. After graduating from Trinity College, he was ordained in the Church of England. A recording exists of Whitfield singing his own composition; I do not know the exact date of the recording, but Whitfield died in 1904. Elvis's version of this hymn was recorded at home and never intended for commercial release.

Oh Little Town Of Bethlehem (Brooks/Redner)
>Recorded by Elvis on Saturday, 7 September, 1957
>Original: Trinity Choir, 1916
>Elvis's version can be heard on Elvis' Christmas Album; If Every Day Was Like Christmas

The number was written by Phillip Brooks and Lewis Redner in 1868, following a visit by Brooks to Bethlehem in 1865: Brooks first wrote a poem and then asked Redner to put it to music. It was first performed on December 27th 1868.

Old MacDonald (Starr)
>Recorded by Elvis on Wednesday, 29 June, 1966
>Original: The Skillet Lickers, 1928
>Elvis's version can be heard on Double Features: Spinout & Double Trouble

Old MacDonald is a popular children's song in English-speaking countries, in which animal sounds are strung together to form a sort of memory game. Fortunately the studio bosses didn't go quite that far with Elvis…A surprising array of artists have recorded various versions of this number, including Frank Sinatra, who had a Billboard Hot 100 charting in 1960 and Tony Curtis, who sang it in the 1963 film *Captain Newman M.D.* together with the neuropsychiatric ward, which seems utterly appropriate.

Old Shep (Foley/Arthur)
>Recorded by Elvis on Sunday, 2 September, 1956
>Original: Red Foley, 1940
>Elvis's version can be heard on Elvis (Rock 'n' Roll no.2); The Complete 50's Masters 2

The story is that Elvis performed this as a ten year old at the Alabama State and Dairy Fair in Tupelo, winning second prize for his performance. Elvis chronicler Bill Burk, however, asserts in his exceelnt book *Early Elvis, The Tupelo Years* that his research proves that Elvis came fifth that day and wore glasses, to boot!

On The Jericho Road (McCrossman/McCrossman)
>Recorded by Elvis on Tuesday, 4 December, 1956
>Original: F.F. Billups & His Kansas City Gospel Singers, 1944
>Elvis's version can be heard on The Complete Million Dollar Session; The Complete Gospel recordings

The song was written by Don and Marguerete McCrossman in 1928. The full title of this gospel song is, *As We Travel Along On The Jericho Road*. (There is another gospel song called simply *On The Jericho Road*, so perhaps the title used for the Elvis recordings is a mistake.)

On Top Of Old Smokey (Traditional)
>Recorded by Elvis on Sunday, 2 July, 1961
>Original: Kate Smith, 1923
>Elvis's version can be heard on From Hollywood to Vegas (unofficial release)

It is not known who wrote the words of *On Top Of Old Smokey*, but the tune is an old folk song from the hills of the American South. Pete Seeger was a member of The Weavers at the time they recorded their version of the song in 1951 and he provided the arrangement. The song became a million seller in the USA, reaching number 2 in the Best Selling Singles chart put out by Billboard. Elvis did not make a full recording of *On Top Of Old Smokey*, providing just about 10 seconds of the song during a scene in his excellent 1962 comedy film *Follow That Dream*.

One Night (Bartholomew/King)
>Recorded by Elvis on Saturday, 23 February, 1957
>Original: Smiley Lewis, 1956
>Elvis's version can be heard on Elvis' Gold Records Volume 2; The Complete 50's Masters 3; ELV1S 30 #1 Hits

Elvis's first recording of this number, entitled *One Night Of Sin* and recorded on January 24, 1957, was not released for almost 30 years, being considered too risqué and therefore possibly damaging to his career. That version used Smiley Lewis's original words, referring to "one night of sin is what I'm now paying for." Elvis re-recorded the number some weeks later, changing this phrase to "one night with you is what I'm now praying for." But you could still understand what he meant…

Only Believe (Rader)
>Recorded by Elvis on Monday, 8 June, 1970
>Original: Harmonizing Four, 1957
>Elvis's version can be heard on Love Letters From Elvis; Amazing Grace (CD2)

This is regarded as Elvis's favorite Hymn from his army days and he had a copy of the Harmonizing Four's recording of it in his German home. Their version was released on the Vee Jay label with Jimmy Jones singing the bass part. Writer Daniel Paul Rader was born in 1878 (though most biographies give 1877 as his year of birth) and lived to be 60 years old. He was a powerful evangelical preacher in the early twentieth century and wrote numerous modern hymns, including *Only Believe*, which dates from 1921.

Only The Strong Survive (Gamble/Huff/Butler)
>Recorded by Elvis on Thursday, 20 February, 1969
>Original: Jerry Butler, 1969
>Elvis's version can be heard on From Elvis in Memphis; From Nashville to Memphis (5)

Jerry Butler, nicknamed "The Iceman" for his cool delivery, had a million-seller with this number in the same year that Elvis recorded his version. Butler is now a Chicago County Commissioner, but also continues to make records and perform.

Out Of Sight, Out Of Mind (Hunter/Otis)
>Recorded by Elvis on Tuesday, 4 December, 1956
>Original: Jimmy Wakely, 1953
>Elvis's version can be heard on The Complete Million Dollar Session

Jimmy Wakely got his break into showbusiness in 1940, when his trio was hired to play in Gene Autry's radio show. He left after two years to pursue his own career in music and films, appearing in well over 30 as a cowboy actor. Wakely died in 1982.

Over The Rainbow (Arlen/Harburg)
>Recorded by Elvis on Friday, 31 March, 1972
>Original: Harold Arlen and Judy Garland, 1939
>Elvis's version can be heard on Backstage with Elvis (unofficial CD)

Created in a moment of inspiration, *Over The Rainbow* almost didn't make it to Oz along with Judy Garland in the fantastic 1939 film *The Wizard of Oz*—

first of all the lyricist, E. Harburg, didn't think that Harold Arlen's tune fitted the film, then MGM deleted the number from the print three times, before deciding to include it in the final version. The song went on to win an Oscar for the best film song and was later chosen as the best song of the 20th century by the American Record Industry. Elvis didn't get too far with the number, singing just one line of it during a performance in 1972.

Padre (Larue/Romans/Webster)

Recorded by Elvis on Saturday, 15 May, 1971
Original: Gloria Lasso, 1956
Elvis's version can be heard on Elvis (The Fool album)

Jacques Larue and Alain Romans composed the original French version of *Padre* in 1956. The original title was *Padre Don José*. English lyrics were provided the following year by Paul Francis Webster. Toni Arden had a million-seller with the number in 1958, reaching number 13 in the Billboard Hot 100. During an interview in 1958, Elvis stated that this was his favourite song. Marty Robbins also had a number 5 hit in 1970. A song called *Padre* was released in 1954 by Lola Dee with Stubby and The Buccaneers (I kid you not!), but as this is two years before the stated copyright for the song sung by Elvis and as I've found no supporting evidence, I can only assume that this is a different number.

Peter Gunn Theme (Mancini)

Recorded by Elvis on Monday, 24 June, 1968
Original: Henry Mancini and His Orchestra, 1958
Elvis's version can be heard on The Complete Dressing Room Session (MS-001)

Elvis would occasionally play a tune on his guitar while hanging around (contrary to popular opinion, he wasn't at all bad on the instrument—it was his solid rhythm, after all that drove the early Sun recordings, a fact sadly forgotten by many commentators!). *Peter Gunn* seems to have been a particularly popular "filler" and the 1968 recording is just the first of several versions available. The original music was the theme tune to a very popular TV show called, surprise surprise, *Peter Gunn* starring Graig Stevens and Lola Albright—who later appeared in Elvis's *Kid Galahad*. Pop guitarist Duane Eddy had a big hit in 1960 with the number

Pieces Of My Life (Seals)

    Recorded by Elvis on Thursday, 13 March, 1975
    Original: Charlie Rich, 1974
    Elvis's version can be heard on Today; Walk A Mile In My Shoes—The Essential 70's Masters Disc 2

Sometime recording artist Troy Seals wrote *Pieces of My Life* in the mid-sixties. Another of Seals' numbers was recorded by Elvis, *There's A Honky Tonk Angel*.

Please Don't Stop Loving Me (Byers)

    Recorded by Elvis on Thursday, 13 May, 1965
    Original: Gigliola Cinquetti, 1964
    Elvis's version can be heard on Double Features: Frankie and Johnny; Paradise, Hawaiian Style

Author David Bret suggests in his *Elvis, The Hollywood Years* that *Please Don't Stop Loving Me* was based on the Eurovision Song Contest entry for Italy in 1964, *Non ho l'Eta* (it won the contest). Strangely, when I was watching *Frankie and Johnny* some time ago, my wife, not an Elvis fan (poor woman), pointed out that *Please Don't Stop Loving Me* sounded like *Non ho l'Eta*. Who am I to argue with two such sources? Indeed, there is a definite resemblance…

Pledging My Love (Washington/Robey)

    Recorded by Elvis on Friday, 29 October, 1976
    Original: Johnny Ace, 1954
    Elvis's version can be heard on Moody Blue; Walk A Mile In My Shoes—The Essential 70's Masters Disc 2

Johnny Ace's recording was released just before he killed himself playing Russian Roulette, on Christmas Eve, 1954.

Polk Salad Annie (White)

    Recorded by Elvis on Wednesday, 18 February, 1970
    Original: Tony Joe White, 1969
    Elvis's version can be heard on On Stage; Walk A Mile In My Shoes—The Essential 70's Masters Disc 5

Tony Joe White himself reached number 8 in the US Hot 100 with this number. When interviewed in 2002 for the excellent *Elvis The Man and His Music* magazine, Tony Joe said that he based Annie on someone he knew! Readers of a culinary bent might be interested to learn that "polk salad" is a corruption of "poke sallet" (or is it the other way round?)—cooked with the green shoots of pokeweed, gathered by rural people in the spring.

Portrait Of My Love (Ornadel/West)
>Recorded by Elvis in 1973
>Original: Matt Monro, 1960
>Elvis's version can be heard on Special Delivery From Elvis Presley (unofficial release)

Matt Monro had a British hit with *Portrait of my love* in 1960. The writers are British: Cyril Ornadel and Norman Newell (pseudonym David West). Steve Lawrence took the number into the top ten of the American Hot 100 in 1961. A recording of Elvis singing this song and accompanying himself on the piano was made at a backstage rehearsal in Las Vegas.

Promised Land (Berry)
>Recorded by Elvis on Saturday, 15 December, 1973
>Original: Chuck Berry, 1964
>Elvis's version can be heard on Promised Land; Walk A Mile In My Shoes—The Essential 70's Masters Disc 2

The master of Rock'n'Roll lyrics wrote this during his stay in prison for allegedly transporting a minor across state boundaries. Like almost all of Berry's numbers, it contains some stunning couplets and inventive rhymes. A masterpiece, really.
Elvis covered numerous Berry numbers—see also *Brown Eyed Handsome Man*; *Johnny B. Goode*; *Long Live Rock And Roll (School Days)*; *Maybellene*; *Memphis, Tennessee*; *Too Much Monkey Business*.

Proud Mary (Fogerty)
>Recorded by Elvis on Monday, 16 February, 1970
>Original: Creedence Clearwater Revival, 1969
>Elvis's version can be heard on On Stage; Walk A Mile In My Shoes—The Essential 70's Masters Disc 5

Writer John Fogerty was lead singer with Creedence Clearwater Revival. They reached number 2 in the US Hot 100 with this track in 1970.

Put Your Hand In The Hand (MacLellan)
>Recorded by Elvis on Tuesday, 8 June, 1971
>Original: Anne Murray, 1970
>Elvis's version can be heard on Elvis Now; Amazing Grace (CD 2)

Like myself, you might be surprised to learn that this number is so young—I thought it was a gospel traditional! I am sure I was singing it as a child, and that's ages ago! Anyway, a group called Ocean had the biggest hit with this number, which they recorded on the Kama Sutra label. Gene MacLellan, who wrote the song, also wrote *Snowbird* for Anne Murray, which was also recorded by Elvis!

Que Sera, Sera (Livingston/Evans)
    Recorded by Elvis on April (?), 1959
    Original: Doris Day, 1956
    Elvis's version can be heard on Greetings From Germany (unofficial CD)

The song was written for Alfred Hitchcock's 1956 remake of his own 1934 film *The Man Who Knew Too Much*. The 1956 version starred James Stewart and Doris Day. The song won the Best Song Oscar. Elvis's version is a home recording, made when he was in Germany during his army service, and was never intended for release. Indeed, it has not been released officially and is available only on the above unofficial CD.

Rags To Riches (Adler/Ross)
    Recorded by Elvis on Tuesday, 22 September, 1970
    Original: Tony Bennett, 1953
    Elvis's version can be heard on Walk A Mile In My Shoes—The Essential 70's Masters Disc 1

Adler and Ross met in 1950 and after some smaller successes, created this huge hit for Tony Bennett in 1953. They went on to write the score for the musical, *The Pajama Game*.

Reach Out To Jesus (Carmichael)
    Recorded by Elvis on Tuesday, 8 June, 1971
    Original: Ralph Carmichael and His Orchestra, 1968
    Elvis's version can be heard on Amazing Grace (CD2)

During his career Ralph Carmichael has worked with such names as Nat King Cole, Bing Crosby and Ella Fitzgerald. He also composed the theme music for the TV show *I Love Lucy* and numerous other programmes. In the early 1960s he helped create Light Records/Lexicon Music to promote contemporary Christian music.

Ready Teddy (Blackwell/Marascalco)
>Recorded by Elvis on Monday, 3 September, 1956
>Original: Little Richard, 1956
>Elvis's version can be heard on Elvis (Rock 'n' Roll no.2); The Complete 50's Masters 2

Elvis covered no less than four Little Richard originals in 1956. In addition to *Ready Teddy*, see also *Long Tall Sally*, *Rip It Up*, and *Tutti Frutti*.

Reconsider Baby (Fulson)
>Recorded by Elvis on Monday, 4 April, 1960
>Original: Lowell Fulson, 1953
>Elvis's version can be heard on Elvis Is Back!; From Nashville to Memphis (1)

Elvis had in fact already recorded this number, though the recording was never really intended for official release. It occurred on Tuesday, December 4, 1956, during the famous Million Dollar Quartet session. That recording can be heard on *The Complete 50's Masters* CD 5 (*Rare and Rockin*') If anyone doubts that Elvis could sing the Blues, then they clearly have not heard either this number or his *Merry Christmas, Baby*.

Release Me (Miller/Yount/Williams)
>Recorded by Elvis on Wednesday, 18 February, 1970
>Original: Eddie "Piano" Miller, 1946
>Elvis's version can be heard on On Stage

Eddie could find no-one interested in his own number, *Release Me*, so he recorded it himself on Four Star Records. It was generally not played because of the apparently risqué number, *Motel Time*, on the flip-side. Perk Williams, the singer with the Jimmy Heap band, found it and had minor a hit with it, but Ray Price covered it, too, and had a number 1 hit with it and the rest, as they say, is history, for everyone and his mother then recorded the number! There is some confusion about the date of Miller's original: some sources indicate 1946, either directly or indirectly, whereas others refer to 1954. The copyright for the number in any case dates from 1954.

Rip It Up (Marascalco/Blackwell)
>Recorded by Elvis on Monday, 3 September, 1956
>Original: Little Richard, 1956
>Elvis's version can be heard on Elvis (Rock 'n' Roll no.2); The Complete 50's Masters 2

Elvis covered no less than four Little Richard originals in 1956. In addition to *Rip It Up*, see also *Long Tall Sally*, *Ready Teddy*, and *Tutti Frutti*. *The Originals* author Arnold Rypens asserts that Elvis was offered this number before Little Richard, but that he refused it!

Roses Are Red (My Love) (Byron/Evans)
>Recorded by Elvis on Saturday, 22 March, 1975
>Original: Bobby Vinton, 1962
>Elvis's version can be heard on Long Lost Songs (unofficial release)

Composed in 1961 by Al Byron and Paul Evans, *Roses Are Red (My Love)* provided Bobby Vinton with a big hit on both sides of the Atlantic and earned him his first gold disc. Elvis never recorded this song in a studio and sang it only very occasionally in concert: he performed it in the Las Vegas midnight show on 22 March 1975; a soundboard recording of this concert exists! It might be that the number was written and recorded earlier—I have found references to it having been the B-side of *Picture In My Wallet*, a 1959 release by Darryl And The Oxfords (a sort of Tokens remnants at the time), but have still to receive confirmation.

Run On (arr. Elvis Presley)
>Recorded by Elvis on Wednesday, 25 May, 1966
>Original: Golden Gate Quartet, 1940(?)
>Elvis's version can be heard on How Great Thou Art; Amazing Grace (CD 1)

The Golden Gate Quartet recorded this number at some date between 1939 and 1943. Originally called the Golden Gate Jubilee Quartet, the group started singing together in the mid-1930s. They gradually moved from a pure gospel repertoire to include pop and jazz numbers. They moved from the USA to France in 1959 where they enjoyed considerable popularity.

Runaway (Crook/Shannon)
> Recorded by Elvis on Friday, 22 August, 1969
> Original: Del Shannon, 1961
> Elvis's version can be heard on On Stage; Collectors Gold—Live In Las Vegas

This debut single for Del Shannon made number 1 on Billboard's Hot 100. See also *(Marie's The Name) His Latest Flame*.

Running Scared (Orbison/Melson)
> Recorded by Elvis on Sunday, 7 June, 1970
> Original: Roy Orbison, 1961
> Elvis's version can be heard on Walk A Mile In My Shoes—The Essential 70's Masters Disc 3

Much like with *Ode To Billie Joe*, Elvis gives us just one line of *Running Scared* prior to cutting *Tomorrow Never Comes*. *Running Scared* was written by Roy Orbison and Joe Melson in 1952. It was Roy's fourth million seller and his first American number one.

San Antonio Rose (Wills)
> Recorded by Elvis in 1966
> Original: Bob Wills And His Texas Playboys, 1938
> Elvis's version can be heard on Home Recordings; Long Lost Songs (on stage)—unofficial release

Bob Wills, the "daddy" of Western Swing wrote and recorded *San Antonio Rose* as an instrumental in 1938, together with his group, the Texas Playboys. It was based on an old fiddle tune called *Spanish Twostep*, Bob Wills took the number and made it his theme song. Two years later Wills rerecorded the number, this time with vocal by Tommy Duncan, as *New San Antonio Rose*. Elvis is known to have sung the song on at least one occasion in concert, in the midnight show on 1 September 1970 in Las Vegas: a recording exists. The version on Home Recordings was made in 1966 at Rocca Place, Hollywood, where Elvis often stayed during filming.

Santa Lucia (Teodoro Cottrau)
>   Recorded by Elvis on Wednesday, 10 July, 1963
>   Original: Caruso, 1916
>   Elvis's version can be heard on Elvis For Everyone

Italian Teodoro Cottrau wrote this number in 1850. Elvis's version was sung in *Love In Las Vegas* (US title *Viva Las Vegas*), but not issued on film soundtrack EP. The text used by Elvis is the most common, but is not the original, which was written in a Neapolitan dialect.

Satisfied (Carson)
>   Recorded by Elvis on Friday, 10 September, 1954
>   Original: Martha Carson, 1952
>   Elvis's version has been lost.

Martha Carson wrote and recorded *Satisfied* in 1952. Johnnie Ray recorded the song the following year. Elvis recorded *Satisfied* at Sun Studios, but RCA has been unable to find the number on its Sun tapes!

Saved (Leiber/Stoller)
>   Recorded by Elvis on Saturday, 22 June, 1968
>   Original: LaVern Baker, 1960
>   Elvis's version can be heard on NBC-TV Special

LaVern Baker was born Dolores Williams in 1929. At the end of the 1940s she won her first recording contract with OKeh Records and later moved to Atlantic. There she scored high with *Tweedle Dee* in 1955. *Saved* was both written and produced by Leiber and Stoller and her recording was nominated for a Grammy for Best Rhythm and Blues Recording of 1960. Further success was limited, however, and Baker's last chart entry was in 1966 on a duet with Jackie Wilson, *Think Twice*. LaVern Baker died in 1997. See also *Tweedlee Dee* and *You're The Boss*.

See See Rider (Conley)
>   Recorded by Elvis on Wednesday, 18 February, 1970
>   Original: Big Bill Broonzy, 1920
>   Elvis's version can be heard on Recorded Live On Stage In Memphis; Walk A Mile In My Shoes—The Essential 70's Masters Disc 5

Big Bill Broonzy's real name was William Lee Conley and he wrote this number. It is often listed as *CC Rider*, which is probably a more correct title, the CC referring to County Circuit. A CC Rider was a County Circuit preacher. However, the number might be considerably older than Big Bill Broonzy's 1920s (exact date unknown) recording suggests, as there seems to have been a popular singer called See See Rider at the turn of the 19th and 20th centuries. The song also appears as *Easy Rider*, so it is not impossible that both *See See Rider* and *CC Rider* are successful attempts to avoid record company censorship, "easy rider" probably referring to someone easy to jump into bed with, or who performs well in bed.

Send Me Some Lovin' (Price/Marascalso)
> Recorded by Elvis on Friday, 17 July, 1959
> Original: Leo Price, 1956
> Elvis's version can be heard on Greetings From Germany (Unofficial CD)

Elvis kept himself amused at times during his army stint in Germany by singing the popular songs of the day or songs that he knew from the past. Occasionally the tape recorder was on and capturing these very informal sessions (similar recordings of Elvis exist from other times and locations, too). On one such occasion, Elvis sung this Rock'n'Roll ballad, written and originally recorded by Leo Price. The number is probably better known in the versions of Little Richard and, of course, Buddy Holly.

Sentimental Me (Cassin/Morehead)
> Recorded by Elvis on Monday, 13 March, 1961
> Original: Ames Brothers, 1950
> Elvis's version can be heard on Something For Everybody; From Nashville to Memphis (2)

The Ames brothers reached number 3 in the US Top 100 with this number in 1950 and both Russ Morgan and Ray Anthony also had hits with it in that same year.

Shake A Hand (Morris)
> Recorded by Elvis on Wednesday, 12 March, 1975
> Original: Faye Adams, 1953
> Elvis's version can be heard on Today; Walk A Mile In My Shoes—The Essential 70's Masters Disc 4

Faye Adams' recording stayed at the top of the Rhythm and Blues charts for nine consecutive weeks in 1953.

Shake, Rattle And Roll (Calhoun)
> Recorded by Elvis on Friday, 3 February, 1956
> Original: Big Joe Turner, 1954
> Elvis's version can be heard on The Complete 50's Masters 2

Charles Calhoun is the pen-name of Jesse Stone, a pioneer R&B songwriter, who was a major influence on the development of Rock'n'Roll. Bill Haley provided a sanitised version of this number for white audiences in 1954. Elvis's 1956 version borrows from both the original and Haley's versions. The first appearance of the phrase, "shake, rattle and roll" on record seems to date back to a number recorded in 1931 by Kansas Joe McCoy and Memphis.

She Thinks I Still Care (Lipscomb/Duffy)
> Recorded by Elvis on Monday, 2 February, 1976
> Original: George Jones, 1962
> Elvis's version can be heard on Moody Blue; Walk A Mile In My Shoes—The Essential 70's Masters Disc 2

George Jones is perhaps less well known outside the USA—I was really only aware of his sixties hit *The Race Is On*—but he has had a long and successful career in C&W music, with the associated ups and down in both his professional and his private life.

She Wears My Ring (Serradell)
> Recorded by Elvis on Sunday, 16 December, 1973
> Original: Rudy Wiedöft (Saxophone), 1926
> Elvis's version can be heard on Good Times

The original title of this number is *La Golondrina*, Spanish for *The Swallow*. The number probably originated in Argentina. Rudy Wiedöft has the distinction of having introduced the saxophone (a Belgian invention) to American jazz. The first vocal recording might be that of soprano Rosa Ponselle in 1934, though this is in fact a radio recording. Felice & Boudleaux Bryant provided the English lyrics. Elvis's version on *Good Times* is an official recording. He had made earlier private recordings of the song, however, and at least one of these, from 1960, has been officially released, this on *Elvis In A Private Moment* on the Follow That Dream collectors label. Elvis must have been quick to pick up on the number then, for the earliest reference I can find to the tune with the more familiar words of *She Wears My Ring* is a recording from that same year by Jimmy Bell.

Show Me Thy Ways, O Lord (Shade)

    Recorded by Elvis probably in 1966
    Original: unknown,
    Elvis's version can be heard on The Home Recordings; Peace In The Valley-The Complete Gospel Recordings

Elvis's home recording of this number was found in Graceland in 1996. It was probably made on Red West's tape recorder about 1966. The words are based on Psalm 25.4, "Show Me Thy Ways, O Lord, Teach me thy paths."

Silent Night (Mohr/Gruber)

    Recorded by Elvis on Friday, 6 September, 1957
    Original: The Haydn Quartet, 1905
    Elvis's version can be heard on Elvis' Christmas Album; The Complete 50's Masters 3

The poem *Stille Nacht, Heilige Nacht* was written in 1819 (some sources list 1816, others 1818!) by Father Joseph Mohr of the Church of St Nicholas (Sankt Nikolaus-Kirche) in Oberdorf (Oberndorf), Austria. The church organist, Franz Gruber, wrote the music. Rev. John Freeman wrote the English words in 1863.

Silver Bells (Evans/Livingston)

    Recorded by Elvis on Saturday, 15 May, 1971
    Original: Bing Crosby & Carol Richards, 1951
    Elvis's version can be heard on Elvis Sings The Wonderful World Of Christmas; If Every Day Was Like Christmas

The number was written for the film, *The Lemon Drop Kid*, in which it was sung by Bob Hope and Marilyn Maxwell. According to a Reuters report at the time of songwriter Jay Livingston's death, *Silver Bells* started out as a routine chore. "Bob Hope needed a Christmas song but we thought they all had been written from *White Christmas* on down," Evans said. "We originally called it *Tinkle Bells*, but realized that had a double meaning. There was a silver bell on the desk at our office at Paramount. We laughed. We said we'd make it *Silver Bells*."

Snowbird (MacLellan)
> Recorded by Elvis on Tuesday, 22 September, 1970
> Original: Anne Murray, 1970
> Elvis's version can be heard on I'm 10,000 Years Old: Elvis Country; Walk A Mile In My Shoes—The Essential 70's Masters Disc 3

A great big hit for Anne Murray, reaching number 8 in the US Hot 100 and number 10 in the Country charts.

So Glad You're Mine (Crudup)
> Recorded by Elvis on Monday, 30 January, 1956
> Original: Arthur "Big Boy" Crudup, 1946
> Elvis's version can be heard on Elvis (Rock 'n' Roll no.2); The Complete 50's Masters 1

Arthur Crudup's original was recorded on February 22, 1946. Unlike the other two Crudup numbers he covered, Elvis's version has a substantially different arrangement, omitting the piano. See also *My Baby Left Me* and *That's All Right Mama*.

So High (Jones)
> Recorded by Elvis on Friday, 27 May, 1966
> Original: LaVern Baker, 1959
> Elvis's version can be heard on How Great Thou Art; Amazing Grace (CD 1)

Elvis greatly admired Jimmy Jones, bass singer with the Harmonizing Four (Elvis had a fascination with bass singers and would occasionally try a bass part himself). He wanted Jones to take part in the *How Great Thou Art* sessions, but the singer could not be located. Nevertheless, Elvis went ahead and recorded Jones's *So High*.

Softly And Tenderly (Thompson)
> Recorded by Elvis on Tuesday, 4 December, 1956
> Original: Miss Florence Hinkle & Mr. Harry MacDonough, 1906
> Elvis's version can be heard on The Complete Million Dollar Session

The earliest known recording was on an Edison 2-min cylinder, number 9367. The words of the number, sung during the Million Dollar Quartet jam session in 1956, are based on the biblical text 1 Corinthians 7:24, "Brethren, let every man, wherein he is called, therein abide with God."

Softly, As I Leave You (de Vita/Calabrese/Shaper)
>Recorded by Elvis on Saturday, 13 December, 1975
>Original: Mina, 1960
>Elvis's version can be heard on Elvis Aron Presley

Softly As I Leave You is the English version of an Italian original, *Piano*, recorded in 1960 by the Italian singer Mina. The original English-language version was recorded in 1962 by British singer Matt Monro.

Soldier Boy (Jones/Williams Jr.)
>Recorded by Elvis on Sunday, 20 March, 1960
>Original: The Four Fellows & Abi Barker Orch., 1955
>Elvis's version can be heard on Elvis Is Back!; From Nashville to Memphis (1)

Although recorded in 1955, this number was written four years earlier in 1951 by David Jones and Larry Banks, when they were serving in Korea (Banks is not credited).

Solitaire (Sedaka/Cody)
>Recorded by Elvis on Tuesday, 3 February, 1976
>Original: Neil Sedaka, 1972
>Elvis's version can be heard on From Elvis Presley Boulevard, Memphis Tennessee

Sedaka's version was an LP release; the first single release was by Andy Williams in 1973.

Somebody Bigger Than You And I (Lange/Heath/Burke)
>Recorded by Elvis on Friday, 27 May, 1966
>Original: The Ink Spots, 1951
>Elvis's version can be heard on How Great Thou Art; Amazing Grace (CD 1)

The Ink Spots might have had the original version, but Elvis was probably more influenced by Jimmy Jones and the Harmonizing Four's version.

Something (George Harrison)
>Recorded by Elvis on Sunday, 14 January, 1973
>Original: Joe Cocker, 1969
>Elvis's version can be heard on Aloha From Hawaii Via Satellite; Walk A Mile In My Shoes—The Essential 70's Masters Disc 5

"Why not The Beatles?" I hear you shout! Well, Joe Cocker, the Sheffield Shrieker, recorded his version before The Beatles, though their version was released first.

Spanish Eyes (Kaempfert/Snyder/Singleton)
> Recorded by Elvis on Sunday, 16 December, 1973
> Original: Freddy Quinn (?), 1966
> Elvis's version can be heard on Good Times; Elvis, Live & Unplugged

German big band leader and composer Bert Kaempfert (he also wrote *Strangers In The Night*) wrote and recorded this melody as *Moon Over Naples* in 1965. Freddy Quinn, a German crooner, released the first English vocal version, now called *Spanish Eyes*, with text by Ted Snyder and Charlie Singleton, in 1965. Elvis's studio recording of this number might date from 1973, but the version on *Elvis, Live & Unplugged* is a home recording and pre-dates the official version by a month; it was recorded at Linda Thompson's home.

Stagger Lee (Traditional)
> Recorded by Elvis on ca. Thursday, 16 July, 1970
> Original: Frank Westphal & His Regal Novelty Orchestra, 1923
> Elvis's version can be heard on Get Down And Get With It (unofficial CD)

What a pity Elvis didn't record this properly—his brief performance during an informal jam session promises so much ("Screw Stagger Lee")! How many titles can a song have? This number probably wins the competition with many variations of *Stagger Lee*, including *Stack O'Lee*, *Stack-a-Lee*, *Stagolee* and several others. The song might well relate to an actual event, though the real story has probably been lost in the retelling. Some versions trace the song back to the James Lee House at 239 Adams, Memphis—another Elvis link!

Stand By Me (Tindley)
> Recorded by Elvis on Wednesday, 25 May, 1966
> Original: Sister Rosetta Tharpe, 1940
> Elvis's version can be heard on How Great Thou Art; Amazing Grace (CD1)

Three legends in a single entry! Charles Tindley, the legendary gospel composer, created this number in 1905—he was also responsible for *By And By* and *I'll Overcome Some Day* (later known as *We Shall Overcome*). Sister Rosetta Tharpe's gospel-singing career spanned more than 50 years, right up until the day before her death in 1973. She was the first gospel singer to tour Europe, her first visit being made in the early 1950s. Elvis needs little introduction, of course, but he was a great admirer of Sister Rosetta Tharpe and recorded a number of Tindley's songs, including *By And By*. An informal home recording of Elvis singing the number, made in April 1959 during his stay in Germany, also exists.

Stay Away (Tepper/Bennett)
>Recorded by Elvis on Monday, 15 January, 1968
>Original: unknown,
>Elvis's version can be heard on Double Features: Kissin' Cousins; Clambake; Stay Away Joe

Some months before his recording was made, Elvis had requested a reworking of *Greensleeves*. An initial attempt, called *Evergreen*, was not recorded, but this one, *Stay Away*, was. The origins of *Greensleeves* are not clear and it is often listed as "traditional" or "anon." One story credits Henry VIII as having composed it for Anne Boleyn. It first appeared in print during the reign of Elizabeth I.

Stay Away, Joe (Weisman/Wayne)
>Recorded by Elvis on Sunday, 1 October, 1967
>Original: Huddie Leadbetter, 1935
>Elvis's version can be heard on Double Features: Kissin' Cousins; Clambake; Stay Away, Joe

Intentionally or not, the writers of this Elvis track seem to have been at the very least inspired by the old slave song, *Pick A Bale O' Cotton*. Huddie Leadbetter is perhaps better known as Leadbelly, who was largely responsible for keeping alive many of America's folk-blues classics, of which *Pick A Bale* is one. Little is known of Leadbelly's early life, other than that it seems not to have been particularly pleasant or lawful. He was imprisoned for murder in 1918, but was pardoned in 1925, only to find himself back in jail in 1930 after a knife-fight. John Lomax, a folklorist, discovered Leadbelly in Angola prison in 1933 and was impressed by his knowledge of folksongs. Leadbelly was released in 1934 and went to work for Lomax, who took him to New York, where he recorded, amongst other numbers, *Pick A Bale O' Cotton*.

Steamroller Blues (Taylor)
>Recorded by Elvis on Sunday, 14 January, 1973
>Original: James Taylor, 1970
>Elvis's version can be heard on Aloha From Hawaii Via Satellite; Walk A Mile In My Shoes—The Essential 70's Masters Disc 2

James Taylor's version was called simply *Steamroller*.

Stranger In My Own Home Town (Mayfield)
    Recorded by Elvis on Monday, 17 February, 1969
    Original: Percy Mayfield, 1963
    Elvis's version can be heard on Back In Memphis; From Nashville to Memphis (4)

Percy Mayfield was born in 1920. He achieved huge US success in 1950 with *Please Send Me Someone To Love*. He is perhaps more remembered as the composer of Ray Charles' international bestseller *Hit The Road Jack*. Mayfield died in 1984.

Such A Night (Chase)
    Recorded by Elvis on Monday, 4 April, 1960
    Original: Clyde McPhatter and the Drifters, 1954
    Elvis's version can be heard on Elvis Is Back!; From Nashville to Memphis (1)

Clyde McPhatter joined Billy Ward and the Dominoes in 1950, but left to form the Drifters in 1953. Other McPhatter originals recorded by Elvis are *Money Honey* and *Without Love*. McPhatter died on June 13, 1971; he was inducted into the Rock'n'Roll Hall of Fame in 1987.

Summertime Has Passed And Gone (Monroe)
    Recorded by Elvis on Tuesday, 4 December, 1956
    Original: Bill Monroe and The Bluegrass Boys, 1946
    Elvis's version can be heard on The Complete Million Dollar Session

Bill Monroe wrote and recorded his *Summertime Has Passed And Gone* in 1946 with his lineup at the time, known as The Bluegrass Boys. Elvis imitated Monroe's delivery during the so-called Million Dollar Quartet session. The number is also listed as *Summertime Is Past and Gone*. Elvis recorded several Bill Monroe originals, including *Blue Moon Of Kentucky, I Hear A Sweet Voice Calling, Little Cabin On The Hill, Sweetheart You Done Me Wrong* and perhaps even *Uncle Pen*.

Surrender (G.D. de Curtis/E de Curtis/Pomus/Shuman)
    Recorded by Elvis on Sunday, 30 October, 1960
    Original: Enrico Caruso, 1911
    Elvis's version can be heard on From Nashville to Memphis (1)

Originally titled *Torna a Surriento* and first published in 1904. The first recorded version was made in 1911 by Enrico Caruso for Victor. Doc Pomus and Mort Shuman wrote new words for Elvis's version in 1960. Versions with different words were recorded earlier, including one by Toni Arden in 1951.

Susan When She Tried (Reid)
>Recorded by Elvis on Tuesday, 11 March, 1975
>Original: Statler Brothers, 1974
>Elvis's version can be heard on Today; Walk A Mile In My Shoes—The Essential 70's Masters Disc 4

Composer Don Reid was a member of the Statler Brothers. Interestingly, none of the Statler brothers was a Statler, the group having taken its name from a box of paper hankies! Their greatest international success came with *Flowers On The Wall* in 1964.

Susie-Q (Hawkins/Lewis/Broadwater)
>Recorded by Elvis on Sunday, 20 July, 1975
>Original: Dale Hawkins, 1957
>Elvis's version can be heard on Susie-Q (unofficial release)

Susie-Q was a hit for Dale Hawkins in 1957. He composed the number, together with Stanley Lewis and Eleanor Broadwater. Elvis's concert guitarist, James Burton played lead on the recording. He explained his own part in its genesis in an interview with Roger Catlin of the Hartford Courant: "I was 15," Burton says. "It was a little instrumental thing I played. When I met Dale Hawkins, he had a blues band. I played this instrumental thing in different places we'd play, and it became so popular—it had such a good dance feel, with a good funky beat in there—Dale said 'I need to write some lyrics to this.' So Dale did." Elvis sang just a small part of *Susie-Q* during the afternoon performance in Norfolk Virginia on July 20th 1975; a recording is known to exist.

Suspicious Minds (Zambon)
>Recorded by Elvis on Thursday, 23 January, 1969
>Original: Mark James, 1968
>Elvis's version can be heard on The Memphis Record; From Nashville to Memphis (4)

Francis Rodney Zambon, the writer of *Suspicious Minds* is the real name of Mark James. See also *Always On My Mind*, *It's Only Love* and *Moody Blue*.

Sweet Caroline (Diamond)
>Recorded by Elvis on Monday, 16 February, 1970
>Original: Neil Diamond, 1969
>Elvis's version can be heard on On Stage

Diamond himself reached number 4 in the US Hot 100 with this number. Elvis also recorded Neil Diamond's *And The Grass Won't Pay No Mind*.

Sweet Inspiration (Pennington/Oldham)
> Recorded by Elvis on Thursday, 20 August, 1970
> Original: Sweet Inspirations, 1968
> Elvis's version can be heard on The Monologue LP (unofficial release)

The group who appeared with Elvis so often during his later years, the Sweet Inspirations, had a number 5 R&B hit with this number in 1968.

Sweet Leilani (Owens)
> Recorded by Elvis in 1960
> Original: Harry Owens and The Royal Hawaiian Band, 1934
> Elvis's version can be heard on In A Private Moment

Though best known for his "Hawaiian" music, Harry Owens was born in Nebraska. However, he became musical director of the Royal Hawaiian Hotel, Honolulu, in 1934, where he mixed traditional instruments with those more commonly used by American dance bands. That same year he wrote *Sweet Leilani* for his daughter, and recorded it with the hotel's band. The number became a big hit for Bing Crosby in 1937, when he sang it in the film *Waikiki Wedding*, earning an Academy Award for Song of the Year and giving Crosby his first gold record.

Elvis's version is a home recording, never intended for release.

Sweetheart You Done Me Wrong (Monroe)
> Recorded by Elvis on Tuesday, 4 December, 1956
> Original: Bill Monroe, 1948
> Elvis's version can be heard on The Complete Million Dollar Session

Bill Monroe is referred to as "the father of Bluegrass." He was born in 1911 and died in 1984 and might have been related to Marilyn Monroe through common descent from US President James Moore! Elvis recorded several Bill Monroe originals, including *Blue Moon Of Kentucky*, *I Hear A Sweet Voice Calling*, *Little Cabin On The Hill*, *Summertime Has Passed And Gone* and perhaps even *Uncle Pen*.

Swing Down Sweet Chariot (Burleigh (or traditional))
> Recorded by Elvis on Monday, 31 October, 1960
> Original: Fisk University Jubilee Quartet, 1910
> Elvis's version can be heard on His Hand In Mine; Amazing Grace (CD 1)

There's a problem with the title of this song! The thing is, another song exists called *Swing Low Sweet Chariot* (it goes, "Swing low sweet chariot, coming for to carry me home...." and is often heard at rugby matches!). It seems that they were both originally part of the same song, but have somehow become separated in time! (The Fisk University Jubilee Quartet's release was titled *Swing Low Sweet Chariot*.) A different version of this number was recorded by Elvis for the film *The Trouble With Girls* and was not officially released until 1995 on the CD, *Double Features: Live a Little, Love a Little; Charro!; The Trouble With Girls; Change of Habit*.

Take Good Care Of Her (Warren/Kent)

    Recorded by Elvis on Saturday, 21 July, 1973
    Original: Adam Wade, 1961
    Elvis's version can be heard on Good Times; Walk A Mile In My Shoes—The Essential 70's Masters Disc 2

A top ten hit for Wade in the USA in 1961. He had two other top ten entries that same year and went on to become a TV show presenter in the USA, becoming the first black host.

Take My Hand, Precious Lord (Dorsey)

    Recorded by Elvis on Sunday, 13 January, 1957
    Original: Thomas A. Dorsey, 1939
    Elvis's version can be heard on Elvis' Christmas Album; Amazing Grace (CD 1)

Thomas Dorsey wrote this number following the deaths of his first wife and baby daughter in 1932 I believe he also recorded it in 1939; if he didn't, then Mahalia Jackson certainly did. Dorsey writes of the song, "This is the greatest song I have written out of near four hundred." The Golden Gate Quartet also recorded the number that same year and the phrasing is very similar to that used by Elvis. Thomas Dorsey died in 1993.

Take These Chains From My Heart (Heath/Rose)

    Recorded by Elvis on Tuesday, 28 August, 1973
    Original: Hank Williams, 1952
    Elvis's version can be heard on Take These Chains From My Heart (unofficial CD)

Written by Hy Heath and Fred Rose, *Take These Chains From My Heart* was first recorded by Hank Williams on 23 September 1952. It was not released until 24 April 1953, almost 4 months after Williams' death on New Year's Day. It reached number one on Billboard's "Country and Western Records Most Played by Disc Jockeys" chart.

Talk About The Good Times (Reed)
> Recorded by Elvis on Friday, 14 December, 1973
> Original: Jerry Reed, 1970
> Elvis's version can be heard on Good Times; Walk A Mile In My Shoes—The Essential 70's Masters Disc 4

Jerry Reed also wrote *A Thing Called Love*, *Guitar Man* and *U.S. Male*, all recorded by Elvis

Tell Me Why (Just A Closer Walk With Thee) (Traditional/Turner)
> Recorded by Elvis on Saturday, 12 January, 1957
> Original: Red Foley, 1950
> Elvis's version can be heard on The Complete 50's Masters 2

Just A Closer Walk With Thee is a traditional American sacred song, which became a million seller for Red Foley in 1950. It is not impossible that Elvis's *Tell Me Why* was based on this tune. Elvis was not the first artist to record *Tell Me Why* as such, either. That honour goes to Marie Knight who had a regional hit with it in early 1956 on the Wing label, prompting a cover version by Gale Storm on Dot. Several different songs have carried the title *Tell Me Why*: The Four Aces in 1951, The Rob Roys in 1959 and The Beatles in 1964, all had totally different numbers by this name. Elvis's version, though recorded in 1957, was not released until 1966 (See also *Old Shep*.)

Tender Feeling (Giant/Baum/Kaye)
> Recorded by Elvis on Monday, 30 September, 1963
> Original: Campbell and Burr, 1918
> Elvis's version can be heard on Double Features: Kissin' Cousins; Clambake; Stay Away Joe

The team of Giant, Baum and Kaye provided many original songs for Elvis's films, but this can hardly be termed "original" as the tune is clearly that of the far older America song, *Shenandoah*. The origin of *Shenandoah* is not known. Some believe it originated among the early American river men or Canadian voyageurs. Others believe it was a land song before it went to sea. Most agree that it incorporates both Irish and African-American elements. The song dates from the early 1800s it tells the tale of a trader who fell in love with the daughter of the Indian chief Shenandoah (other versions also exist)—he presumably had a "tender feeling" for her, so there is some degree of continuity!

Tennessee Waltz (King/Stewart)
>Recorded by Elvis on 1966
>Original: Pee Wee King, 1948
>Elvis's version can be heard on Platinum: A Life In Music

One of *the* country classics, though it is generally associated with Patti Page, who had a no.1 US hit with her more pop version in 1950.

That's All Right Mama (Crudup)
>Recorded by Elvis on Monday, 5 July, 1954
>Original: Arthur "Big Boy" Crudup, 1946
>Elvis's version can be heard on The Sun Sessions CD; The Complete 50's Masters 1

Crudup's original was entitled simply *That's All Right*. Things weren't going too well at Elvis's audition for Sam Phillips, when, during a break in the proceedings, Elvis started messing with this up tempo number—up to then he'd attempted only ballads. Scotty Moore and Bill Black joined in, Sam Phillips was stunned, and the rest, as they say, is history.
Elvis never attempted to "steal" his music from the blacks who developed it. He was the first to give credit where it was due, as witness his remarks in 1956: "The coloured folks been singing it and playing it just like I'm doin' now, man, for more years than I know…I used to hear old Arthur Crudup bang his box the way I do now and I said if I ever got to the place where I could feel what old Arthur felt, I'd be a music man like nobody ever saw." He got there!
Interestingly, Crudup seems to have used the various verses of *That's All Right* separately in other recordings he made in earlier years, so it seems to be an amalgam of remembered, previously composed bits and pieces.
See also *My Baby Left Me* and *So Glad You're Mine*.

That's Amore (Brooks/Warren)
>Recorded by Elvis ion Tuesday, 25 March, 1975
>Original: Dean Martin, 1952
>Elvis's version can be heard on Real Fun On Stage…And In The Studio (unofficial)

Ah, Elvis, the great fan of Dean Martin! Honestly, he was (no, I don't understand it, either!), and so he sang a line of Deano's double-million-seller in a concert in the 1970s, when his idol was in the audience. Actually, Martin wasn't at all keen on the song originally, but changed his mind somewhat when the royalties started to arrive…

That's My Desire (Loveday/Kresa)
>Recorded by Elvis on Tuesday, 4 December, 1956
>Original: Hadda Brooks, 1947
>Elvis's version can be heard on The Complete Million Dollar Session

Pianist Hadda Brooks became known as "Queen of the Boogie" after her first single *Swinging The Boogie* in 1945. She became somewhat typecast with her second release, *Rockin' The Boogie*. In 1951 she became the first black woman to host her own television show in California. She was still recording in the mid-1990s!

That's When Your Heartaches Begin (Raskin/Brown/Fisher)
>Recorded by Elvis on Sunday, 13 January, 1957
>Original: The Ink Spots, 1950
>Elvis's version can be heard on Elvis' Golden Records; The Complete 50's Masters 3

Elvis recorded his first version of this number together with *My Happiness* as a private recording—his very first recording, in fact, in the summer of 1953 (and, no, it wasn't a present for his mother's birthday). It was also included in the jam session that took place at the Sun Studios, Memphis, in December 1956, known to the world as The Million Dollar Quartet. This might have made Elvis think of the song again enough to include it in his next studio session for RCA, which took place at Radio Recorders in Hollywood.

The Eyes Of Texas (Sinclair)
>Recorded by Elvis on Wednesday, 10 July, 1963
>Original: John Sinclair, 1903
>Elvis's version can be heard on Elvis Sings Flaming Star; Double Features: Viva Las Vegas & Roustabout

John L. Sinclair wrote this number in 1903, basing the tune on the traditional *I've Been Working On The Railroad*. Elvis recorded it for the film *Love In Las Vegas* (US title *Viva Las Vegas*) in a medley with *Yellow Rose of Texas*.

The First Noel (arr. Elvis Presley)
>Recorded by Elvis on Sunday, 16 May, 1971
>Original: Mark Andrews (Pipe Organ Solo), 1925
>Elvis's version can be heard on Elvis Sings The Wonderful World Of Christmas; If Every Day Was Like Christmas

This is a seventeenth century Christmas carol, originating from the west of England, where it was originally titled, *The First Nowell* (note spelling!), whose composer is unknown. The oldest printed copy of both music and text appeared in *Christmas Carols*, by William Sandys in 1833. The version by Mark Andrews was a pipe organ solo; the first vocal recording was perhaps by Dick Haymes in 1944.

The First Time Ever I Saw Your Face (MacColl)

    Recorded by Elvis on Monday, 15 March, 1971
    Original: Peggy Seeger, 1958
    Elvis's version can be heard on Walk A Mile In My Shoes—The Essential 70's Masters Disc 1

Long before Roberta Flack's number one version in 1969, *The First Time Ever I Saw Your Face* was recorded by the woman for whom it was written, the sister of Pete Seeger. Flack's version featured in the Clint Eastwood film *Play Misty For Me*.

The Fool (Ford)

    Recorded by Elvis on After April 1959
    Original: Sanford Clark, 1955
    Elvis's version can be heard on A Golden Celebration; Elvis Country

Elvis recorded this number originally at home in Goethestrasse, Bad Nauheim, Germany, whilst on military service. Over ten years later, he used the number again during the *Elvis Country* recording session on Thursday, June 4, 1970.

The Impossible Dream (Leigh/Darion)

    Recorded by Elvis on Saturday, 10 June, 1972
    Original: Jack Jones, 1966
    Elvis's version can be heard on Elvis as Recorded at Madison Square Garden; Walk A Mile In My Shoes—The Essential 70's Masters Disc 5

This number was written for the 1965 musical *The Man Of La Mancha*, in which it was first sung by Richard Kiley.

The Last Farewell (Whittaker/Webster)

    Recorded by Elvis on Monday, 2 February, 1976
    Original: Roger Whittaker, 1975
    Elvis's version can be heard on From Elvis Presley Boulevard, Memphis Tennessee

Yuck! For me (a personal opinion, of course!), this has to be one of the biggest pieces of overproduced false sentimentality that Elvis sang (and I'm a fan!); there isn't a lot of such junk in Elvis's catalogue, I hasten to add! I disliked

Whittaker's original and Elvis's is hardly an improvement—"Tomorrow for old England she sails," my foot!

The Lord's Prayer (Jesus (?))

Recorded by Elvis on Sunday, 16 May, 1971
Original: Traditional,
Elvis's version can be heard on A Hundred Years From Now (Essential Elvis Volume 4)

The Lord's Prayer is, of course, the prayer prescribed by Jesus in the Bible (Matthew 6 and Luke 11). Elvis's version is described in the sleeve-notes of *A Hundred Years From Now* as being an "Informal Performance"—it most certainly is!

The Mickey Mouse Club March (Dodd)

Recorded by Elvis on Tuesday, 1 April, 1975
Original: Jimmy Dodd, 1955
Elvis's version can be heard on Rockin' With Elvis April Fools Day Vol.2 (Claudia unofficial CD)

Elvis as a Mouseteer? Yes, and he wore the mouse ears on stage, too! Well, it was April Fool and the man always enjoyed a laugh! Jimmy Dodd hosted the *Mickey Mouse Club* TV show in the second half of the 1950s. Elvis sang the song during the midnight show during a Las Vegas stint; he sang it again during a Lake Tahoe engagement on 9 May 1976—perhaps April Fool's Day was later that year...Neither of his renditions have been released officially, but the first is available on an unofficial CD.

The Most Beautiful Girl (Bourke/Sherrill/Wilson)

Recorded by Elvis on Sunday, 27 January, 1974
Original: Charlie Rich, 1973
Elvis's version can be heard on Real Fun On Stage...And In The Studio (unofficial)

This number was written in 1968 as *Hey Mister, Did You Happen To See The Most Beautiful Girl In The World*, which was probably too long to fit on a 45 RPM record label! Charlie Rich had a worldwide hit with the song, including a number 1 in the US C&W charts. Elvis sang just one line of the song in a Las Vegas concert in the 1970s. Co-writer Rory Bourke also wrote *Patch It Up* and *Your Love's Been A Long Time Coming*, both recorded by Elvis.

The Twelfth Of Never (Livingston/Webster)
>Recorded by Elvis on Friday, 16 August, 1974
>Original: Johnny Mathis, 1956
>Elvis's version can be heard on Walk A Mile In My Shoes—The Essential 70's Masters Disc 5

As of the time of writing (August 2002), Johnny Mathis is celebrating his 46th year as a recording artist. His album *Johnny's Greatest Hits* spent no less than 490 continuous weeks in the Billboard Top Albums Chart, starting in 1958. Elvis's recording was made during studio rehearsals preceding the August Las Vegas shows.

The Whiffenpoof Song (Sculls/Minnigerode/Pomeroy)
>Recorded by Elvis on Wednesday, 23 October, 1968
>Original: Rudy Vallee, 1937
>Elvis's version can be heard on Double Features: Live a Little, Love a Little; Charro!; The Trouble With Girls; Change of Habit

Guy Sculls (a Harvard man!) wrote the music in 1894 and words were added in 1908 by Meade Minnigerode and George Pomeroy for the Whiffenpoofs (a Yale club!). Apparently, the name of the song is derived from the name of the Yale society that adopted the number as its theme song (and they took their name from that of an imaginary character in the operetta *Little Nemo*!). Rudy Vallee was a Yale graduate and remembered the song from his college days. Elvis's version was recorded in medley with *Violet (Flower of NYU)*.

The Wonder Of You (Knight)
>Recorded by Elvis on Wednesday, 18 February, 1970
>Original: Ray Peterson, 1959
>Elvis's version can be heard on On Stage; Walk A Mile In My Shoes—The Essential 70's Masters Disc 1

Apparently written by Baker Knight for Perry Como, but then given to Ray Peterson, who scored a Top 30 US hit in the summer of 1959 (apparently, Ray had a 4 1/2 octave range at the time). RCA reissued Ray's version in 1964, when it reached number 70 in the US Pop charts. Elvis's version reached considerably higher, but note that the version on the CD *ELVIS 30 #1 Hits* is not that which was released as a single or used on the albums above; instead, it is an inferior version—apparently the compilers didn't notice this error, as there is no indication in the liner notes of it not being the number 1 hit version!

The Wonders You Perform (Chesnut)
>Recorded by Elvis on Wednesday, 25 July, 1973
>Original: Tammy Wynette, 1970
>Elvis's version is probably not available.

The Wonders You Perform was written by Jerry Chesnut and was recorded in 1970 by Tammy Wynette. Her recording reached number 5 on Billboard's country chart. Although an instrumental track for *The Wonders You Perform* was recorded at the Stax Studios, Memphis, on 25 July 1973, it is highly unlikely that Elvis ever recorded a vocal track. Chesnut also wrote *Love Coming Down*, *T-R-O-U-B-L-E* and *Woman Without Love*, all recorded by Elvis.

There Goes My Everything (Frazier)
>Recorded by Elvis on Monday, 8 June, 1970
>Original: Jack Greene, 1966
>Elvis's version can be heard on I'm 10,000 Years Old: Elvis Country; Walk A Mile In My Shoes—The Essential 70's Masters Disc 1

Jack Greene was known as "The Jolly Green Giant" (indeed, his surname often appears as "Green"). Amongst numerous musical incarnations, he appeared as a drummer and vocalist with Ernest Tubb's band. Whilst with the band, he had several solo country hits, including this number, which made a big impact not only on the charts, where it reached the top of the US Country Chart, but also on the 1967 "1st Country Music Association Awards," where it was voted Single of The Year and Song of The Year. Greene was also voted Vocalist of The Year and his LP *There Goes My Everything* was Album of The Year! The number was covered in the UK by Engelbert Humperdinck (and he's lived off it ever since!)

There Is No God But God (Kenny)
>Recorded by Elvis on Wednesday, 9 June, 1971
>Original: Bill Kenny (Ink Spots), 1952
>Elvis's version can be heard on Amazing Grace (CD 2)

The Ink Spots started performing together in 1934. Two years later, Bill Kenny, who became the voice of the Ink Spots, joined and they then went from strength to strength. After an argument in 1951, Bill Kenny's is the only voice heard on subsequent Ink Spots recordings made for the Decca label.

There's A Honky Tonk Angel (Who Will Take Me Back In) (Seals/Rice)
>Recorded by Elvis on Saturday, 15 December, 1973
>Original: Troy Seals, 1973
>Elvis's version can be heard on Promised Land

Co-writer Troy Seals recorded this song for his debut album *Presenting Troy Seals*. Conway Twitty took the number to the top of the US country charts. Cliff Richard's version was withdrawn from the UK market as soon as Cliff discovered exactly what a Honky Tonk Angel was! Seals also wrote *Pieces Of My Life*, recorded by Elvis.

There's No Place Like Home (Payne/Bishop)
>Recorded by Elvis on Tuesday, 4 December, 1956
>Original: John Yorke Atlee, 1891
>Elvis's version can be heard on The Complete Million Dollar Session

This number is also known as *Home Sweet Home*. Originally an operatic aria from Sir Henry Bishop's largely forgotten opera *Clari*, also called *The Maid of Milan*, with words by John Payne. The tune was partly based on a Sicilian Air. The song was the first popular tune to become a "hit," being the first to be intentionally sold so that the "ordinary" person could play it at home (we're talking about the early *19th* century here, remember!). Rossini seemed to like it, too, for he used the tune in his rather better-remembered *Barber of Seville*—more opera! Atlee, also known as "Whistling John Atlee" is sometimes labelled "the first recording star." The earliest vocal recording dates from 1902 and was made by Harry Macdonough & Grace Spencer.

There's No Tomorrow (Hoffman/Corday/Carr)
>Recorded by Elvis on April 1959 (or later)
>Original: Tony Martin, 1949
>Elvis's version can be heard on Platinum: A Life In Music Disc 1

This was a version of *O Sole Mio*, the song Elvis recorded as *It's Now Or Never*. Elvis's home recording, made in Germany during his military service, together with *I'll Take You Home Again Kathleen*, *I Will Be True*, *It's Been So Long Darling*, and *Apron Strings* was released as *Bad Nauheim Medley* on *Platinum: A Life In Music* in 1997.

This Time (Moman)
>Recorded by Elvis on Monday, 17 February, 1969
>Original: Thomas Wayne, 1958
>Elvis's version can be heard on From Nashville To Memphis (Essential 60's Masters) CD 5

Chips Moman wrote this song and went on to have his own recording studio and production company in Memphis. It was at this studio that Elvis recorded some of his very finest work—and for those of you who think that Elvis died in the army, listen to his late 60's work, especially the magnificent *From Elvis In Memphis* LP/CD, and be impressed! Elvis was recorded singing part of this song in combination with *I Can't Stop Loving You* during a session at Moman's studios.

Three Corn Patches (Leiber/Stoller)
>Recorded by Elvis on Saturday, 21 July, 1973
>Original: T-Bone Walker, 1973
>Elvis's version can be heard on Raised On Rock

Aaron Thibeaux Walker—hence the "T-Bone" (sounds like Thibeaux)—was born in 1910. He recorded his first tracks in 1945 and can be regarded as the first electric bluesman, a great influence on the likes of B.B. King, Robert Cray and Stevie Ray Vaughn amongst many others (even Chuck Berry admits to being influenced!). T-Bone Walker died in 1975.

Tiger Man (Louis/Burns)
>Recorded by Elvis on Thursday, 27 June, 1968
>Original: Rufus Thomas, 1953
>Elvis's version can be heard on Elvis Sings Flaming Star; Walk A Mile In My Shoes—The Essential 70's Masters Disc 4

Rufus Thomas's release prior to *Tiger Man* was also animalistic—*Bear Cat*, an answer-song to *Hound Dog*. Joe Hill Louis (or was it Lewis—both forms are used), one of the writers of *Tiger Man*, played on the original recording, though it was credited to Rufus Thomas. *Tiger Man* was Rufus Thomas's follow-up to *Bear Cat*, a sort of answer song to Willie Mae "Big Mama" Thornton's *Hound Dog*. A recording of Elvis rehearsing the number, made on 25 June 1968 has also been released on the set, *Platinum, A Life In Music*.

Time Has Made A Change In Me (Frye)
>Recorded by Elvis on Friday, 31 March, 1972
>Original: Blue Rose, 1972
>Elvis's version can be heard on The Complete On Tour Sessions Vol.2 (unofficial release)

Harkins Frye copyrighted this number in 1948, so it is unlikely that Blue Rose, an all-female Bluegrass group, made the original recording! The number is often listed as "traditional," but this seems not to be the case. Indeed, numerous composer credits can be found, but the consensus seems to be in favour of Harkins Frye, even though his surname is sometimes written "Freye." Confusing!

Today, Tomorrow And Forever (Giant/Baum/Kaye)
>Recorded by Elvis on Thursday, 11 July, 1963
>Original: Johann Strauss Orchester, 1910
>Elvis's version can be heard on Viva Las Vegas EP; Double Features: Viva Las Vegas & Roustabout

Hungarian-born piano virtuoso Franz Liszt wrote three versions of *Liebestraum* between 1847 and 1849, finally publishing in 1850. The third version became the best known and it is on this version that *Today, Tomorrow and Forever* is based. Elvis's original release was a solo number, but an interesting duet featuring Elvis with Ann-Margret, who co-starred with him in *Viva Las Vegas* can be found on the 4-CD set, *Today, Tomorrow And Forever*.

Tomorrow Is A Long Time (Dylan)
>Recorded by Elvis on Thursday, 26 May, 1966
>Original: Ian And Sylvia, 1963
>Elvis's version can be heard on From Nashville to Memphis (3)

Bob Dylan's own version of this beautiful song did not appear until 1971. Elvis's superb version was hidden as a "bonus song" on the film LP *Spinout*— a real scandal that such a track should have been reduced to that status and therefore still remains unknown to the general public. (The same happened with Elvis's own *Suppose* of course, which was on the same album!)

Tomorrow Never Comes (Tubb/Bond)
>Recorded by Elvis on Sunday, 7 June, 1970
>Original: Ernest Tubb, 1945
>Elvis's version can be heard on I'm 10,000 Years Old: Elvis Country; Walk A Mile In My Shoes—The Essential 70's Masters Disc 3

There's another connection between Ernest Tubb and Elvis, apart from this song: Tom Parker, Elvis's (in)famous manager, acted as one of Tubb's advance promo men at the time he made this original.

Tomorrow Night (Coslow/Grosz)
>Recorded by Elvis on Friday, 10 September, 1954
>Original: Horace Heidt and His Orchestra, 1939
>Elvis's version can be heard on Elvis For Everyone; The Sun Sessions CD; The Complete 50's Masters 1

This track was first released on the *Elvis For Everyone* LP in 1963, nine years after its original recording, which is to be found on the collection *The Sun Sessions*. The 1963 release contains overdubs. Horace Heidt might well have had the original version, but Elvis's interpretation sounds as if he was more familiar with Lonnie Johnson's 1947 recording of the number.

Tonight Is So Right For Love (Wayne/Silver/Lilley)
>Recorded by Elvis on Wednesday, 27 April, 1960
>Original: Maud Powell, 1907
>Elvis's version can be heard on G.I. Blues (non-european releases)

The melody is based on (well, copied from...) *Barcarolle* by Jacques Offenbach. For copyright reasons, this track couldn't be released in Europe, so Wayne, Silver and Joe Lilly altered their original lyrics to fit a similar melody taken from *Tales From The Vienna Woods* by Johann Strauss, calling the song *Tonight's All Right For Love*. Copyright problems did not affect release elsewhere in the world, apparently. Indeed, the *Barcarolle* melody had previously been recorded in a "jazzed up" fashion by pianist Frankie Carle and His Sunrise Serenaders in 1940, in purely instrumental fashion. It was an original arrangement by Carle. Carle's version was released on a single with the band's version of Rachmaninov's *Prelude in C sharp minor* (opus 3, No. 2) on the flip. The record was released by Columbia on number 35573. The original recording of the standard music seems to have been made in 1907 by Maud Powell on Victor 17311, quickly followed in 1909 by Marthe Bakkers and Suzanne Brohly on Disque Gramophone GC-34260/1.

Tonight's All Right For Love (Wayne/Silver/Lilley)
    Recorded by Elvis on Saturday, 6 May, 1961
    Original: Marcella Sembrich, 1910
    Elvis's version can be heard on Elvis: A Legendary Performer Vol.1

Because of copyright problems in Europe with the melody used for *Tonight Is So Right For Love*, the words originally written for that song were adapted to fit the similar melody of Opus 325 of *Geschichten aus dem Wienerwald* ("Tales From The Vienna Woods") by Johann Strauss, written in 1868! The working title of Elvis's number was *Vienna Woods Rock and Roll!* Marcella Sembrich was a noted dramatic soprano, born in Austria in 1858; she debuted in Athens in 1877 and later appeared in Vienna, Dresden, London and New York.

Too Much (Rosenberg/Weinman)
    Recorded by Elvis on Sunday, 2 September, 1956
    Original: Bernie Hardison, 1954
    Elvis's version can be heard on Elvis' Golden Records; The Complete 50's Masters 2; ELV1S 30 #1 Hits

Hardison's original was released on Republic 7111 in 1954.

Too Much Monkey Business (Berry)
    Recorded by Elvis on Monday, 15 January, 1968
    Original: Chuck Berry, 1956
    Elvis's version can be heard on From Nashville to Memphis (3)

Elvis covered numerous Berry numbers—see also *Brown Eyed Handsome Man*; *Johnny B. Goode*; *Long Live Rock And Roll (School Days)*; *Maybellene*; *Memphis, Tennessee*; *Promised Land*.

True Love (Porter)
    Recorded by Elvis on Saturday, 23 February, 1957
    Original: Bing Crosby and Grace Kelly, 1956
    Elvis's version can be heard on Loving You; The Complete 50's Masters 3

The original featured in the film *High Society*. Elvis's version appeared on the soundtrack album of his second film, *Loving You*. The first record release of the number, though, was by Grace Powell, also in 1956.

True Love Travels On A Gravel Road (Owens/Frazier)
>Recorded by Elvis on Monday, 17 February, 1969
>Original: Duane Dee, 1968
>Elvis's version can be heard on From Elvis in Memphis; From Nashville to Memphis (4)

Duane Dee was also the first person to record the very well-known country classic, *Before The Next Teardrop Falls*, which he did in 1967. *True Love Travels...* is no slouch in the country stakes, either, having been recorded by The Highwaymen (Waylon Jennings, Kris Kristofferson, Willie Nelson and Johnny Cash) as well as less obvious candidates as Welshman Shakin' Stevens, Nick Lowe and The Grateful Dead!

Trying To Get To You (Singleton/McCoy)
>Recorded by Elvis on Monday, 11 July, 1955
>Original: The Eagles, 1954
>Elvis's version can be heard on Elvis Presley (Rock 'n' Roll no.1); NBC-TV Special

Elvis tried recording this number during a February 1955 Sun session, but the result was unsatisfactory and that particular track has not resurfaced since. Several months later a new, this time successful attempt was made and the number was considered for release as a Sun single, though this never happened. Instead, RCA released the number on its own label, having taken over the track as part of their deal with Sun when they bought out Elvis's contract. (As an aside, it's interesting to note that Roy Orbison also recorded this track in 1955, when it was released on the Je-Wel label as the B-side of his original recording of *Ooby Dooby*, a track he would later re-record at Sun!)

Tumblin' Tumbleweeds (Nolan)
>Recorded by Elvis on ca.1966
>Original: Sons Of The Pioneers, 1934
>Elvis's version can be heard on The Home Recordings

Writer Bob Nolan was leader of the Sons Of The Pioneers. It seems that Elvis also recorded the Pioneers' *Cool Water*, but this has yet to be found.

Turn Around, Look At Me (Capehart)
    Recorded by Elvis on Friday, 28 June, 1974
    Original: Glen Campbell, 1961
    Elvis's version can be heard on In Dreams Of Yesterday (Memory label, CZ)
This was Campbell's first hit. The Vogues made the Top Ten with the number in 1968. Campbell was a frequent session musician in Nashville and even played on some Elvis recordings, notably those from the sessions that gave us the excellent *Viva Las Vegas* soundtrack.

Turn Your Eyes Upon Jesus (Lemmel/Clarke)
    Recorded by Elvis on Friday, 31 March, 1972
    Original: Johnny Hallett, 195?
    Elvis's version can be heard on Amazing Grace (CD 2)
Helen Lemmel was responsible for over 500 hymns during her lifetime (1864-1961). She wrote the hymn *O Soul Are You Weary And Troubled* (the correct title of this number) in 1918, after having read a gospel tract written by Lilian Trotter and based on the biblical passage Matthew 4:1-12. It was first published in 1922. Hallett's version was played on the piano. Elvis's version was made at an informal studio session during the filming of *Elvis On Tou*r, sung together with *Nearer My God To Thee*. It was not included in the film, and was not released until 1994.

Tutti Frutti (Labostrie/Penniman)
    Recorded by Elvis on Tuesday, 31 January, 1956
    Original: Little Richard, 1955
    Elvis's version can be heard on Elvis Presley (Rock 'n' Roll no.1); The Complete 50's Masters 1
Elvis covered no less than four Little Richard originals in 1956. In addition to *Tutti Frutti*, see also *Long Tall Sally*, *Ready Teddy*, and *Rip It Up*.

Tweedlee Dee (Scott)
    Recorded by Elvis on Saturday, 18 December, 1954 (but see comment!)
    Original: LaVern Baker, 1954
    Elvis's version can be heard on The Complete 50's Masters 5 (Rare and Rockin')
LaVern Baker's release was called *Tweedle Dee*. Elvis did not make a studio recording of the number, but three live versions exist: in addition to that on

the set mentioned above, whose sleeve notes indicate not only the date, but also the location as Gladewater, Texas, the CD *Sunrise* has a version supposedly from 22 January 1955 and *The First Live Recordings* (and numerous other CDs) reproduce a recording from 30 April 1955, also purporting to have been made in Gladewater, Texas...But there's a problem, for on 18 December 1954, Elvis was appearing at the Louisiana Hayride in Shreveport, so either he was double-dating, or RCA/BMG have the date incorrect in *The Complete 50's Masters*. Furthermore, Guralnick and Jorgensen's *Elvis Day By Day* provides a list of numbers that Elvis performed on 22 January, 1955—*Tweedlee Dee* is not included! Interestingly, when Elvis appeared in Lubbock in January 1955, he told a young Waylon Jennings that this number would be his next single. See also *Saved* and *You're The Boss*.

U.S. Male (Hubbard)

Recorded by Elvis on Wednesday, 17 January, 1968
Original: Jerry Reed, 1967
Elvis's version can be heard on From Nashville to Memphis (3)

Jerry Hubbard, the author, is the real name of Jerry Reed. He also wrote *A Thing Called Love*, *Guitar Man* and *Talk About The Good Times*, all recorded by Elvis.

Unchained Melody (North/Zaret)

Recorded by Elvis on Sunday, 24 April, 1977
Original: Todd Duncan, 1955
Elvis's version can be heard on Moody Blue; The Great Performances

Theme music for the film *Unchained*, hence the title! Al Hibbler had the first vocal version, reaching number 1 in the US R&B charts in 1955. The song also reached number one in the British charts of that same year, but in a version by Jimmy Young. An earlier recording by Elvis also exists: it dates from 31 December 1976 and can be found on the Follow That Dream collectors label CD *New Year's Eve*.

Uncle Pen (Monroe)

Recorded by Elvis in 1955(?)
Original: Bill Monroe, 1951
Elvis's version can be heard on unofficial 2-Song CD

Uncle Pen is a semi-biographical song about Bill Monroe's uncle and influence, Pendleton Vanderver. There is no absolute certainty that Elvis actually ever recorded this number in the studio. It appeared in the sheet music collection

Elvis' Juke Box Favourites in 1956 and rumours of a recording made while at Sun continue to do the rounds. However, it does seem probable that a recording of Elvis performing the number live does exist (he is known to have sung it live—he did so on his first appearance at the Louisiana Hayride). A recording has been released on the Suedes label (KEYS 1955-578-1), and when the track was played to Scotty Moore a while back in Denmark, after just a few seconds he said, "It is Elvis and it's me playing the guitar." If it's good enough for Scotty, it's good enough for me! (Though I have to say that I still have my doubts!)

Until It's Time For You To Go (Sainte Marie)

Recorded by Elvis on Monday, 17 May, 1971
Original: Buffy Sainte Marie, 1965
Elvis's version can be heard on Elvis Now; Walk A Mile In My Shoes—The Essential 70's Masters Disc 1

UK readers might remember the number 19 UK hit version by The Four Pennies (those of *Juliet* fame). Buffy's own version was only released on a single in 1970, when Neil Diamond also released a single, apparently with rather more success.

Up Above My Head (Tharpe (?))

Recorded by Elvis on Saturday, 22 June, 1968
Original: Southern Sons, 1941
Elvis's version can be heard on NBC-TV Special

Many sources (and, indeed, her own recordings) list Sister Rosetta Tharpe as responsible for both music and words for this number. However, Tharpe's own version was only recorded in 1947, whereas a recording by the Southern Sons from 1941 is clearly the same number. Sister Rosetta Tharpe was one of the very few artists to successfully juggle a career involving both R&B and gospel music. She was a real early rocker, but she was never really happy with her work outside gospel (she also recorded under the name Sister Kati Marie). Her version of *Up Above My Head* was recorded in duet with Marie Knight.

Walk A Mile In My Shoes (South)

Recorded by Elvis on Thursday, 19 February, 1970
Original: Joe South, 1969
Elvis's version can be heard on On Stage; Walk A Mile In My Shoes—The Essential 70's Masters Disc 1

Little success and a lot of session work preceded Joe South's 1968 hit, *Games People Play*, a success on both sides of the Atlantic, soon to be followed by *Walk A Mile In My Shoes*.

We're Gonna Move (Matson/Presley)
>Recorded by Elvis on Friday, 24 August, 1956
>Original: Southern Sons, 1941
>Elvis's version can be heard on Jailhouse Rock (with Love Me Tender)

Vera Matson and Elvis himself are credited for this number, but it seems likely that neither had a great deal to do with its real origins. The musical director of the film *Love Me Tender*, Ken Darby, wrote this along with the other three numbers in the film (one of which was *Love Me Tender*, a reworking of *Aura Lee*), but gave the credit to his wife (Matson) and Elvis. Elvis might well have known a gospel called *There's A Leak In This Old Building*, written by Brother Claude Ely, which is certainly the inspiration for *We're Gonna Move*—same tune and much the same words, too!

Welcome To My World (Winkler/Hathcock)
>Recorded by Elvis on Sunday, 14 January, 1973
>Original: Jim Reeves, 1962
>Elvis's version can be heard on Aloha From Hawaii Via Satellite

Jim Reeves was born in 1923. A "singing disk-jockey," he turned to a full-time singing career in about 1949, but his big break came in 1952 when he stood in for Hank Williams, who had failed to turn up for a show. He became hugely successful in the USA and around the world (especially in South Africa, where he also recorded in Afrikaans). Jim Reeves died on 31 July 1964 when the plane he was piloting crashed outside Nashville during a storm.

What Now My Love (Becaud/Sigman)
>Recorded by Elvis on Sunday, 14 January, 1973
>Original: Jane Morgan, 1962
>Elvis's version can be heard on Aloha From Hawaii Via Satellite; The Home Recordings

Morgan was an American, but first really became popular after having been discovered by a French impresario. She moved to France and enjoyed success throughout Europe before returning to the USA. During her time in France, she recorded a number of Gilbert Bécaud songs, including the first English version of his *Et Maintenant*, as *What Now My Love* (with English lyrics by Carl Sigman) in the same year that Bécaud recorded his original French version. In addition to his frequent on-stage performances, Elvis made a home recording of the song in 1966 and that version can be found on *The Home Recordings*.

What'd I Say (Charles)
>Recorded by Elvis on Friday, 30 August, 1963
>Original: Ray Charles, 1959
>Elvis's version can be heard on Elvis' Gold Records Volume 4; Collectors Gold—Live In Las Vegas

Ray Charles fills many roles: singer, composer, pianist and arranger. Born in 1930, he contracted glaucoma as a child and was completely blind by the age of seven. Despite this, he learned to read and write music and to play several instruments by the time he was 15. His recording career began in 1949, gaining major success in 1954 with *I Got A Woman* (see above).

When God Dips His Love In My Heart (Derricks/Stevenson)
>Recorded by Elvis on Tuesday, 4 December, 1956
>Original: Daniel Sisters & Otis Mccoy, 1949
>Elvis's version can be heard on The Complete Million Dollar Session

Hank Williams and Red Foley also recorded the number. Both Foley and the Daniel Sisters & Otis McCoy recorded this gospel song in 1949. Foley's was probably the very first country gospel hit, but it seems that the Daniel Sisters & Otis McCoy actually made the first recording in June 1949, released on Columbia 20658. Hank Williams' recording dates from late 1950.

When It Rains, It Really Pours (Emerson)
>Recorded by Elvis in November, 1955
>Original: William Robert "Billy The Kid" Emerson, 1954
>Elvis's version can be heard on Elvis For Everyone; The Complete 50's Masters 1

Although recorded in 1955 and handed over to RCA as part of the deal when they bought Elvis from Sun, *When It Rains It Really Pours* was not issued until the *Elvis For Everyone* LP in 1965, in a version that included overdubbed instruments. The original take was first released on *Elvis: A Legendary Performer Vol.4*.

When My Blue Moon Turns To Gold Again (Walker/Sullivan)
>Recorded by Elvis on Sunday, 2 September, 1956
>Original: Wiley Walker and Gene Sullivan, 1941
>Elvis's version can be heard on Elvis (Rock 'n' Roll no.2); The Complete 50's Masters 2

Elvis cuts this number considerably by omitting two verses. The original version was not a success, but in 1944 Cindy Walker reached number 5 in the national charts.

When The Saints Go Marchin' In (Purvis/Black)
>Recorded by Elvis on Tuesday, 4 December, 1956
>Original: Paramount Jubilee Singers, 1923
>Elvis's version can be heard on The Complete Million Dollar Session; Double Features: Frankie and Johnny; Paradise, Hawaiian Style

Elvis sung along on this "traditional" gospel number with Carl Perkins and Jerry Lee Lewis during the Million Dollar Quartet jam session at the Sun Studios in December 1956. It would be almost 10 years, however, before he recorded a more secular version of the number for the soundtrack of the film *Frankie and Johnny*, where it was coupled with *Down By The Riverside*.

When The Snow Is On The Roses (Kusik/Snyder/Last)
>Recorded by Elvis on Monday, 24 August, 1970
>Original: Ed Ames, 1967
>Elvis's version can be heard on Live In Las Vegas

Elvis sings just a couple of lines this number on one of the CDs of the *Live In Las Vegas* box set. Despite singing just two lines of the first verse (and then repeating the same lines), it's clearly a song he likes a lot and fits well into his "melancholy" phase. Kris Kristofferson included the number (in full!) on his 1968 *Jody And The Kid* LP. Ed Ames's original version was released on single and just squeezed into the Cashbox Top 100 in November 1967.

When The Swallows Come Back To Capistrano (Rene)
>Recorded by Elvis at some time in 1960
>Original: Leon T. Rene, 1940
>Elvis's version can be heard on In A Private Moment

In 1939, songwriter Leon Rene was listening to the radio one morning when he heard the announcer say the swallows were about to arrive at the Mission San Juan Capistrano. He got the idea for a song and wrote *When the Swallows Come Back to Capistrano*.
Elvis's version is an informal home recording, never intended for release.

Where Could I Go But To The Lord (Coats)
>Recorded by Elvis on Saturday, 28 May, 1966
>Original: James B Coats, 1940
>Elvis's version can be heard on How Great Thou Art; Amazing Grace (CD 1)

This number again poses the problem of what is an original. K. E. Harvis and J. M. Black wrote the "original" in 1890, but J. B. Coats rewrote the song in

1940, giving us the version we know by Elvis. Red Foley used this song as the B-side of his 1951 release of *Peace In The Valley*.

Where Did They Go, Lord? (Frazier/Owens)
> Recorded by Elvis on Tuesday, 22 September, 1970
> Original: Dallas Frazier, 1970
> Elvis's version can be heard on Walk A Mile In My Shoes—The Essential 70's Masters Disc 1

Perhaps Dallas Frazier's greatest claim to fame is that he wrote *Alley Oop*, a big hit for the Hollywood Argyles in 1960, a track on which he also played. He has been responsible for numerous other hits, however, including *There Goes My Everything* (also recorded by Elvis), O.C. Smith's *The Son Of Hickory Holler's Tramp*, and Charlie Rich's *Mohair Sam*.

Where Do I Go From Here (Williams)
> Recorded by Elvis on Monday, 27 March, 1972
> Original: Paul Williams, 1971
> Elvis's version can be heard on Elvis (Fool)

Writer John Williams's own recording of this number was first issued on his *Life Goes On* LP, released by A&M in 1972. The number reappeared in the 1974 Clint Eastwood film, *Thunderbolt and Lightfoot*.

Where No One Stands Alone (Lister)
> Recorded by Elvis on Thursday, 26 May, 1966
> Original: Mosie Lister, 1955
> Elvis's version can be heard on How Great Thou Art; Amazing Grace (CD 1)

Despite having been tone deaf at a young age, Mosie Lister was studying harmony and composition by the time he was seventeen. By the late 1940s, Lister was writing gospel songs for numerous well-known gospel groups and when the Statesmen used him as an arranger in 1948, Lister introduced harmony techniques that are still in use today in this type of music.

White Christmas (Berlin)
> Recorded by Elvis on Friday, 6 September, 1957
> Original: Bing Crosby, 1942
> Elvis's version can be heard on Elvis' Christmas Album; The Complete 50's Masters 3

White Christmas featured in the film *Holiday Inn* and won an Academy Award as Best Song for Irving Berlin. Crosby sang the song again in a film, this time in the 1954 *White Christmas*. Elvis's version is nothing like the Crosby interpretation, being much closer to the Drifters' 1955 recording.

Who Am I? (Goodman)
Recorded by Elvis on Saturday, 22 February, 1969
Original: Blue Ridge Quartet, 1966
Elvis's version can be heard on Amazing Grace

Charles "Rusty" Goodman wrote numerous popular contemporary gospels during his relatively brief life: he was born in September 1933 and died in November 1990. He recorded this number with his own group, The Happy Goodmans, in 1967, but the original dates from the year before.

Who's Sorry Now? (Snyder/Kalman/Ruby)
Recorded by Elvis on Wednesday, 28 May, 1958
Original: Ishman Jones, 1923
Elvis's version can be heard on Forever Young, Forever Beautiful (unofficial release)

The unofficial release features Elvis's then girlfriend Anita Wood singing, with Elvis accompanying her on piano. The recording was made during a visit by Elvis to Eddie Fadal's home in Waco, Texas, during Elvis's early period in the army.

Whole Lotta Shakin' Goin' On (Williams/David)
Recorded by Elvis on Tuesday, 22 September, 1970
Original: Big Maybelle, 1955
Elvis's version can be heard on I'm 10,000 Years Old: Elvis Country; Recorded Live On Stage In Memphis

Mabel Louise Smith wasn't joking when she recorded *Whole Lotta Shakin' Going On* some time before Jerry Lee Lewis—she weight a hefty 250 pounds! Big Maybelle, as she was professionally known, was plagued with drug-related problems and died in 1972 aged 48.

Why Me Lord (Kristofferson)
Recorded by Elvis on Wednesday, 20 March, 1974
Original: Kris Kristofferson, 1973
Elvis's version can be heard on Recorded Live On Stage In Memphis; Amazing Grace (CD 2)

Former Golden Gloves boxer Kris Kristofferson turned down an offer to teach at the USA military academy at West Point and instead moved to Nashville to become a country musician. A big fan of Willie Nelson, he became one of the on-and-off group The Highwaymen, along with Johnny Cash, Waylon Jennings and Nelson himself. Elvis recorded several Kristofferson numbers, including *Help Me Make It Through The Night* and *For The Good Times*.

Wings Of An Angel (The Prisoner's Song) (Massey)
    Recorded by Elvis on Wednesday, 17 January, 1968
    Original: Vernon Dalhart, 1924
    Elvis's version can be heard on Wings of an Angel (unofficial release, Angel Records EP 10005)

Released as the B-side of his Victor recording of *Wreck of the Old 97*, Vernon Dalhart's version of *The Prisoner's Song* became enormously popular and helped make the single country-music's first million-seller. It went on to be issued on many different labels.

Winter Wonderland (Smith/Bernard)
    Recorded by Elvis on Sunday, 16 May, 1971
    Original: Guy Lombardo and His Royal Canadians, 1934
    Elvis's version can be heard on Elvis Sings The Wonderful World Of Christmas; If Every Day Was Like Christmas

Guy Lombardo was born in Canada in 1902. He formed a dance band with his brothers and moved to the USA, where they performed as Guy Lombardo And His Royal Canadians, enjoying enormous success. Guy Lombardo died in 1977. Listening to Elvis sing this number, I can't help but feel that he is bored out of his mind and probably wondering why he can't do another take of *Merry Christmas, Baby* instead.

Witchcraft (Leigh/Coleman)
    Recorded by Elvis on Saturday, 26 March, 1960
    Original: Gerry Matthews, 1957
    Elvis's version can be heard on From Nashville to Memphis (5)

Gerry Matthews original was an instrumental. Frank Sinatra probably recorded the first vocal version in the same year, however. Elvis sang this number on the Frank Sinatra TV show *Welcome Home, Elvis* as Frank sang along with *Love Me Tender*.

Witchcraft (Bartholomew/King)
>Recorded by Elvis on Sunday, 26 May, 1963
>Original: The Spiders, 1955
>Elvis's version can be heard on Elvis' Gold Records Volume 4; From Nashville to Memphis (2)

A number 5 US R&B hit in 1955. The name of the group The Spiders was the inspiration for the name of Buddy Holly's group, The Crickets. The Beatles, of course (remember them?), continued the tradition.

With A Song In My Heart (Rodgers/Hart)
>Recorded by Elvis probably in May 1965
>Original: Franklyn Baur, 1929
>Elvis's version can be heard on Real Fun On Stage…And In The Studio

Introduced by John Hundley and Lillian Taiz in the 1929 stage musical *Spring is Here*, the song has since been used in a number of Hollywood musical, perhaps the most famous being…*With A Song In My Heart* (the Jane Froman story) in 1952. Baur's recording career ended with a Victor session on 27 December 1929; his final release, early in 1930, was this number. Elvis sang just two lines of the song, probably during a studio recording session for the *Frankie And Johnny* film soundtrack.

Without Him (LeFevre)
>Recorded by Elvis on Friday, 27 May, 1966
>Original: The LeFevres, 1956(?)
>Elvis's version can be heard on Amazing Grace (CD1)

Mylon LeFevre wrote this powerful piece when he was just seventeen years old and might well have recorded it himself. Frankie Laine perhaps recorded it, too, in 1956.

Without Love (There Is Nothing) (Small)
>Recorded by Elvis on Thursday, 23 January, 1969
>Original: Clyde McPhatter, 1957
>Elvis's version can be heard on Back In Memphis; From Nashville to Memphis (4)

Clyde McPhatter joined Billy Ward and the Dominoes in 1950, but left to form the Drifters in 1953: Elvis recorded the Drifters' *Fools Fall In Love, If You Don't Come Back,* and *Money Honey*. Another McPhatter original recorded by Elvis is *Such A Night*. McPhatter died on June 13, 1971; he was inducted into the Rock'n'Roll Hall of Fame in 1987.

Woman Without Love (Chesnut)
>Recorded by Elvis on Wednesday, 12 March, 1975
>Original: Bob Luman, 1968
>Elvis's version can be heard on Today

Jerry Chesnut wrote a number of songs recorded by Elvis, including *Love Coming Down, The Wonders You Perform* and *T-R-O-U-B-L-E*. Although Bob Luman had the original recording of *Woman Without Love*, the first released version was by Johnny Darrell, whose version came out just three days before Luman's.

Wooden Heart (Wise/Weisman/Twomey)
>Recorded by Elvis on Thursday, 28 April, 1960
>Original: Theodore Pusinelli & Hackert (Muss i denn…), 1901
>Elvis's version can be heard on G.I. Blues

Based on a Swabian folk tune, this is an example of an Urbummellied, Abschiedslied, but is better known by its opening lyrics in Swabian dialect, "Muss i denn, muss i denn zum Städtele hinaus." Swabia was a medieval duchy in what is now south-western Germany. The original recording was a clarinet piece.

Words (Gibb/Gibb/Gibb)
>Recorded by Elvis on Monday, 25 August, 1969
>Original: Bee Gees, 1967
>Elvis's version can be heard on In Person

Gibb, Gibb, Gibb? Not an advert for Gibb's toothpaste (although on occasions they looked that way), but a trio of Australian brothers who made some surprisingly good records, writing many of their numbers themselves. Elvis liked their song *Words*, and can be seen in the film *That's The Way It Is* rehearsing it over and over again. The exact date of Elvis's live recording, made during a Las Vegas performance, is hard to track down: some sources list 22 August, some 24 August and others 25 August. I'm going for 25 August, as the number was definitely used during the midnight show of the 24th, if you see what I mean…!

Working On The Building (Hoyle/Bowles)
Recorded by Elvis on Monday, 31 October, 1960
Original: Heavenly Gospel Singers, 1937
Elvis's version can be heard on His Hand In Mine; Amazing Grace (CD 1)

It is possible that someone other than the Heavenly Gospel Singers recorded the original version of this number, for it has appeared in printed form in various gospel songbooks since the early 1900s. Some sources indicate the Blackwood Brothers as the original artists, but also in 1937.

Write To Me From Naples (Alstone/Kennedy)
Recorded by Elvis in 1966
Original: Dean Martin, 1957
Elvis's version can be heard on A Golden Celebration

Elvis, called by many the King of Rock'n'Roll, admired Dean Martin's singing style perhaps as much as anyone else's. He showed it on times, too, and the style is clear in this version of Martin's 1957 hit. Jimmy Kennedy, co-writer of this number, also wrote *Harbor Lights*, one of Elvis's very first recordings. Elvis's version is a home recording, never intended for release.

Yellow Rose Of Texas (J.K.)
Recorded by Elvis on Wednesday, 10 July, 1963
Original: Gene Autry, 1933
Elvis's version can be heard on Elvis Sings Flaming Star; Double Features: Viva Las Vegas & Roustabout

It looks strange, but "J.K." really is the only way the composer of this number is known! The number was written in 1853 and became popular during the American Civil War as *The Gallant Hood of Texas*—a reference to Confederate General John Hood. Mitch Miller had a six-week long Billboard Top 100 number one with his version in 1955. The number was sung by Elvis in a medley with *The Eyes of Texas* (see above) in the film *Love In Las Vegas* (*Viva Las Vegas* in the USA).

Yesterday (Lennon/McCartney)
Recorded by Elvis on Monday, 25 August, 1969
Original: The Beatles, 1965
Elvis's version can be heard on On Stage

As with so many songs credited to both Lennon and McCartney, only one of the pair actually wrote *Yesterday*, Paul McCartney. His working title was

Scrambled Eggs and only he was in the studio when the number was recorded, even though this recording was credited to The Beatles as a whole. The first hit version was sung by Matt Monro in 1965 in the UK. The song was later covered over 2500 times and remains the most played tune on the radio.

You Asked Me To *(Jennings/Shaver)*

>Recorded by Elvis on Tuesday, 11 December, 1973
>Original: Waylon Jennings, 1973
>Elvis's version can be heard on Promised Land; Walk A Mile In My Shoes—The Essential 70's Masters Disc 4

Waylon Jennings was born in 1937. During his youth he became a friend of Buddy Holly and Holly produced his first single, *Jole Blon*, in 1958. Jennings was on the same tour as Buddy when the latter was killed in a plane crash—Jennings had planned to travel in the plane with Buddy, but allowed the Big Bopper (J.P. Richardson) to take his seat. Jennings returned to radio-presenting and playing as a session musician in the 1960s, but returned to big-time performing in the 1970s as part of The Outlaws movement in Country music and became a very big star. Waylon Jennings died in February 2002. The title of Jennings' original was *You Ask me To*.

You Belong To My Heart *(Gilbert/Lara)*

>Recorded by Elvis on Tuesday, 4 December, 1956
>Original: Dora Luz, 1944
>Elvis's version can be heard on The Complete Million Dollar Session; Elvis Latino!

Lyrics and music written as *Solamente Una Vez* in 1941 by Agustín Lara, known as the "Cole Porter of Mexico" for composing some of the country's most beloved classic melodies. The first singer was José Mojica in the 1941 film *Melodia de America*. English lyrics written in 1943 by Ray Gilbert, introduced by the voice of Dora Luz on the soundtrack of Walt Disney's feature-length Donald Duck cartoon *The Three Caballeros* in 1944.

You Better Run *(Traditional)*

>Recorded by Elvis on Friday, 31 March, 1972
>Original: Wiseman Sextette/Quartet, 1923
>Elvis's version can be heard on Amazing Grace (CD 2)

Probably a number that has to be classified as "traditional"—it is at the very least extremely difficult to find any information about it! The first recording I have been able to find dates from 1923, on the Document label, number DOCD-5520, by the strangely named Wiseman Sextette/Quartet.

You Can Have Her (I Don't Want Her) (Cook)
>Recorded by Elvis on Saturday, 11 May, 1974
>Original: Roy Hamilton, 1961
>Elvis's version can be heard on Susie Q (unofficial release)

Bill Cook, who wrote this number, was Roy Hamilton's manager. This was Roy Hamilton's last hit. Hamilton died in 1969, aged just 40, following a stroke. He was a great influence on numerous performers, including Jackie Wilson, Roy Brown and The Righteous Brothers.

You Don't Have To Say You Love Me (Pallavicini/Donaggio)
>Recorded by Elvis on Saturday, 6 June, 1970
>Original: Dusty Springfield (?), 1966
>Elvis's version can be heard on That's The Way It Is; Walk A Mile In My Shoes—The Essential 70's Masters Disc 1

The Italian original is titled *Io Che Non Vivo Piu d'Un Ora Senza Te* and was the entry for the San Remo Song Festival in 1965, sung by Pino Donaggio. Dusty Springfield got Simon Napier-Bell and Vicky Wickham to provide English lyrics and scored a number 1 in the UK and a number 4 in the US Hot 100.

You Don't Know Me (Walker/Arnold)
>Recorded by Elvis on Wednesday, 22 February, 1967
>Original: Eddy Arnold, 1956
>Elvis's version can be heard on Clambake; Command Performances disc 2

Eddy Arnold may have had the first recording of this number, but Jerry Vale's version was released first. The best known version, however, is probably that of Ray Charles who had a huge hit with it in 1962. Elvis recorded the number twice: firstly the film version (used in *Clambake*) and then again on Monday, September 11, 1967, for record release.

You Gave Me A Mountain (Robbins)
Recorded by Elvis on Sunday, 14 January, 1973
Original: Frankie Laine, 1968
Elvis's version can be heard on Aloha From Hawaii Via Satellite; Walk A Mile In My Shoes—The Essential 70's Masters Disc 5

Marty Robbins wrote this number especially for friend Frankie Laine. Laine's recording reached number 24 in 1969 in the Billboard chart and went gold early the following year.

You'll Be Gone (Presley/Hodge/West)
Recorded by Elvis on Sunday, 18 March, 1962
Original: Charles Walters and June Knight, 1935
Elvis's version can be heard on From Nashville To Memphis (CD2)

Cole Porter wrote the number *Begin The Beguine* in the early thirties, basing it on a dance from Martinique. It seems that this was his favourite song. Elvis liked the number, too, but there were problems involved with him recording it, so he decided to rewrite it, which he promptly did, with the help of friends Charlie Hodge and Red West. The tune was also changed, but elements of the Cole Porter "original" (heck, even he wasn't original!) can clearly be heard.

You'll Never Walk Alone (Rodgers/Hammerstein)
Recorded by Elvis on Monday, 11 September, 1967
Original: John Raitt, Christine Johnson, Jan Clayton, and Chorus, 1945
Elvis's version can be heard on You'll Never Walk Alone; Amazing Grace (CD 2)

From the musical, *Carousel*. It is possible that Frank Sinatra recorded the number before the Carousel cast, though also in 1945. Gerry and The Pacemakers topped the UK charts for four weeks with the number in 1965. Elvis probably knew the song from Roy Hamilton's 1954 hit recording.

You're A Heartbreaker (Sallee)
Recorded by Elvis on Friday, 10 December, 1954 (?)
Original: Ray Anthony (?), 1952
Elvis's version can be heard on The Sun Sessions CD

Originally released as the B-side of Sun 215, *Milkcow Blues Boogie*. A number with this title was released by Jimmy Heap in January 1953 on Capitol 2294. However, I've heard a thirty-second extract of Heap's song and I do not think it is the same number! The Ray Anthony orchestra released the title a couple of months later, with vocal by Jo Ann Greer (Capitol 2349)—but is this the same as Elvis's??

According to Guralnick in his book *Last Train To Memphis,* Jack Sallee knew Sam Phillips was looking for an extra number for Elvis, so he wrote *You're A Heartbreaker*—it was the first of Elvis's songs on which Sam Phillips owned the publishing rights.

You're The Boss (Leiber/Stoller)

Recorded by Elvis on Thursday, 11 July, 1963
Original: LaVern Baker and Jimmy Ricks, 1961
Elvis's version can be heard on Elvis Sings Leiber & Stoller; Collectors Gold

Elvis recorded this duet with delicious Ann-Margret for the film, *Viva Las Vegas* or *Love In Las Vegas* (depending on where you live!). See *Saved* and *Tweedlee Dee* for information about LaVern Baker.

You're The Only Star (In My Blue Heaven) (Autry)

Recorded by Elvis on Tuesday, 4 December, 1956
Original: Gene Autry, 1935
Elvis's version can be heard on The Complete Million Dollar Session

Gene Autry wrote this number after receiving a letter from a mentally disturbed fan, who used the title words in her letter. Elvis is heard on the backing vocals of the Million Dollar Quartet recording, with Jerry Lee Lewis taking the lead.

You're The Reason I'm Living (Darin)

Recorded by Elvis on Saturday, 22 March, 1975
Original: Bobby Darin, 1963
Elvis's version can be heard on The Memphis Flash Hits Las Vegas; Live In Las Vegas 4-CD set

The CD on which Elvis's version originally appeared was sold with the book *Growing Up With The Memphis Flash* by Kate Wheeler. The song was later "officially" released.

You've Lost That Lovin' Feelin' (Mann/Weil/Spector)
>   Recorded by Elvis on Monday, 10 August, 1970, etc
>   Original: Righteous Brothers, 1964
>   Elvis's version can be heard on That's The Way It Is; Walk A Mile In My Shoes—The Essential 70's Masters Disc 5

Phil Spector took his "wall of sound" recording technique to its utmost for this US Hot 100 number 1 hit. A rehearsal version of the number being sung by Elvis was recorded on 10 August 1970 and released on the *Elvis Aron Presley* silver set. A version sung on 11 August appeared on the *Live In Las Vegas* set, with the original Elvis release being recorded on 12 August, 1970 and available on the sets indicated above.

Young Love (Joyner/Cartey)
>   Recorded by Elvis on Monday, 24 June, 1968
>   Original: Ric Cartey, 1956
>   Elvis's version can be heard on The Complete Dressing Room Session (MS-001)

Cartey's original was overshadowed by Sonny James' cover, which spent nine weeks at number one in the US Country charts in 1956-57. James started his career at the age of three (!) as a member of his family's band, The Lodens, well-known on the radio throughout the South of the USA. In total, James had 23 number 1's in those charts between 1956 and 1972. The number was also a big hit for Tab Hunter, both in the USA and the UK. Elvis's version has not appeared on an RCA/BMG release (yet!).

Your Cheatin' Heart (Williams)
>   Recorded by Elvis on Saturday, 1 February, 1958
>   Original: Hank Williams, 1952
>   Elvis's version can be heard on Elvis For Everyone; The Complete 50's Masters 4

Hank Williams died in the back of his car on January 1st, 1953. This number was released shortly after, having been recorded on 23 September, 1952. Elvis was not pleased with his own recording and it was not released for seven years.

Artists Index

Artists Index

(Please note that the names listed are those mentioned in the body of the text. You might also wish to check the *Problem Originals* section for a few other titles not included here.)

A. Delcroix	Can't Help Falling In Love
Ada Jones & George Ballard	In The Garden
Adam Wade	Take Good Care Of Her
Al Hibbler	He
Al Martino	Mary In The Morning
Al Rogers And His Rocky Mountain Boys	It Wouldn't Be The Same Without You
Alabama Barn Stormers (Riley Puckett & Hugh Cross)	Come Along
Albert E. Brumley	If We Never Meet Again
Alessandro Moreschi "The Last Castrato"	Ave Maria
Alma Gluck	Carry Me Back To Old Virginia
Ames Brothers	Sentimental Me
Andrae Crouch and The Disciples	I've Got Confidence
Andy Williams	Hawaiian Wedding Song
Ann Cole	Got My Mojo Working
Anne Murray	Put Your Hand In The Hand
Anne Murray	Snowbird
Arthur "Big Boy" Crudup	My Baby Left Me
Arthur "Big Boy" Crudup	So Glad You're Mine
Arthur "Big Boy" Crudup	That's All Right Mama
Arthur Alexander	Burning Love
Arthur Gunter	Baby Let's Play House
Arthur Rubinstein	Five Sleepy Heads

B.J. Thomas	It's Only Love
Band of the Grenadier Guards (Canada)	I Love Only One Girl
Barry Mann	I Just Can't Help Believin'
Beatles, The	Get Back
Beatles, The	Hey Jude
Beatles, The	Lady Madonna
Beatles, The	Yesterday
Bee Gees	Words
Bernie Hardison	Too Much
Big Bill Broonzy	See See Rider
Big Joe Turner	Shake, Rattle And Roll
Big Maybelle	Whole Lotta Shakin' Goin' On
Bill Gaither Trio	He Touched Me
Bill Kenny (Ink Spots)	There Is No God But God
Bill Monroe	Blue Moon Of Kentucky
Bill Monroe	I Hear A Sweet Voice Calling
Bill Monroe	Sweetheart You Done Me Wrong
Bill Monroe	Uncle Pen
Bill Monroe and The Bluegrass Boys	Summertime Has Passed And Gone
Bill Monroe's Bluegrass Boys	Little Cabin On The Hill
Billy Brown	He'll Have To Go
Billy Lee Riley	I've Got A Thing About You Baby
Billy Swan	I Can Help
Billy Walker	Funny How Time Slips Away
Bing Crosby	Blue Hawaii
Bing Crosby	I Apologize
Bing Crosby	White Christmas
Bing Crosby & Carol Richards	Silver Bells
Bing Crosby & Grace Kelly	True Love
Bing Crosby with the John Scott Trotter Orchestra	I'll Be Home For Christmas
Blackwood Brothers, The	I Just Can't Make It By Myself
Blackwood Brothers, The	In My Father's House
Blind Willie Johnson	By And By
Blue Ridge Quartet	Who Am I?

Blue Rose	Time Has Made A Change In Me
Bob Dylan	Blowin' In The Wind
Bob Dylan	Don't Think Twice, It's All Right
Bob Dylan	I Shall Be Released
Bob Luman	Woman Without Love
Bob Wills & His Texas Playboys	Faded Love
Bob Wills & His Texas Playboys	San Antonio Rose
Bobbie Gentry	Ode To Billie Joe
Bobby Bare	Find Out What's Happening
Bobby Darin	I Want You With Me
Bobby Darin	I'll Be There
Bobby Darin	You're The Reason I'm Living
Bobby Vinton	Roses Are Red (My Love)
Bonnie Guitar	Dark Moon
Bread	Aubrey
Brenda Lee	Always On My Mind
Buck Owens	Crying Time
Buddy & Ella Johnson	Alright, Okay, You Win
Buffy Sainte Marie	Until It's Time For You To Go
Campbell and Burr	Tender Feeling
Carl Mann	I'm Comin' Home
Carl Perkins	Blue Suede Shoes
Caruso	Santa Lucia
Charles Walters and June Knight	You'll Be Gone
Charlie Louvin	It Ain't No Big Thing (But It's Growing)
Charlie Porter And The North Carolina Ramblers	Frankie And Johnny
Charlie Rich	Pieces Of My Life
Charlie Rich	The Most Beautiful Girl
Chuck Berry	Brown Eyed Handsome Man
Chuck Berry	Johnny B. Goode
Chuck Berry	Long Live Rock And Roll (School Days)
Chuck Berry	Maybellene

Chuck Berry	Memphis, Tennessee
Chuck Berry	Promised Land
Chuck Berry	Too Much Monkey Business
Chuck Jackson	Any Day Now (My Wild Beautiful Bird)
Chuck Wagon Gang	Hide Thou Me
Chuck Willis	I Feel So Bad
Claiborne Brothers Quartette	If The Lord Wasn't Walking By My Side
Cleavant Derricks	Just A Little Talk With Jesus
Cliff Richard	I Gotta Know
Clovers, The	Fool, Fool, Fool
Clyde McPhatter	Without Love (There Is Nothing)
Clyde McPhatter and the Drifters	Such A Night
Coasters, The	Girls! Girls! Girls!
Coasters, The	Little Egypt
Columbia Band	My Country, 'Tis Of Thee
Connie Smith	Help Me
Cori Sacri in Chiesa	Blessed Jesus (Hold My Hand)
Creedence Clearwater Revival	Proud Mary
Dale Hawkins	Susie-Q
Dallas Frazier	Where Did They Go, Lord?
Damita Jo	Keep Your Hands Off Of It
Daniel Sisters & Otis Mccoy	When God Dips His Love In My Heart
Danny And The Juniors	At The Hop
Danny O'Keefe	Good Time Charlie's Got The Blues
Darrell Glenn	Crying In The Chapel
David Hill	All Shook Up
Dean Martin	That's Amore
Dean Martin	Write To Me From Naples
Del Shannon	(Marie's The Name) His Latest Flame
Del Shannon	Runaway
Dick Haymes	Love Letters
Dobie Gray	Loving Arms
Domenico Modugno	Ask Me
Don Gibson	I Can't Stop Loving You

Don Harris and Dewey Terry	I'm Leaving It Up To You
Don McLean	And I Love You So
Don Robertson	I Really Don't Want To Know
Dora Luz	You Belong To My Heart
Doris Akers	Lead Me, Guide Me
Doris Day	Que Sera, Sera
Doye O'Dell	Blue Christmas Cattle Call
Drifters, The	Fools Fall In Love
Drifters, The	If You Don't Come Back
Drifters, The	Money Honey
Duane Dee	True Love Travels On A Gravel Road
Dusty Springfield	You Don't Have To Say You Love Me
Eagles, The	Trying To Get To You
Ed Ames	When The Snow Is On The Roses
Eddie "Piano" Miller	Release Me
Eddie Boyd	Don't
Eddie Riff	Ain't That Loving You Baby
Eddy Arnold	How's The World Treating You
Eddy Arnold	I'll Hold You In My Heart
Eddy Arnold	It's A Sin
Eddy Arnold	You Don't Know Me
Eddy Howard	I Wonder, I Wonder, I Wonder
Edison Male Quartette	Jingle Bells
Elkins-Payne Jubilee Singers	Down By The Riverside
Elsie Baker & Elizabeth Wheeler	Oh Happy Day
Emile Berliner	Auld Lang Syne
Enrico Caruso	Surrender
Ernest Tubb	I'm With The Crowd (But So Alone)
Ernest Tubb	It's Been So Long Darling
Ernest Tubb	Tomorrow Never Comes
Ernestine Schumann-Heink	Danny Boy
Etta James	Come What May
F.F. Billups & His Kansas City Gospel Singers	On The Jericho Road
Faron Young	Is It So Strange

Fats Waller	End Of The Road
Fats Waller	It's A Sin To Tell A Lie
Faye Adams	Shake A Hand
Fisk University Jubilee Quartet	Swing Down Sweet Chariot
Flatt & Scruggs	A Hundred Years From Now
Four Fellows & Abi Barker Orch., The	Soldier Boy
Four Tunes	I Understand (Just How You Feel)
Frances Farmer	Love Me Tender (Aura Lee)
Frank Sinatra	America The Beautiful
Frank Sinatra	Everybody Loves Somebody
Frank Westphal & His Regal Novelty Orchestra	Stagger Lee
Frankie Laine	High Noon (Do Not Forsake Me Oh My Darlin')
Frankie Laine	You Gave Me A Mountain
Frankie Trumbauer & Band	Blue Moon
Franklyn Baur	With A Song In My Heart
Freddy Quinn	Spanish Eyes
Frederick Whitfield	Oh How I Love Jesus
Gardner and Dee Dee Ford	I Need Your Loving (Every Day)
Gene Autry	Blueberry Hill
Gene Autry	Here Comes Santa Claus
Gene Autry	Yellow Rose Of Texas
Gene Autry	You're The Only Star (In My Blue Heaven)
George Beverly Shea	How Great Thou Art
George Jones	She Thinks I Still Care
Gerry Matthews	Witchcraft
Gigliola Cinquetti	Please Don't Stop Loving Me
Gilbert Bécaud	Let It Be Me
Giuseppe Anselmi	It's Now Or Never
Gladiolas, The	Little Darlin'
Glen Campbell	Turn Around, Look At Me
Gloria Lasso	Padre
Golden Gate Quartet	Bosom Of Abraham

Golden Gate Quartet	I Will Be Home Again
Golden Gate Quartet	Run On
Gordon Terry	Long Black Limousine
Guy Lombardo and His Royal Canadians	Winter Wonderland
Guy Mitchell	My Heart Cries For You
Hadda Brooks	That's My Desire
Hank Snow	(Now And Then There's) A Fool Such As I
Hank Snow	I'm Gonna Bid My Blues Goodbye
Hank Snow	I'm Movin' On
Hank Williams	I Can't Help It (If I'm Still In Love With You)
Hank Williams	I'm So Lonesome I Could Cry
Hank Williams	Jambalaya (On The Bayou)
Hank Williams (as Luke The Drifter)	Men With Broken Hearts
Hank Williams	Take These Chains From My Heart
Hank Williams	Your Cheatin' Heart
Harmonizing Four	Only Believe
Harold Arlen and Judy Garland	Over The Rainbow
Harry Belafonte	Hava Nagila
Harry Macdonough	Nearer My God To Thee
Harry Owens and The Royal Hawaiian Band	Sweet Leilani
Haydn Quartet, The	Silent Night
Heavenly Gospel Singers	Working On The Building
Henry Mancini and His Orchestra	Peter Gunn Theme
Henry Whitter (harmonica solo)	Clambake
Herman "Little Junior" Parker	Mystery Train
Homer Rodeheaver	An Evening Prayer
Horace Heidt and His Orchestra	Tomorrow Night
Hoyt Axton	Never Been To Spain
Huddie Leadbetter	Stay Away, Joe
Ian And Sylvia	Tomorrow Is A Long Time
Ignaz Jan Paderewski	Moonlight Sonata

Impressions, The	Amen
Ink Spots, The	Somebody Bigger Than You And I
Ink Spots, The	That's When Your Heartaches Begin
Ishman Jones	Who's Sorry Now?
Ivory Joe Hunter	I Need You So
Ivory Joe Hunter	I Will Be True
Jack Greene	He Is My Everything
Jack Greene	There Goes My Everything
Jack Jones	The Impossible Dream
Jackie Lomax	How The Web Was Woven
James B Coats	Where Could I Go But To The Lord
James Kokomo Arnold	Milkcow Blues Boogie
James Taylor	Steamroller Blues
Jane Froman	I Believe
Jane Morgan	What Now My Love
Jay McShann	Hands Off
Jerry Butler	Only The Strong Survive
Jerry Reed	A Thing Called Love
Jerry Reed	Guitar Man
Jerry Reed	Talk About The Good Times
Jerry Reed	U.S. Male
Jesse & Marvin	Earth Angel
Jesse Stone and The Clovers	Down In The Alley
Jewels, The	Hearts Of Stone
Jim Reeves	I'm Beginning To Forget You
Jim Reeves	Welcome To My World
Jimmie Rodgers	Froggy Went a'Courtin'
Jimmie Rodgers	It's Over
Jimmie Rodgers Snow	How Do You Think I Feel
Jimmy Clanton	If I'm A Fool (For Loving You)
Jimmy Dodd	The Mickey Mouse Club March
Jimmy Reed	Baby What You Want Me To Do
Jimmy Reed	Big Boss Man
Jimmy Wakely	I'll Never Let You Go (Little Darlin')
Jimmy Wakely	Out Of Sight, Out Of Mind

Joe Babcock	I Washed My Hands In Muddy Water
Joe Cocker	Something
Joe Henderson	After Loving You
Joe South	Don't It Make You Wanna Go Home
Joe South	Walk A Mile In My Shoes
Joe Thomas	I'm Gonna Sit Right Down And Cry (Over You)
Joe Turner	Flip, Flop And Fly
Johann Strauss Rochester	Today, Tomorrow And Forever
John Hartford	Gentle On My Mind
John McCormack & William H. Reitz and male chorus	O Come, All Ye Faithful
John Raitt	If I Loved You
John Raitt, Christine Johnson, Jan Clayton, and Chorus	You'll Never Walk Alone
John Sinclair	The Eyes Of Texas
John Yorke AtLee	There's No Place Like Home
Johnny Ace	Pledging My Love
Johnny Cash	Folsom Prison Blues
Johnny Cash	I Walk The Line
Johnny Darrell	Green, Green Grass Of Home
Johnny Hallett	Turn Your Eyes Upon Jesus
Johnny Mathis	The Twelfth Of Never
Johnny Tillotson	It Keeps Right On A Hurtin'
Jon and Sondra Steele	My Happiness
Joni James	I'll Never Stand In Your Way
Jordanaires, The	I'm Gonna Walk Dem Golden Stairs
Joseph Saucier	Almost Always True
Kate Smith	I Asked The Lord
Kate Smith	On Top Of Old Smokey
Kelly Harrell	I Was Born About Ten Thousand Years Ago
Kenny Loggins and Jim Messina	Mama Don't Dance
Kris Kristofferson	For The Good Times
Kris Kristofferson	Help Me Make It Through The Night

Kris Kristofferson	Why Me Lord
Kuiokolani Lee	I'll Remember You
Larry Gatlin	Bitter They Are, Harder They Fall
LaVern Baker	Saved
LaVern Baker	So High
LaVern Baker	Tweedlee Dee
LaVern Baker and Jimmy Ricks	You're The Boss
Leadbelly (Huddie Ledbetter)	Cottonfields
Lee Denson	Miracle Of The Rosary
LeFevres, The	Without Him
Lefty Frizzell	Give Me More, More, More Of Your Kisses
Leningrad Philharmonic and Academic Choir	Happy Birthday
Leo Price	Send Me Some Lovin'
Leon Payne	I Love You Because
Leon T. Rene	When The Swallows Come Back To Capistrano
Little David (Schroeder)	Apron Strings
Little Jimmy Dickens	I Shall Not Be Moved
Little Richard	Long Tall Sally
Little Richard	Ready Teddy
Little Richard	Rip It Up
Little Richard	Tutti Frutti
Little Walter Jacobs	My Babe
Little Willie John	Fever
Lloyd Price	Lawdy Miss Clawdy
Lonnie Donegan	I'll Never Fall In Love Again
Lowell Fulson	Reconsider Baby
Lulu Belle & Scotty	Have I Told You Lately That I Love You
Lulu Belle and Scotty	Cindy, Cindy
Mahalia Jackson	(There'll Be) Peace In The Valley (For Me)
Marcella Sembrich	Tonight's All Right For Love
Mark Andrews	The First Noel

Mark James	Moody Blue
Mark James	Suspicious Minds
Martha Carson	Satisfied
Marty Robbins	El Paso
Matt Monro	Portrait Of My Love
Matthews' Southern Comfort	I've Lost You
Maud Powell	Tonight Is So Right For Love
Mel Tillis	Detroit City
Mickey Newbury	An American Trilogy
Mighty Faith Increasers	I, John
Mildred Bailey	Fools Rush In (Where Angels Fear To Tread)
Mina	Softly, As I Leave You
Miss Florence Hinkle & Mr. Harry MacDonough	Softly And Tenderly
Morris Albert	Feelings
Morris Brown Quartet	Jesus Walked That Lonesome Valley
Mosie Lister	He Knows Just What I Need
Mosie Lister	Where No One Stands Alone
Musique De La Garde Républicaine	No More
Napua Stevens	Beyond The Reef
Nat King Cole	Mona Lisa
Nat Shilkret	I Apologize
Ned Jakobs	Are You Lonesome Tonight?
Ned Miller	From A Jack To A King
Neil Diamond	And The Grass Won't Pay No Mind
Neil Diamond	Sweet Caroline
Neil Sedaka	Solitaire
Nelstone's Hawaiians	Just Because
Nick Noble	Moonlight Swim
Olivia Newton John	If You Love Me (Let Me Know)
Olivia Newton John	Let Me Be There
Original Hinsons, The	Lighthouse
Paramount Jubilee Singers	When The Saints Go Marchin' In
Pat Boone	Don't Forbid Me

Patti Page	I Don't Care If The Sun Don't Shine
Paul Anka	My Way
Paul Robeson	Joshua Fit The Battle
Paul Whiteman Orchestra, The (vocals Bing Crosby)	Make Believe
Paul Williams	Where Do I Go From Here
Pee Wee King	Tennessee Waltz
Peggy Seeger	The First Time Ever I Saw Your Face
Pepe Guízar	Guadalajara
Percy Mayfield	Stranger In My Own Home Town
Perry Como	It's Impossible
Peter, Paul and Mary	(That's What You Get) For Lovin' Me
Peter, Paul and Mary	500 Miles
Peter, Paul and Mary	Early Morning Rain
Pointer Sisters, The	Fairytale
Ralph Carmichael and His Orchestra	Reach Out To Jesus
Rambos, The	If That Isn't Love
Ray Anthony	You're A Heartbreaker
Ray Charles	I Got A Woman
Ray Charles	What'd I Say
Ray Fox Orchestra, vocal Barry Gray	Harbor Lights
Ray Peterson	The Wonder Of You
Ray Price	Crazy Arms
Ray Price	Make The World Go Away
Razy Bailey	Love Coming Down
Red Foley	Just A Closer Walk With Thee
Red Foley	Mansion Over The Hilltop
Red Foley	Old Shep
Red Foley	Tell Me Why (Just A Closer Walk With Thee)
Red Foley; Eddy Arnold	Just Call Me Lonesome
Rev. J. M. Gates	Amazing Grace
Ric Cartey	Young Love
Richard Harris	MacArthur Park
Richard Harris	My Boy

Righteous Brothers	You've Lost That Lovin' Feelin'
Riz Ortolani	More
Roger Whittaker	The Last Farewell
Rosco Gordon	Just A Little Bit
Roy Acuff & His Smokey Mountain Boys	Blue Eyes Crying In The Rain
Roy Brown with The Bob Ogden Orchestra	Good Rockin' Tonight
Roy Hamilton	Hurt
Roy Hamilton	You Can Have Her (I Don't Want Her)
Roy Orbison	Just Let Me Make Believe
Roy Orbison	Running Scared
Royal Hawaiian Troubadours	Aloha Oe
Rudy Vallee	The Whiffenpoof Song
Rudy Wiedöft	She Wears My Ring
Rufus Thomas	Tiger Man
Sam Cooke and The Soul Stirrers	Must Jesus Bear The Cross Alone
Sanford Clark	The Fool
Simon and Garfunkel	Bridge Over Troubled Water
Sister Rosetta Tharpe	Stand By Me
Skillet Lickers, The	Old MacDonald
Smiley Lewis	One Night
Sons Of The Pioneers	Tumblin' Tumbleweeds
Southern Sons	Up Above My Head
Southern Sons	We're Gonna Move
Spiders, The	Witchcraft
Stamps Quartet	Farther Along
Stan Jones	Ghost Riders In The Sky
Statesmen, The	His Hand In Mine
Statesmen, The	I Believe In The Man In The Sky
Statler Brothers	Susan When She Tried
Stuart Hamblen	It Is No Secret (What God Can Do)
Stuart Hamblen	Known Only To Him
Sweet Inspirations	Sweet Inspiration
T-Bone Walker	Three Corn Patches

Tammy Wynette	The Wonders You Perform
Teddy Redell	Judy
Tex Owens	Money Honey
Theodore Pusinelli & Hackert	Wooden Heart
Thomas A. Dorsey	Take My Hand, Precious Lord
Thomas Wayne	Girl Next Door Went A Walkin'
Thomas Wayne	This Time
Three Blazers	Merry Christmas Baby
Tippy and the Clovers	Bossa Nova Baby
Tito Guízar	Allá En El Rancho Grande
Todd Duncan	Unchained Melody
Tom Jones	Delilah
Tommy Tucker	High Heel Sneakers
Tony Bennett	Rags To Riches
Tony Joe White	For Ol' Times Sake
Tony Joe White	Polk Salad Annie
Tony Martin	There's No Tomorrow
Traditional	The Lord's Prayer
Traditional Polynesian	Drums Of The Islands
Trinity Choir	Oh Little Town Of Bethlehem
Troy Seals	There's A Honky Tonk Angel (Who Will Take Me Back In)
Trumpeteers, The	Milky White Way
Tune Weavers	Happy, Happy Birthday Baby
Unknown	Show Me Thy Ways, O Lord
Unknown	Stay Away
Vernon Dalhart	Wings Of An Angel (The Prisoner's Song)
Vikki Nelson	Like A Baby
Waylon Jennings	You Asked Me To
Wayne Newton	Fool
Wayne Walker	Are You Sincere
Wiley Walker and Gene Sullivan	When My Blue Moon Turns To Gold Again
Will Oakland	I'll Take You Home Again, Kathleen

William Robert
"Billy The Kid" Emerson . . . . When It Rains, It Really Pours
Willie and Ruth. . . . . Love Me
Willie Mae "Big Mama" Thornton . . . . . Hound Dog
Wiseman Sextette/Quartet. . . . . You Better Run
Wynn Stewart . . . . Keeper Of The Key
Young Jessie. . . . . Hot Dog

Writers and Composers Index

Writers and Composers Index

(Please note that the names listed are those mentioned in the body of the text. You might also wish to check the *Problem Originals* section for a few other titles not included here.)

Adler	Rags To Riches
Akers	Lead Me, Guide Me
Albert	Feelings
Allen	Must Jesus Bear The Cross Alone
Allison	He'll Have To Go
Allison	He'll Have To Go
Alstone	Write To Me From Naples
Arlen	Over The Rainbow
Arnold	I'll Hold You In My Heart
Arnold	You Don't Know Me
Arthur	Old Shep
Atkins	How's The World Treating You
Autry	Here Comes Santa Claus
Autry	You're The Only Star (In My Blue Heaven)
Axton	Never Been To Spain
Babcock	I Washed My Hands In Muddy Water
Bach	Ave Maria
Bacharach	Any Day Now (My Wild Beautiful Bird)
Barnes	I Really Don't Want To Know
Bartholomew	One Night
Bartholomew	Witchcraft
Bass	Just A Little Bit
Bates	America The Beautiful
Battersby	An Evening Prayer
Baum	Ask Me

Baum	Down By The Riverside
Baum	Tender Feeling
Baum	Today, Tomorrow And Forever
Baxter	Merry Christmas Baby
Becaud	What Now My Love
Bécaud	Let It Be Me
Beecher	Must Jesus Bear The Cross Alone
Beethoven	Moonlight Sonata
Belvin	Earth Angel
Benjamin	I Will Be Home Again
Bennett	Drums Of The Islands
Bennett	Five Sleepy Heads
Bennett	I Love Only One Girl
Bennett	Stay Away
Bergantine	My Happiness
Berlin	End Of The Road
Berlin	White Christmas
Bernard	Ave Maria
Bernard	Winter Wonderland
Berry	Brown Eyed Handsome Man
Berry	Johnny B. Goode
Berry	Long Live Rock And Roll (School Days)
Berry	Maybellene
Berry	Memphis, Tennessee
Berry	Promised Land
Berry	Too Much Monkey Business
Best	I Understand (Just How You Feel)
Biggs	I'm Gonna Sit Right Down And Cry (Over You)
Bishop	There's No Place Like Home
Black	When The Saints Go Marchin' In
Blackwell	All Shook Up
Blackwell	Just Let Me Make Believe
Blackwell	Long Tall Sally
Blackwell	Ready Teddy

Blackwell	Rip It Up
Blaikley	I've Lost You
Blair	No More
Bland	Carry Me Back To Old Virginia
Bloom	Fools Rush In (Where Angels Fear To Tread)
Boberg	How Great Thou Art
Bond	Tomorrow Never Comes
Bourke	The Most Beautiful Girl
Boutayre	My Boy
Bowles	Working On The Building
Bowman	Hands Off
Broadwater	Susie-Q
Brooks	Bosom Of Abraham
Brooks	I, John
Brooks	Oh Little Town Of Bethlehem
Brooks	That's Amore
Brown	Good Rockin' Tonight
Brown	Just A Little Bit
Brown	That's When Your Heartaches Begin
Brumley	Blessed Jesus (Hold My Hand)
Brumley	If We Never Meet Again
Bryant	How's The World Treating You
Burke	Somebody Bigger Than You And I
Burleigh	Swing Down Sweet Chariot
Burns	Auld Lang Syne
Burns	Tiger Man
Butler	Only The Strong Survive
Byers	Please Don't Stop Loving Me
Byron	Roses Are Red (My Love)
Calabrese	Softly, As I Leave You
Calhoun	Flip, Flop And Fly
Calhoun	Shake, Rattle And Roll
Capehart	Turn Around, Look At Me
Capurro	It's Now Or Never
Carmichael	Reach Out To Jesus

Carr	There's No Tomorrow
Carson	Always On My Mind
Carson	Satisfied
Cartey	Young Love
Cash	Folsom Prison Blues
Cash	I Walk The Line
Cassin	Sentimental Me
Charles	I Got A Woman
Charles	What'd I Say
Chase	Such A Night
Chesnut	Love Coming Down
Chesnut	The Wonders You Perform
Chesnut	Woman Without Love
Christopher	Always On My Mind
Clarke	Turn Your Eyes Upon Jesus
Coats	Where Could I Go But To The Lord
Cochran	Make The World Go Away
Cody	Solitaire
Coleman	Happy Birthday
Coleman	Milky White Way
Coleman	Witchcraft
Conley	See See Rider
Cook	You Can Have Her (I Don't Want Her)
Cooley	Fever
Corday	There's No Tomorrow
Coslow	Tomorrow Night
Cottrau	Santa Lucia
Crane	Hurt
Creatore	Can't Help Falling In Love
Creatore	Froggy Went a'Courtin'
Crook	Runaway
Crosby	Hide Thou Me
Crouch	I've Got Confidence
Crudup	My Baby Left Me
Crudup	So Glad You're Mine

Crudup	That's All Right Mama
Crutchfield	Find Out What's Happening
Currie	I'll Never Fall In Love Again
Cymbal	Mary In The Morning
Darin	I'll Be There
Darin	You're The Reason I'm Living
Darion	The Impossible Dream
Davenport	Fever
David	I Don't Care If The Sun Don't Shine
David	Whole Lotta Shakin' Goin' On
de Curtis, E	Surrender
de Curtis, G.D.	Surrender
de Vita	Softly, As I Leave You
Dee	Moonlight Swim
del Moral	Allá En El Rancho Grande
Delanoë	Let It Be Me
Denson	Miracle Of The Rosary
Derricks	Just A Little Talk With Jesus
Derricks	When God Dips His Love In My Heart
Devine	Keeper Of The Key
di Capua	It's Now Or Never
Diamond	And The Grass Won't Pay No Mind
Diamond	Sweet Caroline
Dilbeck	I'll Hold You In My Heart
Dill	Detroit City
Dixon	Big Boss Man
Dixon	My Babe
Dodd	The Mickey Mouse Club March
Donaggio	You Don't Have To Say You Love Me
Donegan	I'll Never Fall In Love Again
Dorsey	(There'll Be) Peace In The Valley (For Me)
Dorsey	Take My Hand, Precious Lord
Drake	Cindy, Cindy
Drake	I Believe
Duffy	She Thinks I Still Care

Duncan	I Asked The Lord
Dylan	Blowin' In The Wind
Dylan	Don't Think Twice, It's All Right
Dylan	I Shall Be Released
Dylan	Tomorrow Is A Long Time
Emerson	When It Rains, It Really Pours
Evans	I Gotta Know
Evans	Mona Lisa
Evans	Que Sera, Sera
Evans	Roses Are Red (My Love)
Evans	Silver Bells
Faith	My Heart Cries For You
Fisher	That's When Your Heartaches Begin
Flatt	A Hundred Years From Now
Flatt	Little Cabin On The Hill
Flower	Nearer My God To Thee
Fogerty	Proud Mary
Foley	Old Shep
Ford	The Fool
Fosdick	Love Me Tender (Aura Lee)
Foster	Got My Mojo Working
Foster	Keep Your Hands Off Of It
François	My Boy
François	My Way
Frazier	He Is My Everything
Frazier	There Goes My Everything
Frazier	True Love Travels On A Gravel Road
Frazier	Where Did They Go, Lord?
Frizzell	Give Me More, More, More Of Your Kisses
Frye	Time Has Made A Change In Me
Fulson	Reconsider Baby
Gabriel	An Evening Prayer
Gaither	He Touched Me
Gamble	Only The Strong Survive
Gannon	I'll Be Home For Christmas

Gardner	I Need Your Loving (Every Day)
Gates	Aubrey
Gatlin	Bitter They Are, Harder They Fall
Gatlin	Help Me
Gentry	Ode To Billie Joe
George	Long Black Limousine
Giant	Ask Me
Giant	Down By The Riverside
Giant	Tender Feeling
Giant	Today, Tomorrow And Forever
Gibb	Words
Gibb	Words
Gibb	Words
Gibson	I Can't Stop Loving You
Gilbert	You Belong To My Heart
Glenn	Crying In The Chapel
Gold	It's Now Or Never
Goodhart	I Apologize
Goodman	Who Am I?
Gottlieb	Frankie And Johnny
Gounod	Ave Maria
Graham	I Believe
Gray	Milky White Way
Griffin	Just Call Me Lonesome
Grosz	Harbor Lights
Grosz	Tomorrow Night
Gruber	Silent Night
Guízar	Guadalajara
Gunter	Baby Let's Play House
Guynes	Keeper Of The Key
Haldeman	Here Comes Santa Claus
Hall	It Ain't No Big Thing (But It's Growing)
Hamblen	It Is No Secret (What God Can Do)
Hamblen	Known Only To Him
Hammerstein	If I Loved You

Hammerstein	Make Believe
Hammerstein	You'll Never Walk Alone
Handman	Are You Lonesome Tonight?
Hanks	In My Father's House
Harburg	Over The Rainbow
Harris	I Want You With Me
Harris	I'm Leaving It Up To You
Harrison	Something
Hart	Blue Moon
Hart	With A Song In My Heart
Hartford	Gentle On My Mind
Hathcock	Welcome To My World
Hawkins	Susie-Q
Hayes	Blue Christmas
Heath	I'll Never Stand In Your Way
Heath	Somebody Bigger Than You And I
Heath	Take These Chains From My Heart
Hein	A Hundred Years From Now
Hess	Come Along
Heyman	Love Letters
Higginbotham	High Heel Sneakers
Hill	Happy Birthday
Hill	Happy Birthday
Hilliard	Any Day Now (My Wild Beautiful Bird)
Hine	How Great Thou Art
Hinson	Lighthouse
Hodge	Earth Angel
Hodge	You'll Be Gone
Hoffman	Hawaiian Wedding Song
Hoffman	I Apologize
Hoffman	There's No Tomorrow
Holt	I'm Gonna Walk Dem Golden Stairs
Horton	I'll Hold You In My Heart
Howard	I Believe In The Man In The Sky
Howard	I've Lost You

Howard	Keeper Of The Key
Hoyle	Working On The Building
Hubbard	A Thing Called Love
Hubbard	Guitar Man
Hubbard	U.S. Male
Huff	Only The Strong Survive
Hunter	Ain't That Loving You Baby
Hunter	I Need You So
Hunter	I Will Be True
Hunter	Out Of Sight, Out Of Mind
Hutchins	I Wonder, I Wonder, I Wonder
J.K.	Yellow Rose Of Texas
Jackson	Hearts Of Stone
Jacobs	Hurt
James	Always On My Mind
James	It's Only Love
James	Moody Blue
Jans	Loving Arms
Jennings	You Asked Me To
Jesus	The Lord's Prayer
Johnson	Blue Christmas
Johnson	Bosom Of Abraham
Johnson	I, John
Johnson	Long Tall Sally
Jones	Ghost Riders In The Sky
Jones	So High
Jones	Soldier Boy
Joy	It Ain't No Big Thing (But It's Growing)
Joyner	Young Love
Kaempfert	Spanish Eyes
Kalman	Who's Sorry Now?
Karger	Frankie And Johnny
Kaye	Ask Me
Kaye	Down By The Riverside
Kaye	Tender Feeling

Kaye	Today, Tomorrow And Forever
Kennedy	Harbor Lights
Kennedy	Write To Me From Naples
Kenny	There Is No God But God
Kent	I'll Be Home For Christmas
Kent	Take Good Care Of Her
Kern	Make Believe
Kesler	If I'm A Fool (For Loving You)
King	Hawaiian Wedding Song
King	One Night
King	Tennessee Waltz
King	Witchcraft
Knight	The Wonder Of You
Kresa	That's My Desire
Kristofferson	For The Good Times
Kristofferson	Help Me Make It Through The Night
Kristofferson	Why Me Lord
Kusik	When The Snow Is On The Roses
Labostrie	Tutti Frutti
Lane	Everybody Loves Somebody
Lange	I Asked The Lord
Lange	Somebody Bigger Than You And I
Lantz	After Loving You
Lara	You Belong To My Heart
Larue	Padre
Last	Fool
Last	When The Snow Is On The Roses
Ledbetter	Cottonfields
Lee	I'll Remember You
LeFevre	Without Him
Leiber	Bossa Nova Baby
Leiber	Don't
Leiber	Fools Fall In Love
Leiber	Girls! Girls! Girls!
Leiber	Hot Dog

Leiber	Hound Dog
Leiber	If You Don't Come Back
Leiber	Little Egypt
Leiber	Love Me
Leiber	Saved
Leiber	Three Corn Patches
Leiber	You're The Boss
Leigh	The Impossible Dream
Leigh	Witchcraft
Lemmel	Turn Your Eyes Upon Jesus
Lennon	Get Back
Lennon	Hey Jude
Lennon	Lady Madonna
Lennon	Yesterday
Leveen	I Will Be Home Again
Lewis	Blueberry Hill
Lewis	Susie-Q
Lightfoot	(That's What You Get) For Lovin' Me
Lightfoot	Early Morning Rain
Liliuokalani	Aloha Oe
Lilley	Tonight Is So Right For Love
Lilley	Tonight's All Right For Love
Linde	Burning Love
Lipscomb	She Thinks I Still Care
Lister	He Knows Just What I Need
Lister	His Hand In Mine
Lister	Where No One Stands Alone
Livingston	Mona Lisa
Livingston	Que Sera, Sera
Livingston	Silver Bells
Livingston	The Twelfth Of Never
Loggins	Mama Don't Dance
Lopez	Happy, Happy Birthday Baby
Louis	Tiger Man
Loveday	That's My Desire

MacColl	The First Time Ever I Saw Your Face
MacLellan	Put Your Hand In The Hand
MacLellan	Snowbird
Madara	At The Hop
Mancini	Peter Gunn Theme
Mann	I Just Can't Help Believin'
Mann	You've Lost That Lovin' Feelin'
Manning	Hawaiian Wedding Song
Marascalco	Ready Teddy
Marascalco	Rip It Up
Marascalso	Send Me Some Lovin'
Mason	Delilah
Mason	Nearer My God To Thee
Massey	Wings Of An Angel (The Prisoner's Song)
Matson	We're Gonna Move
Mayfield	Stranger In My Own Home Town
Mayhew	It's A Sin To Tell A Lie
Mazzucchi	It's Now Or Never
McCartney	Get Back
McCartney	Hey Jude
McCartney	Lady Madonna
McCartney	Yesterday
McCoy	Trying To Get To You
McCrossman	On The Jericho Road
McCrossman	On The Jericho Road
McFadden	Bosom Of Abraham
McFadden	I, John
McLean	And I Love You So
McShann	Hands Off
Melson	Running Scared
Mercer	Fools Rush In (Where Angels Fear To Tread)
Merritt	It Ain't No Big Thing (But It's Growing)
Messina	Mama Don't Dance
Miles	In The Garden
Miller	Dark Moon

Miller	From A Jack To A King
Miller	Release Me
Miller	After Loving You
Minnigerode	The Whiffenpoof Song
Modugno	Ask Me
Mohr	Silent Night
Moman	This Time
Monroe	Blue Moon Of Kentucky
Monroe	I Hear A Sweet Voice Calling
Monroe	Little Cabin On The Hill
Monroe	Summertime Has Passed And Gone
Monroe	Sweetheart You Done Me Wrong
Monroe	Uncle Pen
Mooney	Crazy Arms
Moore	Merry Christmas Baby
Morehead	Sentimental Me
Morris	Shake A Hand
Morris	I Shall Not Be Moved
Most	How The Web Was Woven
Mullen	He
Nathanson	Hava Nagila
Nelson	Funny How Time Slips Away
Nelson	I Apologize
Newbury	An American Trilogy
Newell	More
Newton	Amazing Grace
Nolan	Tumblin' Tumbleweeds
North	Unchained Melody
Nugetre	Fool, Fool, Fool
O'Keefe	Good Time Charlie's Got The Blues
Oakley	O Come, All Ye Faithful
Oldham	Sweet Inspiration
Oliviero	More
Orbison	Running Scared
Ornadel	Portrait Of My Love

Ortolani	More
Otis	Ain't That Loving You Baby
Otis	Out Of Sight, Out Of Mind
Owens	Cattle Call
Owens	Crying Time
Owens	Sweet Leilani
Owens	Where Did They Go, Lord?
Owens	True Love Travels On A Gravel Road
Pallavicini	You Don't Have To Say You Love Me
Parker	Mystery Train
Payne	I Love You Because
Payne	There's No Place Like Home
Penniman	Long Tall Sally
Penniman	Tutti Frutti
Pennington	Sweet Inspiration
Peretti	Can't Help Falling In Love
Peretti	Froggy Went a'Courtin'
Perkins	Blue Suede Shoes
Peterson	My Happiness
Phelps	I'm Beginning To Forget You
Phillips	Mystery Train
Pierce	How Do You Think I Feel
Pierpont	Jingle Bells
Pitman	Beyond The Reef
Pointer	Fairytale
Pointer	Fairytale
Polynesian Culture Center	Drums Of The Islands
Pomeroy	The Whiffenpoof Song
Pomus	(Marie's The Name) His Latest Flame
Pomus	Surrender
Porter	True Love
Poulton	Love Me Tender (Aura Lee)
Presley	We're Gonna Move
Presley	You'll Be Gone
Presley, adapted	I Was Born About Ten Thousand Years Ago

Presley, arranged	Joshua Fit The Battle
Presley, arranged	Run On
Presley, arranged	The First Noel
Price	Give Me More, More, More Of Your Kisses
Price	Lawdy Miss Clawdy
Price	Send Me Some Lovin'
Purvis	When The Saints Go Marchin' In
Putman	Green, Green Grass Of Home
Rader	Only Believe
Rainger	Blue Hawaii
Ram	I'll Be Home For Christmas
Rambo	If That Isn't Love
Ramos	Allá En El Rancho Grande
Rashkow	Mary In The Morning
Raskin	That's When Your Heartaches Begin
Ray	Hearts Of Stone
Redell	Judy
Redner	Oh Little Town Of Bethlehem
Reed	Baby What You Want Me To Do
Reed	Delilah
Reed	Talk About The Good Times
Reid	Susan When She Tried
Rene	When The Swallows Come Back To Capistrano
Revaux	My Way
Rice	Girl Next Door Went A Walkin'
Rice	There's A Honky Tonk Angel (Who Will Take Me Back In)
Rich	I'm Comin' Home
Richard	I Got A Woman
Richards	He
Rivgauche	It's Impossible
Robbins	El Paso
Robbins	You Gave Me A Mountain
Robertson	I Really Don't Want To Know
Robertson	No More

Robey	Pledging My Love
Robin	Blue Hawaii
Robin	Just Because
Robinson	I Need Your Loving (Every Day)
Rodgers	Blue Moon
Rodgers	Froggy Went a'Courtin'
Rodgers	If I Loved You
Rodgers	It's Over
Rodgers	With A Song In My Heart
Rodgers	You'll Never Walk Alone
Romans	Padre
Rose	Blue Eyes Crying In The Rain
Rose	Blueberry Hill
Rose	I'll Never Stand In Your Way
Rose	It Wouldn't Be The Same Without You
Rose	It's A Sin
Rose	Take These Chains From My Heart
Rosenberg	Too Much
Ross	Rags To Riches
Rostill	If You Love Me (Let Me Know)
Rostill	Let Me Be There
Royale	A Hundred Years From Now
Ruby	Who's Sorry Now?
Sainte Marie	Until It's Time For You To Go
Sallee	You're A Heartbreaker
Schroeder	Apron Strings
Schroeder	It's Now Or Never
Scott	Tweedlee Dee
Scruggs	A Hundred Years From Now
Sculls	The Whiffenpoof Song
Seals	Crazy Arms
Seals	Pieces Of My Life
Seals	There's A Honky Tonk Angel (Who Will Take Me Back In)
Sedaka	Solitaire

Serradell	She Wears My Ring
Shade	Show Me Thy Ways, O Lord
Shannon	Runaway
Shaper	Softly, As I Leave You
Shaver	You Asked Me To
Shepherd	Must Jesus Bear The Cross Alone
Sherrill	The Most Beautiful Girl
Shirl	I Believe
Shirl	Cindy, Cindy
Shuman	(Marie's The Name) His Latest Flame
Shuman	Surrender
Sigman	Fool
Sigman	My Heart Cries For You
Sigman	What Now My Love
Silver	Tonight Is So Right For Love
Silver	Tonight's All Right For Love
Simon	Bridge Over Troubled Water
Sinclair	The Eyes Of Texas
Singer	At The Hop
Singer	I Will Be Home Again
Singleton	Don't Forbid Me
Singleton	Spanish Eyes
Singleton	Trying To Get To You
Slaughter	If The Lord Wasn't Walking By My Side
Small	Without Love (There Is Nothing)
Smith	Big Boss Man
Smith	My Country, 'Tis Of Thee
Smith	Winter Wonderland
Snow	I'm Gonna Bid My Blues Goodbye
Snow	I'm Movin' On
Snyder	Spanish Eyes
Snyder	When The Snow Is On The Roses
Snyder	Who's Sorry Now?
South	Don't It Make You Wanna Go Home
South	Walk A Mile In My Shoes

Spector	You've Lost That Lovin' Feelin'
Stanphill	Mansion Over The Hilltop
Starr	Old MacDonald
Stevenson	When God Dips His Love In My Heart
Stewart	Keeper Of The Key
Stewart	Tennessee Waltz
Stillman	I Believe
Stock	Blueberry Hill
Stoller	Bossa Nova Baby
Stoller	Don't
Stoller	Fools Fall In Love
Stoller	Girls! Girls! Girls!
Stoller	Hot Dog
Stoller	Hound Dog
Stoller	If You Don't Come Back
Stoller	Little Egypt
Stoller	Love Me
Stoller	Saved
Stoller	Three Corn Patches
Stoller	You're The Boss
Stone	Down In The Alley
Stone	Farther Along
Stone	Like A Baby
Stone	Money Honey
Story	I'm With The Crowd (But So Alone)
Stovall	Long Black Limousine
Sullivan	When My Blue Moon Turns To Gold Again
Swan	I Can Help
Sylvia	Happy, Happy Birthday Baby
Tableporter	Come What May
Taylor	Everybody Loves Somebody
Taylor	Steamroller Blues
Tepper	Drums Of The Islands
Tepper	Five Sleepy Heads
Tepper	I Love Only One Girl

Tepper	Stay Away
Terry	I'm Leaving It Up To You
Tharpe	Up Above My Head
Thibaut	My Way
Thomas	I'm Gonna Sit Right Down And Cry (Over You)
Thompson	Just A Little Bit
Thompson	Softly And Tenderly
Thornton	Just A Little Bit
Tillis	Detroit City
Tillotson	It Keeps Right On A Hurtin'
Tindley	By And By
Tindley	Stand By Me
Tiomkin	High Noon (Do Not Forsake Me Oh My Darlin')
Trader	(Now And Then There's) A Fool Such As I
Traditional	Amen
Traditional	Down By The Riverside
Traditional	I Was Born About Ten Thousand Years Ago
Traditional	Jesus Walked That Lonesome Valley
Traditional	Oh Happy Day
Traditional	On Top Of Old Smokey
Traditional	Stagger Lee
Traditional	Tell Me Why (Just A Closer Walk With Thee)
Traditional	You Better Run
Traditional	An American Trilogy
Traditional	Amazing Grace
Traditional	Milkcow Blues Boogie
Tubb	I'm With The Crowd (But So Alone)
Tubb	It's Been So Long Darling
Tubb	Tomorrow Never Comes
Turk	Are You Lonesome Tonight?
Turner	Flip, Flop And Fly
Turner	It's A Sin
Turner	Tell Me Why (Just A Closer Walk With Thee)
Twomey	Wooden Heart

Tyrell	It's Only Love
Unknown	Just A Closer Walk With Thee
Urange	Allá En El Rancho Grande
Wade	O Come, All Ye Faithful
Wakely	I'll Never Let You Go (Little Darlin')
Wakely	It Wouldn't Be The Same Without You
Walker	Are You Sincere
Walker	How Do You Think I Feel
Walker	When My Blue Moon Turns To Gold Again
Walker	You Don't Know Me
Ward	I Just Can't Make It By Myself
Warren	Take Good Care Of Her
Warren	That's Amore
Washington	High Noon (Do Not Forsake Me Oh My Darlin')
Washington	Just A Little Bit
Washington	Pledging My Love
Watts	Alright, Okay, You Win
Wayne	Clambake
Wayne	Girl Next Door Went A Walkin'
Wayne	It's Impossible
Wayne	Stay Away, Joe
Wayne	Tonight Is So Right For Love
Wayne	Tonight's All Right For Love
Weatherly	Danny Boy
Webb	MacArthur Park
Webster	Padre
Webster	The Last Farewell
Webster	The Twelfth Of Never
Weil	I Just Can't Help Believin'
Weil	You've Lost That Lovin' Feelin'
Weinman	Too Much
Weisman	Almost Always True
Weisman	Clambake
Weisman	Frankie And Johnny

Weisman	Moonlight Swim
Weisman	Stay Away, Joe
Weisman	Wooden Heart
Weiss	Apron Strings
Weiss	Can't Help Falling In Love
West	500 Miles
West	Portrait Of My Love
West	You'll Be Gone
Westendorf	I'll Take You Home Again, Kathleen
Westlake	How The Web Was Woven
White	At The Hop
White	For Ol' Times Sake
White	I've Got A Thing About You Baby
White	Polk Salad Annie
Whitfield	Oh How I Love Jesus
Whittaker	The Last Farewell
Williams	Earth Angel
Williams	I Can't Help It (If I'm Still In Love With You)
Williams	I Gotta Know
Williams	I'm So Lonesome I Could Cry
Williams	Jambalaya (On The Bayou)
Williams	Little Darlin'
Williams	Men With Broken Hearts
Williams	Release Me
Williams	Where Do I Go From Here
Williams	Whole Lotta Shakin' Goin' On
Williams	Your Cheatin' Heart
Williams Jr.	Soldier Boy
Willis	I Feel So Bad
Wills	Faded Love
Wills	Faded Love
Wills	San Antonio Rose
Wilmott	Aloha Oe
Wilson	The Most Beautiful Girl
Winkler	Welcome To My World

Wise . . . . Almost Always True
Wise . . . . Wooden Heart
Wiseman . . . . Have I Told You Lately That I Love You
Wyche . . . . Alright, Okay, You Win
Young . . . . Is It So Strange
Young . . . . Love Letters
Yount . . . . Release Me
Zambon . . . . Suspicious Minds
Zaret . . . . Unchained Melody

Problem Originals

Problem Originals

Blues, Stay Away From Me (Delmore/Raney/Glover): I have heard rumours that this number was recorded by someone in December 1954 at Sun Studios, Memphis. Furthermore, Elvis might have sung on the backing vocals! I have searched for the number, with no success, however.

It's No Fun Being Lonely (West): Recorded informally by Elvis, probably in 1966, this number appears on the CD The Home Recordings, but I have been unable to find additional information about its origins. Perhaps it had already been recorded by somebody. On the other hand, as the number is attributed to Elvis's friend, Red West, perhaps they were just trying it out together.

I've Been Blue (West): Recorded informally by Elvis, probably in 1966, this number appears on the CD The Home Recordings, but I have been unable to find additional information about its origins. Perhaps it had already been recorded by somebody. On the other hand, as the number is attributed to Elvis's friend, Red West, perhaps they were just trying it out together.

Lonely Teardrops (Fuqua/Gordy/Davis): There are rumours that Elvis performed at least part of this song during a concert in 1970, but it has not yet surfaced on a recording, either officially or otherwise.

Mary Lou Brown (West): Recorded informally by Elvis, probably in 1966, this number appears on the CD The Home Recordings, but I have been unable to find additional information about its origins. Perhaps it had already been recorded by somebody. On the other hand, as the number is attributed to Elvis's friend, Red West, perhaps they were just trying it out together.

Number Eight (On The Jukebox): a recording of this number appeared on the unofficial CD "Greetings From Germany" in 1998. The number was probably recorded by Elvis at home in 1959. Where did Elvis find the song? I can find it no reference to it having been recorded by anyone else, nor to who wrote it

Rock Around The Clock (Freedman/de Knight): Elvis sang this number live now and then when touring during 1955 and 1956. Performances include unspecified date(s) at the Louisiana Hayride; 22 September, 1955 at Kingsport, TN; 19 November, 1955 at Gladeswater, TX; 9 December, 1955 at Swifton, AR. The number might also have been scheduled for the September, 1956 recording session but there is no record of it being attempted in the studio then. No tape has yet emerged of any of these performances, however.

Teardrop: A recording of Elvis and Linda Thompson, made at Linda's home. Again, I have been unable to find any information about the origins of the song.

Young Dreams (Schroeder/Kalmanoff): I have a suspicion that someone called Cartey first recorded this number in 1956, but am unable to find any more about it.

Your Life Has Just Begun: A recording of Elvis and Linda Thompson singing this number, clearly in the company of others, has appeared on several CDs, usually with the incorrect title, *You're Life Has Just Begun*. The recording was made in 1973 or 1974. I have been unable to find any more information about the song.

Not Included

Not Included

Elvis Presley recorded an enormous amount of material in his 23-year career—it is difficult to know exactly how many titles he recorded (does one include one-liners, home recordings, informal recordings, etc?), but probably close to 800 different titles can be found. You will not find all of these titles in this book: only those numbers originally recorded by someone else are included.

Furthermore, this book does not provide information about numbers performed in an Elvis concert by someone else, on which Elvis?s voice does not feature (such numbers have appeared on some Elvis LPs and CDs, but you won't find them here!). These include:

It's My Time To Praise The Lord, 31 March, 1972, Sung by The Stamps

Steal Away, 31 March, 1972, Sung by The Stamps

Also not included are songs available only on audio- and videotape recordings. These are almost always one-liners, or small parts of songs, thrown in by Elvis on a whim. Here is a list of such titles :

Alfie: 20 February, 1970, Las Vegas

Another Place, Another Time: 22 February, 1970, Las Vegas midnight

Blue Monday: 4 April, 1974, Las Vegas dinner

By The Time I Get To Phoenix: 9 September, 1970, Phoenix evening

Diana: 31 July, 1971, Lake Tahoe dinner and 1 August, 1971, Lake Tahoe midnight

God Calls Me Home: 11 December, 1975, Las Vegas midnight

Goldfinger: 7 September, 1970, Las Vegas closing

Higher and Higher: 30 August, 1974, Las Vegas dinner

Holiday Inn: 23 June, 1973, NY evening

Holly Holy: 21 August, 1970, Las Vegas dinner

I Saw The Light: 1 May, 1976, Lake Tahoe midnight

Just Tired And Lonely: 28 March, 1975, Las Vegas dinner

Kaw Liga: 10 August, 1971, Las Vegas dinner

Lady Of Spain: 30 August, 1973, Las Vegas midnight

Lonesome Like A...(title unknown) 22 February, 1972, Las Vegas midnight

Love Story: 7 May, 1976, Lake Tahoe midnight

My Dreams Are Only Now: 22 February, 1972, Las Vegas midnight

My Woman, My Woman, My Wife: 24 April, 1975, San Diego

Raindrops Keep Falling On My Head: 9 November, 1972, Tucson

Rainy Night In Georgia: 3 July, 1973, Atlanta

Toreador Song (from Carmen): 12 August, 1970, Las Vegas midnight (*That's The Way It Is* video)

Vaya Con Dios: 29 June, 1973, Atlanta

We Shall Overcome: 27 August, 1974, Las Vegas midnight

We Three: September, 1970, Las Vegas dinner

You Are My Sunshine: 27 and 30 August, 1974, Las Vegas midnight and 12 September, 1974, dinner.

Collecting Originals

Collecting Originals

It is interesting not only to know where Elvis's music comes from, but also to be able to listen to those sources. I have to admit that I have been somewhat lax in that I do not know how many originals I possess! I estimate the number to be about 150, however—about one-third of the total, in other words. Some of these numbers are hidden away on LPs and EPs that have not been played for years, as I no longer own a record player! I have found others by searching the Internet, but the quality tends to be rather poor, of course, and this is not really an ethical approach, anyway. A few collections of originals, but then in the very loosest sense of the word, have been released on CD and I provide a list of at least some of these below.

Sadly, the compilers of these collections have generally shown more enthusiasm than accuracy! Nevertheless, the collections remain interesting and all offer at least some genuine originals.

The Roots of Elvis, on Memory 2019-2

    It Is No Secret (The Blackwood Brothers)
    Rock My Soul (Golden Gate Quartet)
    Peace In The Valley (Red Foley)
    Up Above My Head (Sister Rosetta Tharpe)
    Old Shep (Red Foley)
    Have I Told You Lately (Gene Autry)
    Blue Moon Of Kentucky (Bill Monroe)
    I'm So Lonesome I Could Cry (Hank Williams)
    I'm Movin' On (Hank Snow)
    It's A Sin (Eddy Arnold)
    That's All Right, Mama (Arthur Crudup)
    This Train (My Babe) (Sister Rosetta Tharpe)
    Sorrento (Mario Lanza)
    There's No Tomorrow (O Sole Mio) (Tony Martin)
    I Don't Care If The Sun Don't Shine (Dean Martin)

My Happiness (Ella Fitzgerald)
Sentimental Me (Ames Brothers)
That's When Your Heartache Begins (sic) (The Ink Spots)
Sentimental Journey (Ruth Brown)
Beyond The Reef (Bing Crosby)
Good Rockin' Tonight (Wynonie Harris)
Rocket 88 (Bill Haley's Saddlemen)
Bump Miss Susie (Big Joe Turner)
Don't Knock (The Spiders)
Careless Love (Fats Domino)
Stack-a-Lee (Dave Bartholomew)

The Originals, on EVA 7895622

That's All Right (Arthur Crudup)
Baby Let's Play House (Arthur Gunter)
Mystery Train (Little Junior & The Blue Flames)
Hound Dog (Big Mama Thornton)
I Love You Because (Leon Payne)
Old Shep (Red Foley)
All Shook Up (David Hill)
That's When Your Heartaches Begin (The Ink Spots)
Blue Christmas (Russ Morgan & His Orchestra)
One Night (Smiley Lewis)
(Now And The There's) A Fool Such As I (Hank Snow)
O Sole Mio (Emilio De Gogorza)
Are You Lonesome Tonight? (Al Jolson)
Bossa Nova, Baby (Tippie & The Clovers)
Crying In The Chapel (Darrell Glenn)
Love Letters (Dick Haymes)
Guitar Man (Jerry Reed)
The Wonder Of You (Ray Peterson)
I Just Can't Help Believing (Bobby Vee)
Burning Love (Arthur Alexander)
Steamroller (James Taylor)
Loving Arms (Dobie Gray)

The Roots Of Elvis Presley, on Catfish KATCD184

    I Love You Because (Leon Payne)
    That's All Right (Arthur Crudup)
    Blue Moon Of Kentucky (Bill Monroe)
    Tomorrow Night (Lonnie Johnson)
    Just Because (The Shelton Brothers)
    Good Rockin' Tonight (Wynonie Harris)
    My Baby Left Me (Arthur Crudup)
    Down By The Riverside (Sister Rosetta Tharpe)
    Little Cabin On The Hill (Bill Monroe)
    Precious Lord (Golden Gate Quartet)
    I Need You So (Ivory John Hunter)
    So Glad You're Mine (Arthur Crudup)
    Frankie And Johnny (Various Artists)
    I'm Movin' On (Hank Snow)
    Faded Love (Bob Wills)
    I'm So Lonesome I Could Cry (Hank Williams)
    See See Rider (Wea Bea Booze)
    Aura Lee (The Shelton Brothers)
    Milk Cow Blues (Jonnie lee wills)
    Old Shep (Red Foley)
    Blueberry Hill (Gene Autry)

The King's Record Collection Vol.1, on Hip-O HIPD-40082

    That's All Right (Arthur "Big Boy" Crudup)
    Blue Moon Of Kentucky (Bill Monroe)
    I Love You Because (Leon Payne)
    Good Rockin' Tonight (Wynonie Harris)
    Just Because (Shelton Brothers)
    Baby Let's Play House (Arthur Gunter)
    Mystery Train (Little Junior Parker)
    Money Honey (Drifters)
    Lawdy Miss Clawdy (Lloyd Price)
    Shake, Rattle And Roll (Joe Turner)

Blue Suede Shoes (Carl Perkins)
Hound Dog (Big Mama Thornton)
That's When Your Heartaches Begin (Ink Spots)
One Night (Smiley Lewis)

The King's Record Collection Vol.2, on Hip-O HIPD-40083

(Now And Then There's) A Fool Such As I (Hank Snow)
Such A Night (Drifters)
Fever (Little Willie John)
Reconsider Baby (Lowell Fulson)
Crying In The Chapel (Orioles)
I Feel So Bad (Chuck Willis)
Love Letters (Ketty Lester)
Big Boss Man (Jimmy Reed)
Guitar Man (Jerry Reed)
You Don't Know Me (Eddy Arnold)
High Heel Sneakers (Tommy Tucker)
The Wonder Of You (Ray Peterson)
There Goes My Everything (Jack Greene)
The Promised Land (Chuck Berry)

Acknowledgements, etc.

Acknowledgements, etc.

The Books

In searching for original versions, I have used numerous books, including:

    The Encyclopedia of Rock Vols. 1-3; Phil Hardy & Dave Laing; 1977

    Encyclopaedia Britannica; 1978

    Million Selling Records From The 1900s To The 1980s; Joseph Murrells; 1984

    Elvis, His Life From A to Z; Fred L. Worth & Steve D. Tamerius; 1989

    Hits of the '60s: Million Sellers; Demitri Coryton & Joseph Murrells; 1990

    Good Rockin' Tonight; Colin Escott with Martin Hawkins; 1991

    Mystery Train; Greil Marcus; 1991

    Lost Highway; Peter Guralnick; 1992

    Feel Like Going Home; Peter Guralnick; 1992

    This Day In African-American Music; Ted Holland; 1993

    The History of Blues; Frank Davis; 1995

    The Originals; Arnold Rypens; 1996

    Go, Cat, Go!; Carl Perkins and David McGee; 1996

    Elvis Presley: A Life In Music; Ernst Jorgensen; 1998

(Year shown indicates publication year of the edition I used.)

The above list is certainly not exhaustive—many of the books I have used are listed among my Elvis In Print and Popular Music In Print sites, but these were certainly my early sources. LP covers and CD inserts have also provided the occasional hint, though these are frequently inaccurate.

Elvis In Print: http://users.pandora.be/davidneale/elvis/books/

Popular Music In Print:
http://users.pandora.be/davidneale/music/books.html

The Web

The World Wide Web is a remarkable source of information, but there is a huge amount of duplication and misinformation, too. Considerable patience is often required to find exactly what one requires and this was certainly the case for many of the titles included in this book. I found the following sites particularly useful:

AMG Music Guide: http://www.allmusic.com/

Early Blues: http://www.earlyblues.com/

The Iceberg Artists Directory:
http://www.theiceberg.com/artist_directory.html

The Mudcat discussion Forum: http://www.mudcat.org/threads.cfm

Oldies.com: http://www.oldies.com/index.cfm

The Rock and Roll Hall of Fame and Museum:
http://www.rockhall.com/

I have endeavoured to at least double-check all information shown for each title. In some cases, doubts still exist and these are indicated in the relevant entries. Checking the information is done with both traditional material (books, etc) and through searching the Web, dropping questions in discussion boards, and mailing people I think might be able to help—often family members or associates of the supposed original artist.

The People

A number of people have sent me corrections and additions to my Elvis Presley, The Originals site, upon which this book is based: Garth Bond (UK), Sebastiano

Cecere (Italy), Chris Deakin (UK), Stig Ericsson (Sweden), Joop Jansen (Netherlands), Torben Jensen (Denmark), Robin Jones (Saudi Arabia), Rami Poutiainen (Finland), Aad Sala (Netherlands), Leroy Smith (Netherlands), Kris Verdonck (Belgium).

If I've forgotten anyone, please forgive me! Thanks to all who have taken the trouble to contact me in this respect.

If you wish to pass on suggestions, comments, corrections, additions, or whatever, please feel free to do so via email: david.neale@pandora.be

Supplementary Index

Supplementary Index

The main section of this book is indexed by both the Artists Index and the Writers and Composers Index. These offer a good way to cross-reference the various entries, but are built with only the information from each entry's title and writers' credits, together with the artists listed as having performed the original version. The following index is built from the comments of each entry and therefore also references alternative titles and performers whose names perhaps do not appear in the other two indices.

A

A Life In Music, 11-12, 16, 25, 42, 48, 52, 61-62, 65, 71, 83, 117, 123-124, 205

Adeste Fideles, 92

Ahbez, Eden, 39

All My Trials, 15

Alouette, 13

Ann-Margret, 125, 144

Anthony, Ray, 105, 143, 160

Arden, Toni, 97, 112

Army Blue, 82

As You Like It, 17

As We Travel Along The Jericho Road, 95

Atkins, Chet, 50

Auprès de Ma Blonde, 55

Aura Lee, 82, 132, 154, 172, 180, 201

B

Bach, J.S., 18

Bad Nauhcim Medley, 16, 71, 123

Bad Penny Blues, 77

Bailey Gospel Singers, The, 54

Bakkers, Marthe, 126

Barber of Seville, 123

Barcarolle, 126

Bare, Bobby, 11, 29, 34, 80, 151

Barney, Take Me Home Again, 62

Bassey, Shirley, 71

Battle Hymn Of The Republic, 15

Bear Cat, 124

Begin The Beguine, 143

Bell, Freddie, 49

Bell, Jimmy, 106

Bethany, 91

Bible
- Corinthians 7:24, 108
- Luke 1:28, 18
- Luke 11, 120
- Matthew 4, 1-12, 129
- Matthew 6, 120
- Psalm 19:12-13, 15
- Psalm 25.4, 107
- Revelations 21, 66

Big Texas, 73

Bigger They Are, Harder They Fall, 20

Blackwell, Otis, 34

Blackwood Brothers, The, 15, 55, 68, 140, 150, 199

Blue Barron Orchestra, 17

Boberg, Carl, 49

Boleyn, Anne, 111

Boone, Pat, 12, 29, 41, 159

Bossa Nova, 23, 162, 176, 184, 200

Bowie, David, 91

Bradley Film & Recording Studio, 11

Brahms, Johannes, 34-35

Brohly, Suzanne, 126

Brown, Alex, 54

Bula Lai, 31

Burk, Bill, 94

C

Caminos de Ayer, 42

Cannon, Hughie, 38

Captain Newman M.D., 94

Carle, Frankie, 126

Carlisle, Cliff, 75

Carousel, 66, 143

Carr, Vikki, 71

Carroll, Jimmy, 78

Carter Family, 91

Carter, C.C., 15

Castel, Lili, 71

Chanson de Marie Antoinnette, 90

Cher, 71

Clari, 123

Clark, Dick, 17

Clayton, Paul, 30

Coleman, Cynthia, 41

Coleman, Robert, 43

Come and Get It, 82

Comme d'Habitude, 91

Como, Perry, 15, 71, 121, 160

Cool Water, 128

Corey, Jill, 78

Crickets, The, 138

Curtis, Tony, 94

D

Damone, Vic, 90

Darby, Ken, 82, 132

Darin, Bobby, 9, 58, 60, 144, 151

Dark Was The Night, 24

Darryl And The Oxfords, 102

Davis, Skeeter, 83

de Florian, Jean-Pierre Claris, 24

Deary, Joan, 28, 90

Dee, Lola, 97

Delcroix, A., 24-25, 149

Diamonds Are A Girl's Best Friend, 21

Dixie, 15, 22

Do The Bop, 17

Dolan, Robert Emmett, 26

Domino, Fats, 22-23, 77, 200

Donaggio, Pino, 142

Donald Duck, 141

Done He Me Wrong, 38

Dorsey, Thomas A., 10, 115, 162

Dorsey, Tommy, 37, 81

Duke Of Bucclugh's Tune, 18

Duncan, Tommy, 103

Dykes, John, 91

E

Early Elvis, 94

Eastwood, Clint, 119, 135

Edwin Hawkins Singers, 93

Elizabeth I, 111

Ellington, Duke, 45

Elvis Monthly, 3, 17

Ely, Claude, 132

Emmett, Dan, 15

Ertegun, Ahmet, 36

Estes, Sleepy John, 19, 85

Et Maintenant, 132

Etting, Ruth, 71

Even A Fool Learns To Know, 91

Evergreen, 111

F

Fabares, Shelley, 70

Fabian, 54

Fadal, Eddie, 43, 52, 57, 136

Fairport Convention, 65

Farmer, Frances, 82, 154

Flatt and Scruggs, 11, 22, 154

Flatt and Scruggs, 22

Flowers On The Wall, 113

Foley, Red, 10, 74, 76, 83, 94, 116, 133, 135, 160, 199-201

Follow That Dream, 5, 25, 95, 106, 130

Four Aces, The, 59, 116

Four Pennies, The, 131

François, Claude, 89, 91

Freddie and The Dreamers, 57

G

Gasté, Louis, 33

Gates, David, 18

Gerry and The Pacemakers,, 60, 143

Geschichten aus dem Wienerwald, 127

Go, Johnny, Go, 66

God Save The King/Queen, 89

Goldsboro, Bobby, 15

Gonna Raise A Ruckus Tonight, 26

Good Morning To All, 43

Grammy Award(s), 23, 32-33, 35, 82, 93, 104

Grateful Dead, 128

Green, Rita, 15

Greensleeves, 111

Greer, Jo Ann, 144

Grob, Dick, 76

Growing Up With The Memphis Flash, 144

Guten Abend, Gute Nacht, 34

H

Hallelujah, 32

Hamilton IV, George, 80

Hand, Albert, 17

Harlow, Jean, 21

Harmonizing Four, The, 96, 108-109, 155

Harris, Wynonie, 41, 200-201

Harvard, 121

Haymes, Dick, 81, 119, 152, 200

Heap, Jimmy, 101, 143

Hein, Silvio, 11

Henderson, Joe, 11, 157

Henry VIII, 111

Hess, Jake, 48, 52, 67-68, 77

Hey Mister Did You Happen..., 120

Higginbotham, Robert, 48

Highgwaymen, The*****

High Society, 127

Hi-Heel Sneakers, 92

Hill, David, 12, 72, 152, 200

Hilo Hawaiians, 13

Hit The Road Jack, 112

Hobart, George V., 11

Holiday Inn, 135, 196

Holliday, Billie, 71

Holly, Buddy, 46, 105, 138, 141

Hollywood Argyles, The, 135

Home Sweet Home, 123

Hope, Bob, 107

Hopkins, Lightnin', 53

Hornbury*****

Howe, John*****

Hubbard, Jerry, 11, 42, 130

Humes High School, 40

Humperdinck, Engelbert, 122

Humphrey Lyttleton Band, The, 77

Hunter, Tab, 145

Husky, Ferlin, 42

I

I John Saw A Mighty Number, 65

I Love Lucy, 100

I'll Fly Away, 20, 67

I'll Overcome Some Day, 24, 110

I've Been Working On The Railroad, 118

I've Got A Woman, 54

I've Got A Savior, 54

I Got A Break Today*****

Imperials, The, 67-68

Io Che Non Vivo Piu d'Un Ora Senza Te, 142

Ives, Burl, 39

J

Jackson, Mahalia, 10, 15, 51, 115, 158

James, Etta, 26, 153

James, Sonny, 145

Jennings, Waylon, 128, 130, 137, 141, 162

Je t'Appartiens, 78

John Brown's Body, 15

John Saw a Mighty Number, 65-66

John Saw De Holy Number, 66

Johnson, Lonnie, 126, 201

Jolson, Al, 16, 200

Jones, Corky, 49

Jones, Jimmy, 96, 108-109

Jordanaires, The, 23, 58, 63, 157

Jorgenson, Ernst*****

Joshua Fit De Battle of Jericho, 74

Joshua Fit The Battle of Jericho, 74

Joshua Fought The Battle of Jericho, 74

Jules, Hey, 47

K

Ke Kali Nei Au, 44

Keep The Fire Burning In Me, 78

Keisker, Marion, 53

Kiley, Richard, 119

King, Ben E., 24, 36, 67

Kirby, Kathy, 71

Knight, Marie, 116, 131

L

La Golondrina,, 106

La Mano de Dios, 42

La Paloma, 92

Lamperez, Julius, 73

Last Train To Memphis, 144

Last, James, 36

Lawrence, Steve, 99

Le Feu Aux Poudres, 34

Leadbelly, 27, 111, 158

Leavin' Home, 37

Lee Conley, William, 104

Lee, Peggy, 13, 32, 34

Leighton Brothers, The, 38

Lewis, Jerry Lee, 27, 29-30, 42, 57, 75, 134, 136, 144

Liebestraum, 125

Lightfoot, Gordon, 10, 31

Lindsay, Mark, 15

Lister, Hovie, 48

Lister, Mosie, 45, 48, 135, 159

Liszt, Franz, 125

Little Miss Broadway, 55-56

Little Nemo, 121

Loch Lomond, 14

Lomax, John, 111

Lombardo, Guy, 18, 137, 155

Londonderry Air, 28

Lopez, Trini, 25

Lowe, Nick, 128

Lynn, Vera, 71

M

Maddox, Rose, 80

Macdough, Harry*****

Manhattan Melodrama, 22

Manzanero, Armando, 71

Martini, Johann Paul Aegidius, 24

Materna, 14

Matson, Vera, 82, 132

Matthews' Southern Comfort, 65, 159

Maxwell, Marilyn, 107

Mayfield, Curtis, 14

McCoy, Kansas Joe, 106

McCracklin, Jimmy, 75

McEnery, David L., 11

McGuire Sisters, The, 45

Melodia de America, 141

Mercer, Johnny, 26

Mickey Mouse Club, 120, 156, 171

Miller, Glenn, 22, 37

Miller, Jody, 80

Miller, Mitch, 140

Million Dollar Quartet, 27, 29-30, 32-33, 57, 67, 69, 75, 79, 101, 108, 112, 118, 134, 144

Milsap, Ronnie, 16

Mojica, José, 141

Monroe, Marilyn, 21, 54, 114

Monroe, Vaughn, 39

Moon Over Naples, 110

Moore, Johnny, 36, 67

Moore, President James, 54, 114

Moreno, Dario, 34

Morgan, Russ, 105, 200

Muss i denn, 139

Must Jesus Bear This Cross Alone?, 88

N

Nearer My God To Thee, 88, 91, 129, 155, 172, 178

Nelson, Ricky, 25, 37

Nelson, Willie, 21, 38, 128, 137

New World Singers, 20

No Words, 36

Non ho l'Eta, 98

North Carolina Ramblers, 37, 151

O

O Mother Dear Jerusalem, 14

O Sole Mio, 72, 123, 199-200

O Soul Are You Weary And Troubled, 129

O Store Gud, 49

Ocean, 100

Offenbach, Jacques, 126

Oh Dem Golden Slippers, 25

Orbison, Roy, 72, 76, 103, 128, 161

Otis, Clyde, 12

Owens, Buck, 28, 49, 151

P

Paderewski, Ignaz, 87, 155

Page, Patti, 53, 117, 160

Papa Cairo And His Boys, 73

Parce-que Je T'aime Mon Enfant, 89

Parker, Tom, 16, 50, 60, 70, 126

Parsons, Bill, 34

Pate, John W., 14

Paul Revere and the Raiders, 15

Peter, Paul and Mary, 10-11, 31, 160

Penguins, The, 31

Petrie, George, 28

Phillips, Sam, 53, 63, 75, 90, 117, 144

Piano, 48, 52, 73, 77, 99, 101, 108-109, 125, 129, 136, 153

Pick A Bale O' Cotton, 111

Pierce, Webb, 60

Pike's Peak, 14

Plaisir d'Amour, 24

Play Misty For Me, 119

Porter, Charles*****

Porter, Cole, 141, 143

Pour Toi, 34

Powell, Grace, 127

Prayer, 15, 21, 51, 120, 155, 162, 167, 172, 175

Preston, Billy, 39

Price, Ray, 27, 37, 60, 63, 83, 101, 160

Princess Kamekeha Liliuokalani, 13

Pryor, Arthur, 13

Puckett and Cross, 26

R

Ray, Johnnie, 104

Red River Dave, 11

Red, Ida, 73

Red, Tampa, 10

Reed, Jerry, 5, 11, 42, 116, 130, 156, 200, 202

Reed, Mama, 19

Reeves, Jim, 15, 46, 62, 132, 156

Richard, Cliff, 12, 16, 54, 123, 152

Rivers, Johnny, 84

Rob Roys, The, 116

Rockin' The Boogie, 118

Rock Of Ages, 47

Rodgers, Jimmie, 9, 38, 49, 63, 72, 76, 156

Rogers, Rock, 56

Romance du Chevrier, 24

Ross, Shirley, 21

Royale, Edwin, 11

Ruffin, Edward, 12

S

Scarlet Ribbons For Her Hair, 30

Schwarzendorf, 24

Scrambled Eggs, 141

Seeger, Pete, 95, 119

Shakespeare, William, 17

Shannon, Del, 9, 103, 152

Shelton Brothers, The, 76, 201

Shelton, Robert, 30

Shenandoah, 116

Shields, Ren, 38

Shilkret, Nat, 51, 159

Shore, Dinah, 90

Shortnin' Bread, 26

Shostakovich, 43

Showboat, 83

Sinatra, Frank, 14, 32, 37, 81, 94, 137, 143, 154

Slack, Freddy, 74

Snow, Hank, 9, 49, 60, 63-64, 155, 199-202

Solamente Una Vez, 141

Somos Novios, 71

Sonata quasi una Fantasia, 87

Sovine, Red, 49

Spencer, Grace, 123

Spiders, The, 138, 200

Spring is Here, 138

Stack-a-Lee, 110, 200

Stack O'Lee, 110

Stack o' Dollars, 19

Stagolee, 110

Stamps, The, 24, 33, 161, 195

Stevens, Shakin' 128

Stille Nacht, Heilige Nacht, 107

Stone, Jesse, 31, 35, 79, 106, 156

Stookey, Noel, 10

Storm, Gale, 28, 116

Strauss, Johan*****

Stubby and The Buccaneers, 97

Sullivan, Ed, 10

Sunrise Serenaders, The, 126

Sutch, Screaming Lord, 66

Sweet, Sweet Spirit, 78

Swingin' The Boogie, 118

Swing Low Sweet Chariot, 114-115

T

Tales From The Vienna Woods, 126-127

Tavers, Mary, 10

Taylor, Eddie, 19

Temple, Shirley, 43

Ti Guardero' Nel Cuore, 88

The Bad In Every Man, 22

The Bragging Song, 58

The Death Of Bill Bailey, 38

The First Nowell, 118

The Gallant Hood of Texas, 140

The Joy of Love, 24

The Lemon Drop Kid, 107

The Louvin Brothers, 69

The Maid of Milan, 123

The Man Of La Mancha, 119

The Man Who Knew Too Much, 100

The One-Horse Open Sleigh, 73

The Originals, 4, 35, 55, 77, 102, 200, 205-206

The Pajama Game, 100

The Prisoner's Song, 137, 162, 178

The Reno Brothers, 82

The Three Caballeros, 141

The Trouble With Girls, 115, 121

The Tupelo Years, 94

The Way Of Love, 71

The Wizard of Oz, 96

There's A Leak In This Building*****

Thornhill, Claude, 44

Three Dog Night, 92

Thunderbolt and Lightfoot, 135

Titanic, 91

Todlen Hame, 14

Tolentino, Federico Arturo Guízar, 12

Toots Paka Hawaiians, 13

Torna a Surriento, 112

Trumpeteers, The, 23, 86, 162

Twitty, Conway, 123

U

Undertakers, The, 75

V

Vee, Bobby, 9, 55, 200

Versailles, Treaty of, 87

Vienna Woods Rock and Roll, 127

Vogues, The, 129

Voice, 3, 5, 10, 18, 22, 29, 54, 63, 79, 112, 114, 122, 141, 150, 179, 195

Volare, 17

W

Wagoner, Porter, 42

Waikiki Wedding, 21, 114

Waiting At The End Of The Road, 32

Wakely, Jimmy, 19, 61, 96, 156

Walker, Aaron Thibeaux, 124

Walker, Cindy, 133

Ward, Billy, 87, 112, 138

Ward, Samuel, 14

Washington and Lee Swing, 75-76

Washington, Dinah, 32

Waters, Muddy, 41, 89

We'll Raise a Ruckus Tonight, 26

We'll Understand It Better By and By, 24

We Shall Not Be Moved, 57

We Shall Overcome, 24, 110, 196

Weavers, The, 10, 95

Wheeler, Kate, 144

When You Were Sweet Sixteen, 55

Whiteman, Paul, 32, 83, 160

Whiting, Margaret, 19

Who'll Buy Your Chickens When I'm Gone, 30

Williams, Andy, 17, 44, 109, 149

Williams, Dolores, 104

Williams, Perk, 101

Wilson, Jackie, 104, 142

Winterhalter, Hugo, 25

Wiseman, Scott, 44

Wood, Anita, 52, 136

Woodstock, 65

Worried Man Blues, 91

Y

Yale, 121

Yarrow, Peter, 10

You'll Miss Me, 75

You Ask Me To, 141

You Got To Walk That Lonesome Valley, 73

Young, Jimmy, 130

Young, Vicki, 12

Yradier, Sebastián, 92

Yuro, Timi, 83

Addendum

After this book had been set, I was amazed to receive information about two additional songs that had been recorded prior to Elvis's own versions. This would have been less of a surprise had it concerned one-liners or private, informal recordings that had just surfaced on an unofficial release, but the songs are full studio recordings, officially released many years ago, that all Elvis fans know. Perhaps there are others!

Stop, Look And Listen (Byers)
    Recorded by Elvis on Wednesday, 16 February, 1966
    Original: Rick Nelson 1964
    Double Features: Spinout, Double Trouble

Born in 1940, Rick Nelson appeared with his parents in their 1950s TV show, The *Adventures Of Ozzie And Harriet*. His recording career began in 1957 and the following year he formed his own band, which included James Burton, who would later become a fixed member of Elvis's band. His soft version of rock'n'roll and clean ballads left him without hits after the early 1960s. He continued recording, forming a new group called *The Stone Canyon Band*, but was disappointed by the reception to his new style when he performed in Madison Square Garden in 1971. As a reaction, he wrote and released *Garden Party* in the early 1970s, a song that ironically became a million-seller and his last hit. Ricky Nelson died in a plane crash on 31 December 1985.

Thrill Of Your Love (Kesler)
    Recorded by Elvis on Monday, 4 April, 1960
    Original: Carl McVoy 1958
    Elvis's version can be heard on Elvis is Back!; The Essential 60's Masters 1, CD1

Stan Kesler wrote five songs recorded by Elvis: *I'm Right, You're Left, She's Gone, I Forgot To Remember To Forget, If I'm A Fool For Loving You, Playing For Keeps* and this gospel-like *Thrill Of Your Love*. Carl McVoy was an older cousin of Jerry Lee Lewis and seems to have given him some early piano-playing lessons!

His 1958 version of *Thrill Of Your Love* was called *A Woman's Love* and remained unissued at the time, but has since appeared on compilations.

If you, dear reader, can provide any information about songs you think should appear in *Roots Of Elvis*, or wish to provide corrections to entries, please contact me by email at david.neale@pandora.be

For further information, visit http://users.pandora.be/davidneale/elvis/originals/

0-595-29505-3